GREAT BATTLES OF THE ROYAL NAVY

AS COMMEMORATED IN THE GUNROOM, BRITANNIA ROYAL NAVAL COLLEGE, DARTMOUTH

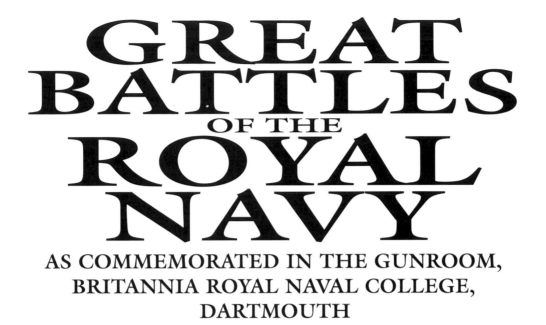

GREAT BATTLES OF THE ROYAL NAVY

AS COMMEMORATED IN THE GUNROOM, BRITANNIA ROYAL NAVAL COLLEGE, DARTMOUTH

EDITOR-IN-CHIEF ERIC GROVE

FOREWORD BY THE ADMIRAL OF THE FLEET HIS ROYAL HIGHNESS, THE PRINCE PHILIP, DUKE OF EDINBURGH, K.G., K.T.

ARMS AND ARMOUR

Arms and Armour Press
A Cassell Imprint
Wellington House, 125 Strand, London WC2R 0BB.

First published in 1994
This paperback edition 1997

British Library Cataloguing-in-Publication Data:
a catalogue record for this book is available from the British Library

ISBN 1-85409-4173

Cartography by Cilla Eurich.

Designed and edited by DAG Publications Ltd.
Designed by David Gibbons; layout by Anthony A. Evans.
Printed in Singapore by Craft Print Pte Ltd

Jacket illustration: *Drake Battling the Armada* by Donald Macleod.
Reproduced by courtesy of the artist, St Ives Gallery, Cornwall,
and PRC Studios, Mansfield-Woodhouse, Notts, England.

The paintings on pages 42, 50, 52-3, 62,
70, 86, 98, 102-3, 106, 142-3, 148 and 151 are reproduced
courtesy of The National Maritime Museum, London
and those on pages 97 and 111 courtesy of the
Anne S K Brown Collection, Brown University Library, USA.

CONTENTS

The introduction to the Naval Discipline Act begins with these resounding words "Whereas it is expedient to amend the law relating to the government of Her Majesty's Navy, whereon, under the good Providence of God, the wealth, safety and strength of the Kingdom so much depend;'. These words acknowledge the fact that an island realm depends for its freedom and security on naval defences, but they also suggest that those defences had been tested more than once in our long history and proved to be effective.

The major decisive battles of the Royal Navy are appropriately commemorated at the Royal Naval College at Dartmouth. This is where the future leaders of the Royal Navy are trained and prepared for their responsibilities, and there can be no better training than learning from the examples of the most successful leaders of the past. Not all the battles described in this book were directly in defence of the realm, but they were all fought to promote the best interests of the nation.

Not all the leaders in these battles displayed exactly the same talents. Some were better tacticians than others, some were able to inspire exceptional initiative and bravery, while others had an instinctive grasp of the broad strategic issues. What they all had in common was a burning ambition to serve their country. I have no doubt that this same ambition will continue to inspire all future leaders of the Royal Navy.

LIST OF CONTRIBUTORS

Dr. DAVID D. ALDRIDGE was educated at Repton and Corpus Christi College, Oxford. On graduation in 1951 (and having done National Service between school and Oxford) he spent three years in the London fine art trade, with which he retains links, before starting a spell of eight years in university administration, in West Africa, Oxford and East Anglia. After researching for his London doctorate, his field of research being the British naval presence in the Baltic during the reign of George I (as yet unpublished), in 1965 he was appointed to a lectureship at the University of Newcastle-upon-Tyne; from which he retired in 1993. He has reviewed books on naval, diplomatic, and Scandinavian history in the leading English historical periodicals and has published a substantial number of articles in dictionaries, encyclopedias, and in journals cognate to his interests. He also contributed to the Navy Records Society centenary volume for 1993, *British Naval Documents 1204–1960*. He lives in Leicestershire.

BILL ALLARD was educated at Paston Grammar School, Norfolk, and King Alfred's College, Winchester, where he specialised in Anglo-Saxon and early mediaeval history. He has worked extensively in a number of museums and the heritage industry, including archaeological excavation on Roman and Saxon sites, conservation and renovation of listed buildings and, more recently, museum documentation and gallery development. Since 1990 he has worked as a Curator for the National Maritime Museum in Greenwich, and was project officer on the Museum's new Twentieth-Century Seapower gallery.

KENNETH BREEN joined the History Department of St. Mary's College, Strawberry Hill, following service in the Royal Signals, mostly in the Far East. From 1983 until his retirement in January 1993 he was head of the department. He has served on the Councils of the Navy Records Society and the Society for Nautical Research. At present he is a member of the British Commission for Maritime History. He has contributed to the United States Naval Academy Naval History Symposium at Annapolis. His main interest is in the naval side of the American War of Independence, and he has written numbers of articles on this, including 'A Reinforcement Reduced? Rodney's Flawed Appraisal of French Plans, West Indies, 1781' in *Selected Papers from the Ninth Naval History Symposium*, 1991; 'Divided Command: The West Indies and North America, 1780–1781' in *The British Navy and the use of Seapower in the Eighteenth Century*, 1988 and 'Graves and Hood at the Chesapeake' in the *Mariners' Mirror*, February 1980.

Lieutenant Commander The Hon. MICHAEL COCHRANE, RN is a great-great-grandson of Admiral Lord Cochrane, 10th Earl of Dundonald. After education at Glenalmond, he joined the Royal Navy in 1978. His early sea appointments included HMS *Beachampton* based in Hong Kong, HMS *Upton* in Northern Ireland, and HM Yacht *Britannia*, which circumnavigated the globe as part of the Royal Tours of Australia and the Pacific Islands. After two years in the frigate *Ambuscade*, he served as ADC to the Governor of Gibraltar, during a period that saw the normalisation of relations with Spain. From 1987 to 1989 he was appointed to the frigate *Scylla*, which operated in the Persian Gulf at the height of the Iran-Iraq tanker war. In 1989–91 he navigated the ice patrol ship *Endurance*, undertaking two fascinating deployments to the Antarctic. In 1991 he joined HMS *Coventry*, flagship of the senior naval officer, Middle East, in the immediate aftermath of the Kuwait War, before becoming navigator of the Amphibious Assault Ship *Fearless*. In 1991 he was awarded the Shadwell Testimonial Prize for work submitted to the Hydrographic Department, which included his claiming an Indian ocean island for HM The Queen. In October 1993, he assumed command of the minehunter HMS *Brecon*. He lives in Hampshire.

PATRICIA K. CRIMMIN was educated at Aberdare Girls Grammar School and the University College of Wales, Aberystwyth, and at the University of London. Since 1967 she has been a lecturer, and since 1990, senior lecturer in the department of History at the Royal Holloway College, University of London. She has been a member of the Council of the Society for Nautical Research and is a member of the editorial board of its journal, *The Mariner's Mirror*. She is a member of the Council of the Navy Records Society and has contributed to its current volume, *British Naval Documents 1204–1960* (ed, J. B. Hattendorf *et al*, 1993) and to *The Naval Miscellany*, vol V (ed, N. A. M. Rodger, 1984). She is a Fellow of the Royal Historical Society and Treasurer of the British Commission for Maritime History. She has written a number of articles on aspects of naval and maritime history and is currently working on a major study of prisoners of war held by Britain during the French Revolutionary and Napoleonic Wars. She lives in Surrey.

Dr J. D. DAVIES was educated at Llanelli Grammar School and Jesus College, Oxford. After teaching in Cornwall for several years, he returned to Oxford to undertake research into the personnel of the later Stuart navy. The doctoral thesis that resulted became the basis of his book, *Gentlemen and Tarpaulins: The Officers and Men of the Restoration Navy* (1991). He won the Julian Corbett essay prize for naval history in 1986, has written widely on political, strategic and administrative aspects of the seventeenth-century navy and is a council member of the Navy Records Society. Since 1987 he has taught History at Bedford Modern School, where he serves as an officer in the Royal Navy section of the Combined Cadet Force, and is also a chief examiner for A-level History. He is currently working on a study of the Anglo-Dutch wars and an edition of Samuel Pepys's Admiralty letterbooks. He lives in Bedfordshire.

Dr. MICHAEL DUFFY was educated at Price's School, Fareham, and Lincoln College, Oxford. In 1969 he joined the Department of History and Archaeology at Exeter University where he is now a Senior Lecturer and Director of its Centre for Maritime Historical Studies. Author and editor of many books and articles including *Soldiers, Sugar and Seapower* (1987), *Parameters of British Naval Power 1650–1850* (1992) and the *New Maritime History of Devon* (2 vols, 1992, 1994), He is a vice-president of the Navy Records Society and the Hon. Editor of *The Mariner's Mirror, The Journal of the Society For Nautical Research.*

Cdr JAMES GOLDRICK joined the Royal Australian Naval College at the age of fifteen in 1974. He holds a BA and an MLitt from Australian universities. A Principal Warfare Officer (PWO) and anti-submarine warfare sub-specialist, his sea service has included HMA ships *Stalwart, Vendetta, Tarakan* and *Darwin* and exchange service with the Royal Navy in HM Ships *Alderney, Sirius* and *Liverpool*. He commanded HMAS *Cessnock* in 1990–91 and, after a year as a Research Fellow at the US Naval War College in Newport, Rhode Island, is presently in charge of the RAN's PWC training and tactical development at HMAS *Watson* in Sydney. He is married with one child. Publications include *The King's Ships Were At Sea* (1984), as well as editing *With The Battle Cruisers* (1987), *Reflections on the RAN* (1990) and *Mahan is Not Enough* (1993).

ANDREW GORDON gained his first degree in International Politics at Aberystwyth before studying for his PhD in War Studies at King's College, London. The author of *British Seapower and Procurement Between the Wars* (1988) and a forthcoming study of naval command at Jutland, he works for the Cabinet Office Historical Section. A lieutenant commander in the Royal Naval Reserve, he lives in south London.

ERIC GROVE was a civilian lecturer at the Britannia Royal Naval College, Dartmouth from 1971 to 1984, with a year away in 1980–1 as visiting professor at the United States Naval Academy, Annapolis. After leaving as Deputy Head of Strategic Studies he spent a year as Senior Research Officer with the Council for Arms Control before becoming a freelance defence analyst and naval historian. His activities included directing the naval research of the Adderbury-based Foundation for International Security, teaching at the Royal Naval College Greenwich and Cambridge University and appointment as a research fellow at the University of Southampton. In 1993 he was appointed Lecturer in International Politics and Deputy Director of the Centre for Security Studies at the University of Hull. His books include *Vanguard to Trident*, the standard account of post-war British naval policy, *The Future of Sea Power* and *Fleet to Fleet Encounters*, a comparative study of twentieth century fleet actions.

Professor JOHN B. HATTENDORF is the Ernest H. J. King Professor of Maritime History and Director of the Advanced Research Department at the US Naval War College, Newport, Rhode Island. As an officer in the United States Navy, 1965–73, he served in both Atlantic and Pacific Fleet destroyers as well as on the staff of the Naval Historical Center and the faculty at the Naval War College. He is a member of the faculty of the Munson Institute of American Maritime History at Mystic Seaport and has been visiting professor in military and naval history at the National University of Singapore and at the German Armed Forces Military History Research office. He is the corresponding member from the United States for the Society of Nautical Research, a corresponding member of the Royal Swedish Society for Naval Science and a corresponding member of the Academie du Var (France). He has contributed a number of essays on naval and maritime history to books and scholarly journals and is the general editor the US Naval Institute's 'Classics of Sea Power' series and the John Carter Brown Library's series of facsimiles of rare books on Maritime History 1485–1815. He is the author of numerous books, including *England in the War of the Spanish Succession* (1987) and co-editor on many more.

Dr. GERALD JORDAN served for ten years in the British merchant navy before entering academic life. In 1974 he received a PhD from the University of California and joined the faculty of York University, Toronto, Canada, where he is currently Associate Professor of History. In 1989–90 he was a Visiting Professor at the National University of Singapore and during 1991–2 held a Visiting Fellowship at the Institute of South-East Asian Studies in Singapore. He is a member of the Canadian Committee for the History of the Second World War, on whose executive committee he served from 1981 to 1984, and of the Canadian Sub-Commission for Maritime History. He has edited and contributed to several books, including *Naval Warfare in the Twentieth Century* (1977) and *British Military History: A Guide to the Sources* (1988). He has published numerous articles on aspects of British naval history and on the maritime history of south-east Asia.

Dr. ANDREW D. LAMBERT Educated at the Hammond School, City of London Polytechnic and King's College, London. BA Law, MA and PhD War Studies (1982). Taught at Bristol Polytechnic, The Royal Naval College, Greenwich, Royal Military Academy Sandhurst, and since 1991, Lecturer in War Studies, King's College, London. Fellow of the Royal Historical Society, Councillor the Society for Navy Records and the SS The Great Britain Trust. Books published: *Battleships in Transition: The Creation of the Steam Battlefleet 1815–1860* (1984); *Warrior: The First Ironclad* (1987); *The Crimean War: British Grand Strategy Against Russia 1853–1856* (Manchester 1990); *The Last Sailing Battlefleet: Maintaining Naval Mastery 1815–1850* (1992); *The War Correspondents: The Crimean War* (1994). He lives in Kew with his wife and daughter.

BRIAN LAVERY was born in the shipbuilding town of Dumbarton and educated at Dumbarton Academy, Glasgow University, Edinburgh University and Moray House College of Education, graduating with an MA in Politics from Edinburgh, 1969. He taught History for four years in Stirlingshire and spent eleven years working in the printing industry before leaving to become a freelance consultant in 1985. He did the historical research and the initial design for the *Susan Constant* replica in Jamestown, Virginia. For two years he was Assistant Curator, Chatham Historic Dockyards, and worked on the award-winning 'Wooden Walls' exhibition. He is a member of the Research, Technical and Programme Committee of the Society for Nautical Research, and the Victory Advisory Technical Committee, which advises on the restoration of the historic ship at Portsmouth. He was appointed Deputy Head of Ship Technology, National Maritime Museum, in 1991 and became Head of Ship Technology in April 1992. Responsible for the collection of models, boats, ships' fittings, ships' plans, historic photographs, archaeology and ordnance, he is also responsible for developing museum-wide policies on the modern period, post-1950. Author of numerous books and articles including *Dean's Doctrine of Naval Architecture 1670* (1981), *Anatomy of the Ship: Bellona* (1985) and *Nelson's Navy* (1989).

Dr. PETER LE FEVRE was educated at St George's College, Weybridge, Surrey. He worked for a number of years in the Civil Service and for an international synthetic rubber manufacturer before going to Lancaster University, where he obtained a degree in History. While working for his PhD, he lectured part-time at Brighton Polytechnic. From 1988 to 1992 he worked for the early seventeenth-century section of the *History of Parliament*, researching, writing and preparing biographies for eventual publication. He was a council member of the Navy Records Society from 1989 to 1993. His interest in the Navy was inspired by his grandfather, an ex-sailor, and also by the discovery that a group of late seventeenth-century admirals had retired to Weybridge, Surrey. He has written a large number of articles on the late seventeenth-century navy, and is writing a book on one of the admirals who settled at Weybridge, Arthur Herbert, Earl of Torrington, (1648–1716), who was present at the St. James's Day Fight.

D. J. LYON has spent his working life at the National Maritime Museum, Greenwich. Here he worked on the world's largest collection of ship plans for more than twenty years before running the Ordnance and then the Enquiries sections. He is now one of the leading lights of the Authorship section. He was an officer in the Naval Reserve, where he learned to dive. He was joint founder of both Maritime Archaeological Surveys and of the Ordnance Society. He is the author of several books (of which the latest is the monumental *Sailing Navy List*) and many articles on ships and naval history.

Dr. RUDDOCK MACKAY was born in Auckland, New Zealand, in 1922. He went to Wanganui Collegiate School, served as a rating in the RNZN (Pacific and Atlantic), 1942–6, and by external study graduated BA (NZ, history, economics, etc.) in 1945. His other degrees comprise MA (Oxon., PPE, 1948); BA (London external, French, 1952); and D. Litt. (St. Andrews, 1975). He taught history (etc.) at RNC, Dartmouth, in 1954–65 and then Modern History at St. Andrews University (Reader, 1974–83). At OUP he published *Admiral Hawke* (1965); *Fisher of Kilverstone* (1974); and *Balfour: Intellectual Statesman* (1985). He also edited *The Hawke Papers* (NRS, 1990).

Dr. COLIN J. M. MARTIN was born in Edinburgh and educated at Aberdeen Grammar School. After working as a flying instructor, he joined the Army on a Short Service Commission and was posted to Cyprus, where he learned to dive. Since 1968 he

has been an underwater archaeologist, and has worked on three Armada wrecks - *Santa Maria De La Rosa* (off south-west Ireland), *El Gran Grifon* (Fair Isle), and *La Trinidad Valencera* (off Donegal). In 1972 he founded the Institute of Maritime Archaeology at the University of St Andrews, where he now holds a Readership. In 1975 he published a general account of his work on the Armada wrecks, *Full Fathom Five*, and in 1988 re-examined the 1588 campaign in *The Spanish Armada*, written jointly with Geoffrey Parker. He is currently investigating a Cromwellian shipwreck off Mull.

Admiral of the Fleet Sir JULIAN OSWALD joined the Navy at the age of thirteen and retired as First Sea Lord in 1993. He served in ten ships, commanded three and specialised in gunnery and air weapons. He had six appointments in the Ministry of Defence covering Naval Plans, NATO, Rest of the World, Defence Programmes, Defence Policy and Nuclear affairs. From 1980 to 1982 he was Captain of the Britannia Royal Naval College, Dartmouth. He has a special interest in the aspects of British naval history featured in this book.

SUSAN ROSE read history at Lady Margaret Hall, Oxford, graduating in 1958. She began research into the history of the mediaeval navy while bringing up a young family and received her PhD from the University of London in 1974 for a thesis concerning the navies of Henry V and Henry VI. She has been connected with the Society for Nautical Research for many years, recently as a Trustee and currently as a Vice-President. She has also served on the Council of the Navy Records Society, which published her *Navy of the Lancastrian Kings* in 1982. She also contributed to the mediaeval section of the Society's centenary volume, *British Naval Documents 1204–1960*, published in 1993. She divides her time, apart from research, between a lectureship in History at the Roehampton Institute of Higher Education and work for the Open University. She has written on the French revolution and the history of London as well as on mediaeval naval matters. She lives in London.

Captain A. B. SAINSBURY was educated in Liverpool, joined the Liverpool Fire Service and was a Bevin Boy before going to Trinity College, Oxford. He retired in 1988 from a career in academic administration after taking the Julia Cortill essay prize from the University of London for a study of Admiral Sir John Duckworth, whose biography he is soon to complete. He is a Trustee of the *Naval Review*, a Vice-President of the Society for Nautical Research and recently retired from the Navy Records Society as Senior Vice-President. He published *The Royal Navy Day by Day* (1993) and a celebratory publication for the centenary of the NRS. Both books had the accepted dedication of the Lord High Admiral of the United Kingdom, Her Majesty Queen Elizabeth II. He lives in Blackheath, London, which is handy for the National Maritime Museum and the Public Record Office.

JON SUMIDA received his BA from the University of California, Santa Cruz, and his MA and PhD from the University of Chicago. He has been a fellow-commoner of the Archives Centre at Churchill College, Cambridge, and a fellow of the Wilson Center and the Guggenheim foundation. His articles have appeared in the *Journal of Modern History, International History Review* and *Journal of Military History* and in several volumes of conference proceedings. His books include *The Pollen Papers: The Privately Circulated Printed Works of Arthur Hungerford Pollen, 1901–1916* (1984), and *In Defence of Naval Supremacy: Finance, Technology and British Naval policy, 1889–1914* (1989; paperback edition, 1993). Sumida is presently an associate professor of history at the University of Maryland, College Park.

Professor GEOFFREY TILL is Professor and Head of the Department of History and International Affairs at the Royal Naval College, Greenwich. He also teaches in the Department of War Studies at King's College, London, and before that taught in the Department of Management and Systems at the City University. In addition to many articles on various aspects of defence, he is the author of a number of books including *Air Power and the Royal Navy* (1979) and *Modern Sea Power* (1987). Educated at Salisbury and then at King's College London, he obtained a first degree in Modern History in 1966, a Postgraduate Certificate in Education in 1967 and an MA in War Studies in 1968. His PhD on 'The Development of Naval Aviation in the 1920s' was successfully completed in 1976 for the University of London. He has been a member of the History Department of the Britannia Royal Naval College at Dartmouth and the Department of History and International Affairs at the Royal Naval College, Greenwich, becoming Professor and Chairman there in 1989. He has also lectured in the Department of Systems Science at the City University, London, and for the Open University. He is currently Chairman of the Board of War Studies at King's College. He lives in Kent.

CHRIS WARE has been employed as a historian at the National Maritime Museum since 1977. He has published papers on the Navy and the Plantations and the Royal Navy in the Mediterranean at the start of the Revolutionary War. He has also written reviews for *The Journal for Underwater Archaeology* and *The Journal of the Society for Nautical Research*. At present he is completing a book on bomb vessels.

PREFACE

This book was stimulated by Great Battles of the British Army as Commemorated in the Sandhurst Companies. It seemed appropriate to produce a companion for the Royal Navy, but this presented some problems. The Dartmouth divisions are named after admirals, not engagements. The obvious alternative lay in the impressive Senior Gunroom at the west end of the College. There around the walls are commemorated thirty-two naval battles, from Alfred versus the Danes to Stopford's bombardment of Acre, which took place sixty-five years before the College opened. Interestingly, the unknown hand that selected these battles to inspire the Cadets did not think any battles of the Russian War or such recent events as the bombardment of Alexandria to be worthy of note.

Here was a collection that could form the basis for a book; but there were still snags. A volume that stopped in 1840 would not perhaps have as much appeal as the Army volume, which contained a great deal of twentieth century material. The number of battles in any case was too many. It was decided therefore to cut out more of the earlier battles and select some of the twentieth century engagements one would expect a designer of a College opened in 2005 to choose. The obvious candidates seemed the Falkland Islands, 1914; Jutland, 1916; the River Plate, 1939; Taranto, 1941; Matapan, 1941; North Cape, 1943; and the Falklands, 1982. The choice of which admiral to place by each victory was suggested by the idiosyncratic approach of the Gunroom itself. Attributing Copenhagen to Nelson and Basque Roads to Cochrane would meant that Taranto should go to the officer in operational command rather than to the C-in-C, Cunningham (who gets his own battle anyway). The same principle also suggested the attribution of the Falklands to the Carrier Task Group commander rather than to Admiral Fieldhouse, who was based in Northwood in overall command of the Task Forces engaged. To make this point more strongly, the chapter covers the campaign very much from TG 317.8's point of view.

Many people have assisted in the production of this volume. First, thanks must be extended to Admiral of the Fleet His Royal Highness the Duke of Edinburgh for graciously consenting to provide a foreword and to Admiral Sir Julian Oswald, one of the most distinguished former Captains of the College, for providing an epilogue. Then great thanks must be expressed to Captain and Mrs Simon Moore of Britannia Royal Naval College, who allowed not only the full use of the College by the book production team but even the use of the collection of battle prints in the Captain's house. Evan Davies, BRNC's archivist, provided truly vital assistance and liaison as well as the up-to-date history of the College with which the book ends. All the authors must be thanked for their excellent contributions, which were produced both on schedule and to specification, but Peter Le Fevre deserves special mention for his rapid production of a replacement chapter when the Editor discovered he had asked him for an account of the wrong battle! The National Maritime Museum showed great generosity and assistance in filling the gaps in illustrations after the College's collection of paintings and prints had been exhausted. My wife Elizabeth showed her usual forbearance in putting up with a preoccupied husband at a time of considerable personal upheaval. Finally, the editor must add a personal note of thanks to Rod Dymott and Peter Burton of Arms & Armour Press, who have shown remarkable patience and forbearance with the various delays that have overtaken the production of the volume.

The dates for the earlier battles are in the old Julian style used in Britain before 1751; this seemed the best approach for a book discussing the engagements from a British perspective. Eleven should be added to the date figure in order to convert to the new Gregorian style used from 1582 in Spain, Portugal and France.

GENERAL INTRODUCTION
by Eric Grove, Editor-in-Chief

The first four battles covered in this book pre-date the existence of the Royal Navy, which in its modern form dates back only to the Restoration of 1660. The first engagement, Alfred versus the Danes, described by Bill Allard in an illuminating account, pre-dates even the existence of the English kingdom itself. To the Victorians and Edwardians who built the College, 897 could be interpreted romantically as the first event in a thousand years of naval history. Evan Davies' point seems a sound one: that the prominence of this particular inscription in the Gunroom – over the main door – means that it was seen to have this specific and inspirational relevance, and perhaps was even meant to raise echoes of the 1897 Diamond Jubilee Review, one of the major naval occasions of the period of BRNC's construction. Whatever that motivation was, it had to be the starting-point for this survey of major engagements involving the Royal Navy and its forebears. Now we can see this first battle in its true light, an episode in what was more a civil war in modern terms, a battle between north and south in which the ancestors of modern Englishmen were on both sides.

Sluys was the largest naval battle of the mediaeval English Navy, and was the clear choice to represent the engagements of this period, with an account written by the leading historian of the mediaeval English Navy, Susan Rose. Fought by a fleet mobilised from all the ships of the realm and fitted out for war, Sluys has all the characteristics of the classic 'land battle at sea' that was representative of mediaeval naval warfare in Atlantic waters. Indeed the French threw away the advantage that might have been provided by the presence on their side of more sophisticated Mediterranean-type naval forces.

The choice for the Elizabethan era had to be the Armada, especially as an impressive portrait of Lord Howard of Effingham dominates the Gunroom. Again this is a battle fought by the entire 'Navy of England', with private as well as Royal ships playing their part. Thanks to that naval enthusiast, Henry VIII, the Royal fleet was much stronger than it had been before, with its own dockyard infrastructure, but it was still as much the private property of the Crown as a modern state Navy, to be contributed to naval expedition in hope of profit just as private citizens contributed their assets. Colin Martin's account of the battle draws on the latest work carried out by himself and Geoffrey Parker in the best account of the battle, published to mark the 1988 four-hundredth anniversary.

The victory of Parliament in the Civil War led to the creation of the first 'British' Navy with Cromwell's temporary unification of the entire British Isles and, indeed, the first real 'Navy' in its modern sense as a national maritime fighting force. Blake, a name commemorated in one of Dartmouth's divisions, was the major figure of this era. He never served a king but is rightly honoured as a great British naval leader. Rather than the hard-fought engagements of the First Dutch War, Blake's victory against Spain at Santa Cruz, rated at the time the greatest success since the Armada, was chosen to commemorate this great man in the Gunroom.

In his typically thorough and thoughtfully argued account, seventeenth-century expert David Davies argues that Santa Cruz played a part in Cromwell's refusing the crown; the 'Royal Navy' had therefore to wait two more years to be re-created, until the Stuarts were restored in 1660. As Royal administrators, notably Samuel Pepys, struggled to maintain the Republican standard of efficiency, English admirals fought more major battles against the first-class sea power of the Netherlands. Victory was difficult to achieve against probably the Royal Navy's most formidable opponents ever, but perhaps the finest was the St James's Day Fight of 1666. This is covered here by Peter Le Fevre, the other leading expert on the period. It was regrettable that the sequel to this fine victory was the Dutch descent on the Medway and the capture of some of the vessels that had taken part – a useful warning that battles do not always settle everything.

The Revolution of 1688 made England and the Netherlands allies against the common enemy of Louis XIV's France, the beginning of more than a century of confrontation with our cross-Channel neighbour. The dual victory of Barfleur and La Hogue, commemorated under the latter title in the Gunroom, was the high spot of this first war for the Navy. As David Aldridge emphasises, victory prevented invasion but it could not prevent other forms of naval pressure on England, notably commerce raiding, that contributed to the War of the League of Augsburg's indecisive result.

The next battle, Cape Passaro, the first included in this book fought by Great Britain after the Act of Union of 1707, was not part of a declared war but was a piece of large-scale 'gunboat diplomacy', the subtlety of which Professor John Hattendorf makes clear. It took place in the longest lull in the struggle with France for world domination. When this conflict was renewed, Lord Anson developed the strategy of the Western Squadron that led to classic engagements off Finisterre such as that described so well by Pat Crimmin. Hawke won a similar battle the same year, which is briefly described both in the Appendix – for it appears at Dartmouth – and in Ruddock Mackay's account of Quiberon Bay, perhaps the finest all-round victory in all the annals of the Royal Navy. The greatest expert on this fine admiral is able to describe succinctly what made Hawke such an excellent sea officer as well as why he and his 'heart of oak' men and ships were able to 'have something more' of the 'wonderful year' of 1759.

The War of American Independence was the most dismal part of the 'Second Hundred Years War', but it was saved towards the end by the activities of the Royal Navy and its most controversial of successful flag officers, Rodney. Ken Breen gives us a judicious description of his great victory at Les Saintes, without taking sides in the debate over whether the breaking of the French line was intentional or mere accident. What is not in doubt is the importance of the battle in helping Britain hang on to the colonies that really mattered to her – the West Indies.

The wars with France culminated in the battles of the Revolutionary and Napoleonic Wars, the golden age of British sea power. The French Navy was not what it had been, but at the beginning of the war it

could still put up a fierce fight, a point made by Chris Ware in his account of the Glorious First of June. Michael Duffy then demonstrates his excellent mastery of the subtleties of naval warfare under sail in his description of the Battle of Cape St. Vincent, a remarkable victory of British skill against the decayed might of Spain. Jervis became Lord St. Vincent, a name still honoured in a Dartmouth Division (and the one to which the Editor was attached as a tutor during his time on the staff there).

St. Vincent also helped make the name of Nelson, whose figure gazes out over his successors from the west end of the Gunroom; indeed the room appears to have been called 'Nelson' in its early days, precluding the name's being applied to a specific term, house or division. In their highly professional contributions, Brian Lavery, David Lyon and Gerry Jordan next cover Nelson's own three classic victories, Aboukir Bay (referred to as 'The Nile' in the Gunroom), Copenhagen (ascribed at Dartmouth to Nelson rather than to the less aggressive C-in-C, Hyde Parker) and finally Trafalgar, where the charismatic little man met the end he had been chasing for much of his career in the context of a remarkable tactical success.

The war did not end, however. There was still room for more action against the French Navy in battles that are too often forgotten in the tendency to over-emphasise Trafalgar's decisiveness. Tony Sainsbury, the expert on Sir John Duckworth, covers his success at San Domingo in the year after Trafalgar. Then Lieutenant Commander Michael Cochrane, a former student of the Editor at Dartmouth and currently commanding the mine-hunter HMS *Brecon*, provides an exceptionally creditable description of his ancestor's troubled success at Basque Roads. His point about the battle's being mentioned at Dartmouth in vindication of Lord Cochrane is a particularly interesting one.

The last battle to be mentioned in the Gunroom is Stopford's successful bombardment of Acre, and there is no one better able to describe this action than the doyen of historians of the mid-nineteenth century navy, Andrew Lambert. Like Professor Hattendorf, he clearly describes the complex political background to another exercise in 'gunboat diplomacy'. He also shows that the power of warships against forts should not be underestimated, and that Acre's demonstration of this fact made it a more decisive battle than some might think. Palmerston, that arch-exponent of the art of gunboat diplomacy, certainly thought so, as the quotation ending Dr Lambert's fine piece makes clear.

We now move to the twentieth century and the Editor's choice of engagements. This seemed to be conditioned by the clarity of the victory, the historical significance of the battle, both as to context and participants, and finally the existence of commemorative material at the College. Sturdee's revenge for the disaster of Coronel seemed the obvious first choice as well as an opportunity for Jon Sumida, the leading historian of the period, to explain the significance of Fisher's battlecruisers. A fine portrait of Fisher hangs in the Gunroom.

Jutland had to be covered if for no other reason than the use of Jellicoe as a Divisional name for a time by the College and that of Beatty for the rating's accommodation. Frustrating and costly though Jutland was, Andrew Gordon, the today's leading expert on the battle, is able to explain that the engagement was in part at least a success for the Royal Navy. His account benefits from the interesting and important new work on the battle that he has been carrying out in the last few years.

The River Plate was the first real naval success of the Second World War and is illustrated in the photographic collection commemorating the Royal Navy's more recent achievements in 'D' Block main corridor. This is a battle that has not often been fully explained, and the account that follows uses German sources to provide the full picture of how Captain Langsdorff's ill-advised exercise in risk taking went horribly wrong.

Taranto is a name almost to rival Trafalgar in Royal Navy tradition, and there is no one better able to describe it than former Fleet Air Arm officer and Head of Naval Historical Branch, David Brown. It was truly a remarkable demonstration of the economical use of force as well as the utility of carrier air power, a decisive new component of naval operations. It is a victory that will always be celebrated by the Royal Navy's aviators. Andrew Cunningham, that greatest of Second World War Commanders-in-Chief, whose picture hangs in the Gunroom and whose bust stands in the main corridor, was in overall command of the fleet that carried out the attack, but he was in more direct control of that classic night action of Matapan a few months later. Commander James Goldrick, RAN, brings to bear his unique combination of historical skill and professional insight in a new critical account of a

battle that was successful enough but which might have gone still better.

The last battle between gun-armed capital ships in the Royal Navy's history was fought off North Cape in the murk of an Arctic winter on Boxing Day 1943. It was a classic and dramatic success, and Bruce Fraser, that most thoughtful of C-in-Cs, took it as his title in the tradition of great sea officers before him. It is commemorated in the 'D' Block corridor photographs. Professor Till of the Royal Naval College, Greenwich, and a former Dartmouth lecturer himself, explains the dynamics of this final clash of the titans in his typically lucid way.

Finally, the Falklands had to be included, the last great success in combat of the Navy to date, and a battle fought while the Editor was actually at BRNC by officers known to him both as colleagues and students. It was important as a vindication of a politically beleaguered service and in making the Royal Navy perhaps the only fully battle-hardened naval service of the modern era. It has been commemorated at BRNC by two fine paintings. Although eyebrows may be raised as to the attribution of the battle to Admiral Woodward, it seemed a good way of emphasising the naval portion of the operations, rather than the campaign as a whole. It was also in the spirit of previous Gunroom attributions that emphasised the role of the commander on the spot. In no way is it meant to belittle the role of the late Lord Fieldhouse, who was in command of the Task Forces as a whole, or indeed of Lord Lewin, who was the key politico-military link in the campaign and whose portrait now graces the Gunroom.

Tradition can be a sterile thing, but if properly interpreted as a reputation for excellence it can give the present members of an institution high standards to live up to. It can also instill confidence, a tradition of winning that is one of the Royal Navy's most important attributes. As they look up at the names around the Gunroom and at the other relics of the past that surround them at BRNC, the officers of the future begin to sense both those positive aspects of the Royal Navy's long story of success. Not all battles were won; even when they were, they were often not sufficient conditions of victory. But the fact that many victories were achieved by some of the greatest sea officers of all time gives the Royal Navy a matchless record of success and the basis for the maintenance of a level of British naval power that allows the country still to 'punch above her weight' in the councils of the World.

ALFRED THE DANES, 897

by W. A. Allard

'Once he had taken over the helm of his kingdom, he alone, sustained by divine assistance, struggled like an excellent pilot to guide his ship laden with much wealth to the desired and safe haven of his homeland.'
Biographer of King Alfred, Asser

'Once he had taken over the helm of his kingdom, he alone, sustained by divine assistance, struggled like an excellent pilot to guide his ship laden with much wealth to the desired and safe haven of his homeland...' It is perhaps not surprising that King Alfred's biographer, the Welsh monk Asser, should describe him in such glowing nautical terms. Much of his reign was taken up with the defence of the West Saxon kingdom against Viking raids, many of which came by sea from their great bases in Northumbria and East Anglia. Alfred, the master diplomat and warlord, cannot have missed the importance of a naval force to the defence of his realm. Indeed, the Anglo-Saxon Chronicle, our main contemporary source for this period of history, mentions a number of occasions when Alfred either leads or orders a small fleet against Danish attack, well before his victory of 897. Yet he was not the first of the Anglo-Saxon kings to maintain a fleet. King Athelstan 'fought in ships' in 851, destroying 'a great host' off Sandwich in Kent. Many historians view this as the first great naval victory of 'the English', but the record is too vague to draw any firm conclusions, and some would question too much identification of the West Saxons with 'England' as a whole.

In 875, only four years after becoming king, Alfred is recorded as having taken a fleet to sea against seven Danish vessels; the outcome to this engagement is uncertain. Seven years later Alfred again went to sea to confront four Danish ships, and in 885 a rather larger engagement seems to have taken place. Alfred ordered a naval force from Kent into the heartland of Danish East Anglia and engaged sixteen vessels, killing all the crews and capturing the ships. If we take the *Chronicle* at its word, this would have required a fleet of some considerable size, manned with competent crews. Unfortunately the success was somewhat soured when the West Saxons were intercepted on their return to the south coast by another Danish force. As the historical text draws close to the end of Alfred's reign, the problem of Danish warships seems to play an increasingly important role. In 892 Haesten, one of the great Danish warlords, set up a fleet of 80 ships at Milton Royal, near the mouth of the Thames. Alfred set about constructing forts to control the river, and in 894 the trapped Danish fleet was either burnt or taken by the men of London.

Three years later, in 897, Danish ships from East Anglia and Northumbria harassed all along the south coast of Wessex and into Devon. This prompted Alfred to order the construction of warships to meet the Danes. These ships were: 'almost twice as long as the others, some had sixty oars, some had more; they were both swifter, steadier, and with more freeboard than the others; they were built neither after the Frisian design nor after the Danish, but as it seemed to himself that they could be most serviceable.' This description of the new warships is perhaps more accurate than at first appears and gives us a fair idea of the

Left: The superbly carved memorial of the action with the Danes in 897 as commemorated in the Dartmouth Gunroom.

ALFRED : THE 𝔅 DANES · 897

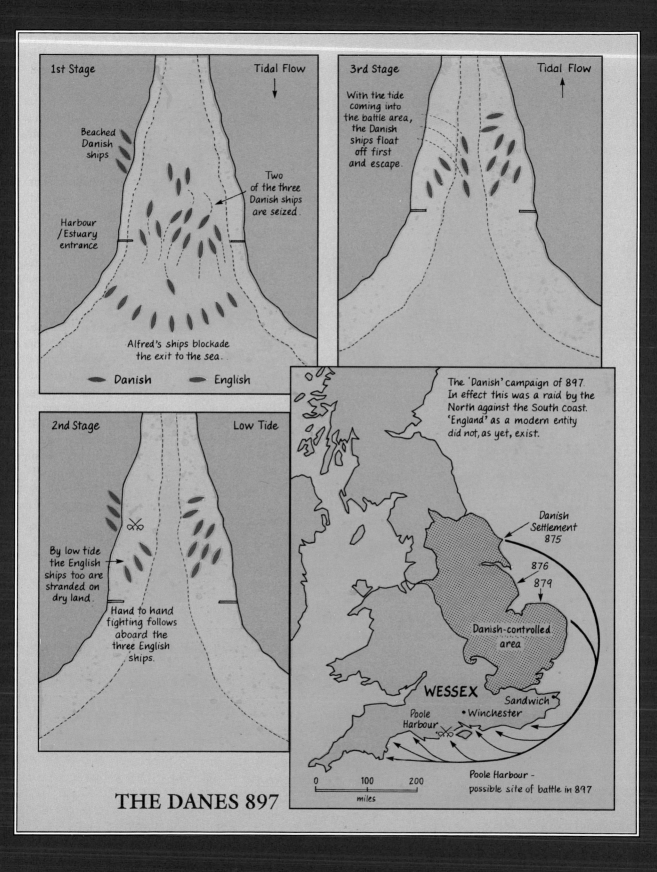

1st Stage

Tidal Flow

Beached Danish ships

Two of the three Danish ships are seized.

Harbour / Estuary entrance

Alfred's ships blockade the exit to the sea.

Danish   English

2nd Stage

Low Tide

By low tide the English ships too are stranded on dry land.

Hand to hand fighting follows aboard the three English ships.

3rd Stage

Tidal Flow

With the tide coming into the battle area, the Danish ships float off first and escape.

The 'Danish' campaign of 897. In effect this was a raid by the North against the South coast. 'England' as a modern entity did not, as yet, exist.

Danish Settlement 875

876

879

Danish-controlled area

WESSEX

Sandwich

Poole Harbour

• Winchester

Poole Harbour - possible site of battle in 897

0   100   200

miles

THE DANES 897

oars with numbers of men. As for what the ships actually looked like, we can be less sure; but the English vessels depicted on the Bayeux Tapestry, about 200 years later, are probably similar to the type of ship that Alfred ordered. They were most likely a cross between the old Frisian merchantmen and the Danish long-ships, and, if recovered Viking ships can be used as a guide, about 100ft long. (Some scholars have conjectured that after Alfred's trips to Rome as a young man there may have been a Mediterranean galley influence in his designs.)

The nine West Saxon ships, probably led by Alfred himself, found the Danish raiders in an inlet or bay and 'blockaded the entrance from the open sea.'. Here we are at the mercy of the Old English language, for the original text is extremely vague about the actual site of the battle. The use of words such as 'entrance', 'open sea' and, later, 'upper harbour' and 'channel' have led scholars to suggest that the action all took place in the vicinity of Southampton Water, perhaps at the point where the River Hamble enters the main channel. However, for many years the engagement has been referred to as the 'Battle of Poole Harbour' and there is every possibility that this was the site of the engagement battle.

'Then the Danes sailed out with three ships against them [the West Saxons, referred to as 'the English' by the Chronicler], and three of their ships [the Danes] were beached on dry land at the upper end of the harbour, and their crews had gone off inland. Then the English seized two of the three ships at the entrance to the estuary, and slew the men, but the other escaped; in her all but five were slain; and they escaped because the ships of the others [the 'English'] were aground...'

This section of the text is extremely important, since it begins to hint at the actual time-scale involved in the whole conflict. The nine West Saxon ships engaged the three Danish vessels left afloat – these were perhaps left to guard the estuary or may have simply been waiting for a suitable high tide to beach alongside their companions. The method of engagement was probably to join broadside with the enemy while exchanging missiles, and carry out hand-to-hand fighting until the enemy was overpowered. In this instance the increased crew numbers of the English vessels would have given them the upper hand. Consequently two Danish ships were captured and their crews killed; the third escaped with only five men, owing to the West Saxon ships becoming 'very

Above: King Alfred's greatest naval assets were his appreciation of the sea spirit and sea interest, and his ability to turn rather unpromising material to good use.

number of men involved in the battle described below. As the *Chronicle* puts it: 'came six [Danish] ships to the Isle of Wight and did much harm there, both in Devon and almost everywhere along the coast. Then the king ordered nine of the new ships to put out...'

If the English ships, with sixty oars, were twice as long as the Danish vessels, we can assume the latter had approximately fifteen oars per side, with a crew of between 30 and 50 men per ship. In total the English force was probably more than 600 men and the Danes something like half that figure. This certainly fits in with the numbers of men reportedly lost in the action, but we must be careful not to confuse the numbers of awkwardly aground; three had gone aground on the side of the channel where the Danish ships were aground, and all the others on the other side...'. The third Danish vessel is not mentioned again, and we can only presume that it escaped to some unknown destination. Running aground seems to have been extreme bad luck for the West Saxons, though it is entirely possible that they were inexperienced in handling their somewhat unwieldy craft in a tidal channel, especially in the heat of the battle. Alan Binns' extremely detailed work on this subject has produced perhaps the best scenario for explaining the run of events described, suggesting that the action took place some two hours before low water. Considering tidal flows along the south coast, the channel would have been low enough at this point for the West Saxon vessels, with their deeper hulls, to ground and allow the tide to have 'ebbed many furlongs from the ships [the beached Danish vessels]...'. The subsequent

Below: A rather stylized interpretation of combat between the Saxons and their Danish enemies.

action turned from a naval engagement to a land battle: 'the Danes went from the three ships to the other three [the West Saxon vessels] which were stranded on their side, and then there they fought.'

In the ensuing fighting, 62 of Alfred's men were killed, including Lucumon, the King's reeve, Aethelfrith of the King's household, and a number of Frisians – possibly experienced naval mercenaries. Asser tells us that the King had a number of skilled and learned men in his court from around Europe, and it would not be unreasonable to expect that such men advised Alfred on the construction of his ships, as well as actually manning them. The Danes, in contrast, are recorded as having lost 120 men in the action. If the calculations of numbers of men involved are roughly accurate, the Danish losses must have left their force severely depleted and may have prompted the decision to abandon the fighting and take advantage of the flood tide to escape. As the *Chronicle* puts it: 'The tide, however, came first to the Danes, before the Christians [the West Saxons] could push off theirs.'

This section has proved somewhat difficult for historians to understand. It would not be unreasonable to assume that the three beached Danish vessels described at the beginning of the action were above the high water mark, 'on dry land'. This would have ensured that they would not be refloated by any subsequent flood tide. Since the naval battle took place as the tide was ebbing, the West Saxon vessels must have beached some way below the Danish vessels. How then could the Danes have refloated their ships first? Again Alan Binns has suggested an answer – that the Danish vessels were in fact set upon a series of rollers or runners to ensure easy access back to the water. This argument holds some weight, since the depleted Danish crews, tired from the fierce hand-to-hand fighting, would have found it impossible to man-handle ships weighing around two tons over the beach to the rising tide. The rollers or runners would have provided a speedy and effective route to the channel, especially since the bulkier West Saxon vessels, with their inexperienced crews, would have had more trouble reaching open water. Indeed, the Danes managed to escape completely to row away to the open sea – even, it seems, against the flood tide. However, out of the surviving three Danish ships, only one managed to escape back to the safety of East Anglia. 'They were so sorely crippled that they were unable to row past Sussex, but there the sea cast two

Left: An impression of the attacking tactics used by King Alfred against the Danes. The key aspects are to attack with greater numbers from a larger and higher deck.

of them ashore; the men were led to the King at Winchester, and he had them hanged there. The men who were on the single ship reached East Anglia badly wounded.'

The *Chronicle* is again very vague at this point and does not tell us where, exactly, the two Danish ships were forced ashore. Some historians have suggested that the Danes were beached near Selsey Bill, where a series of sandbanks and strong currents are well known to navigators, and would have provided a stiff challenge to the already weakened mariners. This area is also, conveniently, within a day or two of Winchester, though it would be unwise to read too much into such theories.

The result of the battle was a victory for the West Saxons. We can assume that, as the tide flooded the channel, Alfred's ships were able to refloat and return to their base, possibly at Sandwich, well known later in Saxon times as a naval centre. As for the subsequent history of the fleet itself, the *Chronicle* makes no mention, though Alfred's successors seem to have taken the idea of a standing naval force seriously. Edward and Athelstan both maintained fleets, and in 973 King Edgar's fleet was on hand to receive the submission of the Scottish and Welsh kings. Thirty-five years later Ethelred ordered each land area of 300 hides to provide a 'large warship', together with a 'cutter' from each ten hides. These vessels were to supply a standing fleet based at Sandwich. In the event, the idea was eventually abandoned – not for the last time would the financial burden of naval power prove too great.

It seems therefore, in one sense, that King Alfred's victory over 'the Danes' set some form of precedent for his successors to follow. It must, however, be remembered that these 'Danes' from the North and East were in modern terms probably as 'English' as the West Saxons. One must be as careful about calling Alfred the 'Father of the Royal Navy' as one must be about Alfred's general claims to rule a kingdom he clearly did not control. Nevertheless this little skirmish is the first occasion that a fleet we know to be purpose-built for defence was used by a king who claimed to be a 'King of England'. As such, it is not a bad starting-point for a survey of 'great battles of the Royal Navy'.

BIBLIOGRAPHY

Keynes, S., and M. Lapidge, *Alfred the Great: Asser's Life of Alfred*, 1983. Excellent volume that provides a very readable translation of Asser's original work and gives some insight on Alfred, with examples of his own writings.
Garmonsway, G. N., *The Anglo-Saxon Chronicle*, 1990. Many versions of the Chronicle have been published; more recent editons tend to include current discussion on the subject.
Binns, A., Article in *Fifth Viking Conference*, 1968. Brief, but provides a more reasoned practical analysis than in Magoun, F. F.,

'King Alfred's beach Battle with the Danes' in *Modern Language Review*, vol 37, which remains useful but now somewhat outdated.
Stenton, F. M., *Anglo-Saxon England*, 1987. A large volume encompassing the fall of Roman Britain to the Norman Conquest, still the definitive work on the subject.
Wilson, D., *The Anglo-Saxons*, 1966. Another excellent general work on the subject, which addresses the main themes of Anglo-Saxon Britain and provides archaeological background.

EDWARD III: SLUYS, 1340

by Susan Rose

'A fleet of British ships at war are the best negotiators...'
Nelson, 1801

In what would now, perhaps, be viewed as an inspired piece of public relations, after the Battle of Sluys Edward III issued a gold noble which depicted on the obverse himself on board a ship (a cog prepared for war and displaying the quartered arms of England and France). Gold coins were a rarity at the time, and this image has served to fuel the conviction that the Battle of Sluys was not only a great victory for the English but an engagement of lasting importance, the first major encounter of the Hundred Years War, which had a measurable effect on the conduct of the war between the French and the English in subsequent years. Indeed Sir Nicholas Harris Nicolas, the great early nineteenth century naval historian, roundly declared: 'The name of Edward III is more identified with the naval glory of England than that of any other of her sovereigns.' Can this conviction be sustained by a closer look at the battle and its results?

There is no doubt that the English, particularly those who lived in the counties by the sea, needed a victory in 1340. For the past two years, as relations had worsened between Edward and Philip VI, the French had raided up and down the Channel coast meeting little effective opposition and causing severe harm to the inhabitants of some of the port towns. Edward's strategy had been to pursue alliances energetically with the rulers of the Low Countries and with the Empire so that he could mount a counter-offensive in France. The Count of Hainault was already his father-in-law, and embassies were dispatched to the courts of other rulers likely to be friendly or capable of being induced to favour the English cause through the payment of subsidies – more than 300,000 florins, for example, were paid to the Emperor, Lewis of Bavaria. The Flemish cloth merchants were threatened with ruin by the imposition of an embargo on the export of English wool to Flanders and wooed to abandon their already unpopular Count, a close ally of France.

The French were well placed to mount raids on English coastal towns. The *Clos des Gallées* had been established at Rouen some time before 1294 to build, under Genoese supervision, galleys on a broadly Mediterranean pattern for the French king. These mainly oar-propelled vessels, long and low in the water, were not much good for trading voyages in the

Channel, but they could be used very effectively for raids in the confined spaces of harbours and estuaries where the sailing ships of the period (which could sail only with the wind astern or on a very broad reach) were only too likely to find themselves unable to manoeuvre. In 1337, Philip VI had built a further base at La Rochelle. The French galleys under the command of Hue Quiéret and Nicolas Béhuchet posed an obvious threat to south coast towns. In September of the same year sheriffs in this area were calling on the 'keepers of the maritime lands' (whose duty it was to raise a militia for defence) to have warning beacons ready and for the people to be aware of the sinister import of sudden unexpected ringing of church bells.

In the summer of 1338 local forebodings were proved correct. Portsmouth was burnt by French

KING EDWARD THE III.rd

Right: Edward III gained a reputation as a sea-king in his search for military glory while neglecting the merchant marine.

raiders in June. In October, Southampton suffered even more severely. Chroniclers record how more than 50 galleys appeared off the town; the crews landed and plundered at will, carrying off their booty to the galleys. The next morning, seeing that the local people were at last beginning to organise resistance, the town was put to the torch; but not before, apparently, the women of the leading families had been raped and their menfolk hanged in their own houses. These dramatic events left their mark on royal actions, and immediate efforts were made to provide Southampton with a wall. An urgent inquiry was ordered into the only too evident failure of those charged with the defence of the town. In March 1339, those inhabitants who had fled and who, perhaps, were not thoroughly reassured by all this activity, were ordered immediately to return to the town. The order was repeated in stronger terms in July, an indication of the lack of security on the coast. Since March, in fact, the French galleys had attacked Harwich (where a change in the wind prevented the fire they had set spreading very far); they had also burnt down the fishermen's huts on the beach at Hastings. Other reports of their activities came from Thanet, Dover, Folkestone, Sandwich, Rye, the west country

and Bristol. Only the virtually octogenarian Earl of Devon had had much success in beating them off when he trapped a raiding party on shore at Plymouth and caused the French heavy casualties.

At sea the English response to these events had been somewhat muted. In the autumn of 1337, Walter Manny had defeated pro-French forces on the island of Cadzand opposite the port of Sluys, but the following year brought near-disaster. Several (five according to the chronicle of Adam Murimuth; other chroniclers are less specific) of the King's largest ships were lost to an opportunist stroke by the French galleys. The English ships were in port in Flanders (either at Middelburg or Sluys; the sources do not agree), having discharged their cargoes. Their crews were ashore when the French arrived and made off with the English ships to Normandy. It is certain that *Christopher*, one of the largest and best found of the King's ships, was in this group – lost to the French without a blow being struck. Even if this ship did not carry cannon (the belief that she did so is founded on the mis-dating of a fifteenth-century account by Nicolas), she was still the pride of the small group of ships in royal ownership.

The men of the Cinque Ports did better in 1339. They slipped across the Channel in a fog and conduct-

Above: Sluys was essentially a foot soldiers' battle fought from ships.

from England on the King's business. Wool exports were suspended in April on the King's return, for fear that they would fall into enemy hands. An attempt by the English to hire a force of galleys in the Mediterranean, presumably to take on the French, seems to have ended in dismal failure when Nicholas Flisco, the chosen envoy, was arrested in the Papal enclave of Avignon and smuggled into France sometime before the beginning of June. Edward's clear intention to be absent from England for some time was finally signalled when, on 27 May, Edward, Duke of Cornwall (the King's eldest son), was appointed Regent during his absence. By the middle of June the King was based at Ipswich while the fleet was being gathered together, probably with some difficulty, in the estuary of the Orwell. His own vessel, the *Cog Thomas*, under the command of Richard Fille, had been ready since 17 May when Fille received £32 16s 3d to pay the crew of 120 men for the voyage to Flanders.

All the chroniclers agree that the fleet, numbering somewhere around 160 vessels, finally set sail on 22 June. There is also, of course, no disagreement about the result of the engagement, which took place on 24 June in the estuary of the River Zwyn, off Sluys. The English utterly defeated the French fleet, which took very heavy casualties and lost the great majority of its ships.

We know very little for certain, however, about the actual course of the battle. Our best source is the terse letter written by the King himself to the Duke of Cornwall on 28 June while still on board the *Thomas*. He tells how the fleet sailed from Orwell and reached the Flemish coast near Blankenburgh the following day. They knew the French fleet was massed in the port of 'Swyn' (Sluys) but could not attack immediately because the tide was against them. The next day, with the tide under them, the English attacked the French, who had drawn up their ships 'in a very strong formation'. Despite a stout defence, the French were beaten and the English took 180 ships, leaving only 24 to take refuge in flight. The French losses in manpower were very high – Edward gives the figure of 30,000 dead and paints a gruesome picture of corpses being washed up all along the neighbouring coasts. With quiet satisfaction he records the re-taking of his great ship *Christopher* and the others lost, he says, at Middelburg. He also mentions the welcome help of the Flemings, probably from Cadzand.

The various chroniclers add further, often picturesque, details to this account, but much of what

ed a successful raid on Boulogne, setting fire to the lower town and destroying a large warehouse full of naval stores and arms. According to the report (maybe a rather optimistic one), nineteen galleys, four great ships, and twenty small ones were also destroyed.

In early 1340, Edward III was in Flanders. He had at last successfully concluded an alliance with Jacob van Artevelde, the leader of the Flemish burghers, who recognised his claim to the French throne. Edward then challenged France by proclaiming this title at a great assembly in Ghent before leaving for England.

In the previous November, when in Brussels, the King had already authorised commissioners to raise a loan of £20,000 to pay for naval expenses despite his serious financial difficulties. Further commissioners were also sent out to arrest shipping for a fleet to sail

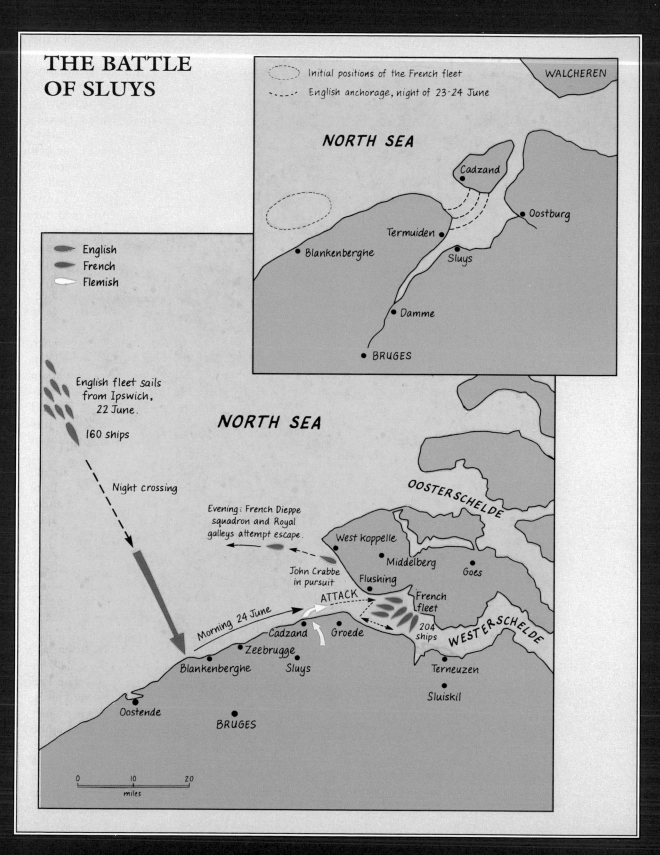

THE BATTLE OF SLUYS

WALCHEREN

Initial positions of the French fleet

English anchorage, night of 23-24 June

NORTH SEA

Cadzand

Oostburg

Termuiden

Blankenberghe

Sluys

Damme

BRUGES

English
French
Flemish

English fleet sails from Ipswich, 22 June.

160 ships

NORTH SEA

Night crossing

Evening: French Dieppe squadron and Royal galleys attempt escape.

West koppelle

OOSTERSCHELDE

Middelberg

Goes

John Crabbe in pursuit

Flushing

French fleet

ATTACK

204 ships

WESTERSCHELDE

Morning 24 June

Cadzand

Groede

Zeebrugge

Sluys

Terneuzen

Blankenberghe

Sluiskil

Oostende

BRUGES

0   10   20

miles

they say must be treated with caution. We must not forget the location of the battle, about which there is little controversy, and the technical limitations of fourteenth-century ships. The estuary of the Zwyn, where the battle took place, was encumbered with sandbanks; it was not the easiest place for the vessels of the day to manoeuvre, given their limitations. The galleys of the French would have had the advantage here in this respect and, if it is true, as one chronicler states, that the French had chained their ships together into three large floating platforms, they seem to have thrown away this advantage with almost crim-

Left: Armour was very much in evidence during the fourteenth century, putting a soldier in deepest peril if he were to fall into the sea.

inal negligence. There is a report that the Genoese galley commander, Barbavera, present with three ships, remonstrated with the French leaders when he realised their tactics; when they refused to change their minds, he slipped away just as the fighting commenced. He would seem to have had a better grasp of the realities of fighting at sea at this date than did his employers.

It is also often stated that the English came on with both the wind and the sun behind them. We have no direct evidence of the wind direction, but it must have been sufficiently from a westerly direction to allow the English fleet to sail up the Zwyn. If, however, the two fleets met near to midday, as they would have had to do for the English to take advantage of the tide (high tide in the Zwyn being at 11.23 a.m. on 24 June 1340), it would be impossible for the English to have had the sun behind them, since they were approaching from the north-west.

Walsingham states that Edward received late reinforcements when Robert Morley's northern squadron joined his forces off Blankenburgh. This seems more likely than the story found in Froissart concerning the French sinking an English ship bearing the most noble and most beautiful ladies of England on their way to the Queen's court at Ghent; there is no trace of such a disaster in English sources, and ladies would have been unlikely to have set out on what was clearly a war expedition rather than a pleasure trip.

French sources include a full list of the ships in the French fleet; apart from the French royal ships, mainly galleys, and the three Genoese galleys already mentioned, these came exclusively from French ports along the Channel coast. There is no trace of the Castilian ships often said to have been present. A hero in one French chronicle is a Norman knight, as strong as a giant, who with eight companions held out in the castle of a French barge and was not finally overwhelmed until a hundred English dead lay at his feet. Towards evening a squadron from Dieppe, including royal galleys, fled from the disaster that had overtaken the French fleet, pursued by John Crabbe, a Flem-

Above: A late fourteenth century French raid on the Kent coast.

ing supporting the English. In his letter, Edward refers to this escape but hints that few of this squadron reached their home ports in safety.

We can be certain that the fighting would have consisted largely of a bitter struggle, hand-to-hand on the decks of ships grappled together with hooks and iron chains. The mastheads were equipped with fighting tops or castles from which a variety of missiles would have been hurled to the decks beneath. Where possible both sides would have used archers – crossbowmen for the French, longbowmen for the English – but their effectiveness may have been limited once opposing vessels had grappled each other.

After the battle the English royal ships put into Sluys; the *George, Cog Thomas, Message, Philip, Robinet, Margaret Spinace,* and *Barge d' Abbeville* (probably a galley despite her name), waited there for orders and arrangements were made to pay the crews. The King himself had also landed and was soon involved in an inconclusive but expensive advance to Tournai. By 25 September, only three months after this crushing

victory at sea, Edward and Philip had concluded a truce. What, then, were the effects of this battle? Did it give Edward 'command of the sea' or, more modestly, 'of the Channel'? It is hard to maintain that such concepts had any validity at this period. French raids did not entirely cease after Sluys, and coastal defence depended as much on stout walls and well-prepared defenders on shore as upon ships at sea. Allmand states categorically in *The Hundred Years War* that 'although [the victory] broke the threat of a possible French invasion of England, the victory in itself brought little immediate advantage to the English'. It is hard to disagree with this verdict, but one should not forget the image on the *noble* with which we began. Sluys may not have achieved a great deal in itself, but it decisively associated the image of national glory and military success with victory at sea – something that did have importance for the future.

BIBLIOGRAPHY

Fowler, K. (ed), *The Hundred Years War*, London, 1971. A collection of essays that includes Colin Richmond's The War at Sea, the best easily accessible account of the naval aspects of the war.

Allmand, C., *The Hundred Years War*, Cambridge, 1988. Includes a very useful discussion of the naval objectives pursued by English sovereigns.

Sumption, J. *The Hundred Years War*, vol I, *Trial by Battle*, London, 1990. A new narrative with a vigorous description of Sluys closely following chronicle sources.

Hewitt, J., *The Organisation of War under Edward III*, Manchester, 1966. Invaluable on the logistics of fourteenth-century warfare at sea as well as on land.

Froissart, J. *Chronicles*, edited by G. Brereton, Harmondsworth, 1968. The best known of the contemporary chronicles in an accurate but fluent translation.

Hattendorf, J. B., et al, *British Naval Documents 1204–1960*, Aldershot, 1993. Includes a translation of Edward III's own account of the battle; the mediaeval section of this book allows one to form a good idea of the reality of the mediaeval navy of England.

LORD HOWARD: THE ARMADA, 1588

by Colin Martin

'There must be a beginning of any great matter,
but the continuing unto the end until it be
thoroughly finished yields the true glory.'
Sir Francis Drake, 1587

'Some made little account of the Spanish force by sea, but I do warrant you, all the world never saw such a force as theirs was.' So wrote Charles, Lord Howard of Effingham, Lord Admiral of England, on 7 August 1588. The enormity of the threat posed by Philip II of Spain's task force, which attempted to invade England that year, was not underestimated by contemporary naval commanders. Lord Admiral Howard's sober assessment of that threat was echoed by his senior subordinates. 'This [the Armada] is the greatest and strongest combination, to my understanding, that ever was gathered in Christendom', wrote John Hawkins from his flagship Victory, when her guns were barely cool after the final encounter off Gravelines. A few days later, Francis Drake reminded Elizabeth's ministers that even with the Armada scattered into the northern seas the threat was by no means past, for the Duke of Parma's invasion troops still lay on the Flemish coast, poised to embark for England. 'Being so great a soldier as he is', wrote Drake, 'he will presently, if he may, undertake some great matter... my poor opinion is that we should have a great eye unto him.' The comfortable legends of Spanish incompetence, crassness and inevitable defeat, spawned in the euphoria of deliverance and carried forward by popular perception ever since, are not borne out by informed naval opinion of the day. The Armada was a force to be reckoned with. Had circumstances been only slightly different, it might even have succeeded.

The Spanish invasion plan was rooted in traditions of amphibious warfare that had their origins in the Mediterranean. Here the galley reigned supreme, and it functioned as an extension of terrestrial military operations. Its primary role was to seize and hold bases, so expanding the zones of latent striking power through which states exercised their authority. Even the rare full-scale galley engagements, such as Lepanto in 1571, had this underlying goal and employed formation tactics akin to those of armies on land. Galley warfare was thus highly structured, dependent on good and sustained logistical support, and primarily the preserve of military men. Within the confines of the Mediterranean, and the struggle for domination between Christianity and Islam, it was highly effective.

In 1580, Spain's annexation of Portugal brought this kind of amphibious warfare into the Atlantic. At first it was extremely successful. Lisbon was seized with a textbook assault by an army supported on its flank by galleys. Leading the galley force was Don Alvaro de Bazan, Marquis of Santa Cruz, who a decade earlier had commanded the Christian reserve at Lepanto. His experience and competence in the conduct of such operations was immense. Three years later, from the secure Atlantic base of Lisbon, he mounted an invasion of Terceira in the Azores, the final core of Portuguese resistance. His strategy was simple but effective. He assessed the strength of the Terceiran garrison, calculated the number of troops and supporting services he would need to overwhelm it, and organised a task force to take it there. This force, which consisted of sailing ships as well as galleys, was arranged so that its component parts could provide mutual support without breaking formation or becoming deflected from their purpose. When the landing zone was reached, the troops stormed ashore, with the galleys engaging coastal targets and landing heavy artillery by backing directly on to the beaches. Deployed in fully supported formations, the troops quickly seized their assigned objectives and Terceira fell.

These successes, reinforced by a growing belief that it was God's purpose to bring Elizabeth and her people back to the Catholic fold, prompted Philip II to consider a similar operation against England. He had more worldly motives for such an enterprise, too. English support for the Dutch revolt was becoming ever more blatant and extensive, while increasing (and to his eyes illegal) activity by English seafarers in the New World had become intolerable. Accordingly, in 1586, he directed the Marquis of Santa Cruz to draw up a plan for the invasion of England. Santa Cruz's response was swift and predictable: he proposed a self-contained amphibious operation on the Terceira model, expanded to match the magnitude of the new task: 55,000 troops, he reckoned, would be needed to mount a *blitzkrieg* assault on London from a beachhead somewhere in east Kent. Nearly 80,000 tons of shipping would be required to get them there, and the task force would be supported by 40 galleys, six galleasses and 200 landing craft. A heavy siege train of 48 battery cannons would be put ashore to take out the relatively weak static defences – most of them built a generation earlier by Henry VIII – during the advance to London. The overwhelming virtue of the plan was its simplicity. If the logistics of assembling such a force could be overcome, no complex tactics would need to be employed. It would simply make its ponderous way to its objective, rolling over any oppo-

Right: The *Ark Royal*, the first warship to bear the name, was the English Admiral's Flagship.

sition whether that opposition came from land or sea.

Santa Cruz's plan might well have worked, but he was not allowed to put it into effect. Philip II had also consulted his nephew, the Duke of Parma, who commanded the formidable Army of Flanders in the Low Countries, as to how England might be invaded. Parma's plan was quite different from that proposed by Santa Cruz, but potentially just as viable. It depended entirely on speed and secrecy. If sufficient troops could be mobilised along the Channel coast, and barges mustered in the network of canals and waterways just behind them, the whole force could slip out past the blockading squadrons of Dutch and English warships and be in England within a matter of hours. Parma's veterans, once ashore, would certainly have made short work of any resistance Elizabeth's ramshackle land forces might have put up.

Both plans were good ones, on their own terms. It was the misfortune of the two commanders that Philip II decided to combine their two proposals in a single operation. A reduced Armada would sail from Lisbon, carrying the supplies, support equipment, and second-wave troops necessary to back up a direct assault from Flanders. The two forces would rendezvous off the Flemish coast, and the Armada's ships would ensure the localised sea supremacy necessary to escort Parma's invasion barges across the Channel. Parma and Santa Cruz were outraged by the King's plan, and told him so in forthright terms. They pointed out that an operation that depended upon the pre-

cise synchronisation of two large forces mustering a thousand miles apart without effective communication was military lunacy, especially when the rendezvous was in shallows dominated by Dutch inshore squadrons and the narrow part of the Channel was the focus of England's naval defence. With courteous reasonableness, but absolute authority, Philip rejected his subordinates' pleas: the operation was in God's cause, and He would ensure that all difficulties would be overcome. The combined operation would proceed as the King directed.

Therein lay the seeds of the Armada's failure. In January 1588, Santa Cruz, worn out by the burden of organising an operation he knew would fail, died at Lisbon. The Armada had already suffered many delays. Problems with shipping, supplies and, most of all, the health of the mustering soldiery, led to a cycle of attrition that was constantly eroding the fleet's hard-won resources. With its formidable commander gone, it seemed that the Armada's logistical base, and the morale of its participants, were in terminal decline. But all Europe knew of the preparations and the delays, and the King's prestige demanded that the fleet must sail, whatever the cost.

Philip now made his only sensible move in the whole unhappy affair. He appointed a landsman, the Duke of Medina Sidonia, to the command of the Armada. Though denigrated by many historians, Medina Sidonia was an inspired choice. First, he was Spain's senior nobleman, so none of the socially sen-

Above: The victor against the Armada, Lord Howard of Effingham.

Below: After many delays the Spanish fleet set sail from Ferrol, 12 July 1588.

sitive squadron commanders could object to serving under him. More to the point, he was a top-line administrator, versed in running his own enormous estates in Andalusia and in organising the trans-atlantic fleets to Spain's possessions in the New World. Perhaps most important of all, he possessed that forceful but friendly and approachable disposition that inspires teamwork (Eisenhower being a good modern parallel). For all his apparent inexperience, moreover, the test of battle was to prove his competence as a commander – not to mention his physical courage – to the full.

In the three months that elapsed between his appointment and the fleet's sailing in the middle of May, the Armada was transformed. The state of its ships and provisions were improved beyond measure, and the once-abysmal morale of its men was replaced (or so, at least, it seemed) by a pious fervour to sail. On 18 May the Armada warped out of Lisbon and the 'Enterprise of England' was under way. In a muster held a few days earlier, 130 ships were listed, totalling some 60,000 tons. They carried about 30,000 men, two-thirds of whom were soldiers. There were 2,431 guns aboard, including a siege train to support Parma's march on London, together with provisions and munitions for a three-month campaign.

Contrary weather scattered the fleet off Corunna,

THE ARMADA

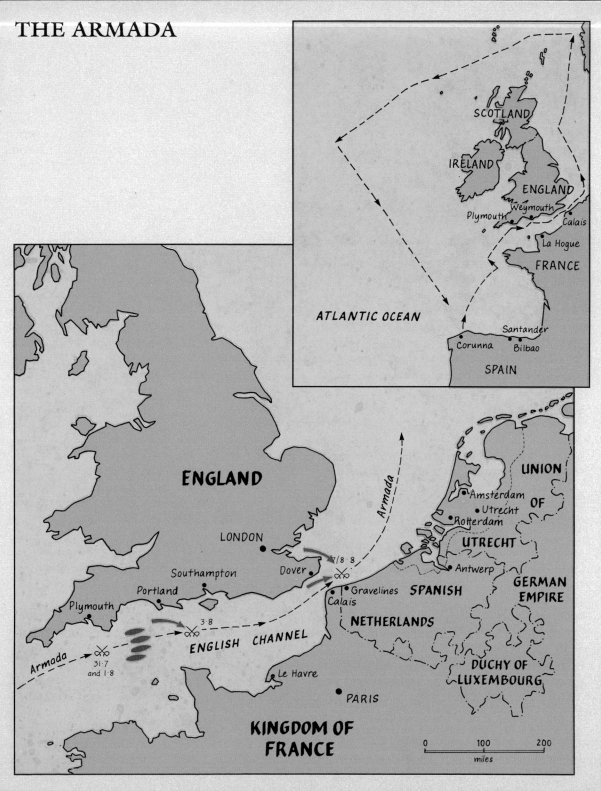

Left: The English fleet engages the Spanish fleet for the first time and disrupts the Spanish formation

and its regrouping in that port caused further delay. But Medina Sidonia put the time to good use in strengthening and replenishing his force, and when it sailed for the Channel on 10 July it was at a high state of operational efficiency. Even so, Medina Sidonia knew as well as his predecessor that the enterprise was probably destined to fail, and he had written to the King urging him to call the whole thing off. Philip's response was courteous but firm: at all costs the Armada must sail for England.

Off Plymouth, Medina Sidonia arrayed his force in battle order. The fleet formation was based on the precedents of galley warfare, with their strong military undertones. Its core was the main battle, headed by four galleasses and a force of strong warships, including Medina Sidonia's flagship, *San Martin*. Another group of fighting ships under Don Pedro de Valdes brought up the rear. Herded between these two groups were the bulk of the supply ships and heavy transports. To the main battle's left was the vanguard under Don Alonso de Leiva, strung out like an extended wing; to its right was Juan Martinez de Recalde's rearguard, similarly arrayed. Thus ordered, the fleet prepared for its advance up-Channel towards the rendezvous with Parma.

The Armada's defensive strategy was brilliantly simple and effective. Since the fleet's purpose was to reach an objective rather than bring an opposing fleet to battle, it was essential that its progress should not be impeded or its cohesion lost. The primary duty of each ship was therefore to keep to its appointed station on the flagship – failure on any captain's part to do so was a capital offence. However, discretion to act on their own initiative was given to a small group of powerful and nobly-officered ships, no more than twenty in number, which were dispersed throughout the formation. Any attack on the formation as a whole would therefore draw an immediate response from these 'troubleshooters', which would move from their allotted stations to deal with it. The remainder would plod on as before, leaving gaps to which the troubleshooters would return when the action was over. The system was self-regulating and required no coordinating command structure once the order to advance had been given.

That part of the English fleet, under Lord Admiral Howard and Sir Francis Drake, which first encountered the Armada off Plymouth could see no obvious way of breaking the Spanish formation or deflecting its progress. 'We durst not adventure to put in amongst them', wrote the Lord Admiral, 'their fleet being so strong.' Henry White, captain of the auxiliary warship *Bark Talbot*, expressed himself more bluntly: 'The majesty of the enemy's fleet, the good order they held, and the private consideration of our own wants did cause, in mine opinion, our first onset to be more coldly done than became the value of our nation and the credit of the English navy...' These are harsh words, and perhaps not entirely justified. In truth, there was a tactical stalemate between the two sides. The Spanish ships were essentially floating fortresses, packed with troops, designed to prevail in close-quarter boarding engagements. Since the time of Henry VIII, however, the English had moved away from this concept, and had developed their warships as gun-platforms which sought to exploit fine sailing characteristics to bring artillery to bear at ranges beyond the threat of boarding by clumsier troop-car-

Right: The giant *Nuestra Señora del Rosario* was bombarded into submission by the *Revenge*, captained by Drake, and Don Pedro de Valdez was taken prisoner. The Spanish fleet regained formation and left the huge warship to her fate.

rying adversaries. The problem was that at such ranges smooth-bore artillery was incapable of inflicting serious damage on a wooden hull. All the Spaniards had to do was grit their teeth, stoically accept the long-range fire, and maintain progress towards their objective.

One factor above all deterred the English from closing to effective range. The Spaniards, it seemed, carried a heavy armament themselves, and some of their guns were certainly extremely large. If an Englishman approached too close he might expect to be disabled by the short-range Spanish artillery, after which he would be easy meat for boarding by the Spanish troops with their short pikes, firearms and specialist incendiary weapons. This perhaps explains why the first English attacks were 'more coldly done' than the fire-eating Henry White thought proper.

In fact the English knew remarkably little about their enemy and how he intended to fight. It was the acquisition of this information that lay at the heart of their subsequent response, and the Armada's downfall. The key figure is Drake. It was he who, a few years earlier, had cut through the archaic and divisive social distinctions that had previously dogged command at sea: a ship's complement, he said, must 'all be of a company' and must work under the unified command of a single sea captain. This attitude certainly prevailed on the Queen's ships in 1588. Equally certainly, it did not prevail aboard the ships of the Armada. Early in the seventeenth century an Englishman could still write of the Spanish that they had 'more officers in their ships than we... This breeds a great confusion, and is many times the cause of mutiny among them.'

Most of the actions that took place as the rival fleets moved eastwards through the Channel were desultory skirmishes. The Armada kept steadfastly to its advance towards the rendezvous with Parma. Howard's ships kept to windward, uncertain yet of how they might halt the Spanish advance. But the skirmishes produced vital information for the English. Most important, perhaps, was Drake's controversial capture of the Andalusian flagship, *Nuestra Senora del Rosario* – his brother-officers, rightly, accused him of being after her treasure – and his subsequent conversations with her embittered commander, Don Pedro de Valdes. This gave England's foremost seaman a chance to see at first hand the operational realities of a front-line Armada unit, and to recognise that its artillery, though superficially formidable, was not designed for sustained action in a mobile fight. The Spanish guns, like those aboard a galley, were preloaded for a crippling close-range salvo, which would be delivered seconds before a boarding assault; neither their ponderous two-wheeled trailed carriages nor the soldiers who served them were suited to the skilled and arduous business of working guns in action.

But the English sea-gunners were. At least as early as 1545 (the wreck of the *Mary Rose* having provided examples of them) English naval guns were mounted on compact four-wheeled truck carriages, which could be worked time and again within the cramped area of a ship's deck. So long as they avoided actual contact with a Spanish ship, the English realised, they could deliver repeated broadsides at as close a range as they liked. They had little to fear from the virtually ineffectual Spanish guns.

Above: Open decks were typical of the galleons used by English against the Armada.

Their ammunition stocks, however, were perilously low, and Howard (advised, no doubt, by Drake) wisely decided to conserve them until they could be used most effectively. His chance came when the Armada, still uncertain about the precise location or state of readiness of Parma's task force, anchored off Calais. It was a classic opportunity for fireships, and the English seized it. For once, Spanish discipline broke, and most of the Armada scattered. But Medina Sidonia and his loyal troubleshooters stood firm, forming a line to face the oncoming English attack. A providential change of wind saved the Armada from destruction on the Flemish Banks, but off Gravelines it received the full force of a close-range English artillery assault. Nevertheless Medina Sidonia managed to regroup his scattered force and formed a protective rearguard to cover its retreat. Individual units of the Armada received serious damage and casualties, but the fleet as a whole remained unbroken to the end. The Spaniards, wrote a contemporary, Emanuel van Meteran, 'had many great vantages of the English,

namely the extraordinary bigness of their ships, and also for that they were so nearly conjoined, and kept together in so good array, that they could by no means be fought withall one to one.' It is a worthy epitaph.

After Gravelines the English had no further capacity to engage the Armada, because they had expended all their ammunition and could neither attack nor defend themselves against any further Spanish assault. Had the Armada been a self-contained assault force, as Santa Cruz had intended, it is difficult to see what could now have prevented a successful invasion. But without Parma's troops the Spanish fleet was impotent. It had no option but return home. So it was unseasonable weather off the Scottish and Irish coasts, not the English, that turned Philip II's great enterprise from failure to disaster.

Right: The *Ark Royal* engaged in combat with the *San Martin*.

Below: The refreshed English men-of-war renew the assaualt off Gravelines, 30 July 1588.

Above: Sir William Wynter's squadron attacks the Spanish ships.

Below: A Local tradition states that one of the Armada ships was wrecked on the rocks at Collieston, Aberdeenshire, some of the survivors settling in the region and marrying local women.

Yet the event was not without significance to England as a burgeoning sea power. The great amphibious task forces that had conditioned naval warfare for centuries (though they would be seen again in such operations as Normandy and the Falklands) had been replaced by that formidable combination – the sailing ship and the broadside gun – which would dominate England's global destiny for the next 250 years.

BIBLIOGRAPHY

Laughton, J. K., *State Papers Relating to the Defeat of the Spanish Armada, 1588*, London 1895.

Martin, Colin, and Geoffrey Parker, *The Spanish Armada*, London 1988. New account based on a re-examination of documentary sources and the archaeological investigation of Armada shipwrecks.

Thompson, I. A. A., 'Spanish Armada Guns' in *Mariner's Mirror*, no 61, 1975. An assessment based on Spanish sources of the Armada's gun strength, which entirely succeeds Michael Lewis's *Armada Guns* (London, 1961).

Thompson, I. A. A., 'The Appointment of the Duke of Medina Sidonia to the Command of the Spanish Armada' in *Historical Journal*, no 12, 1969.

BLAKE:
SANTA CRUZ, 1657

by J. D. Davies

'The advantage of time and place in all martial actions
is half a victory, which being lost is irrecoverable.'
Sir Francis Drake, 1588

'A signal victory, and which is here considered the greatest which they have had against the Spaniards since that of 1588 in the time of Queen Elizabeth...' This assessment of the battle of Santa Cruz by the Venetian ambassador at Oliver Cromwell's court indicates the significance contemporaries assigned to Robert Blake's greatest victory. To the leaders and propagandists of the English republic, it was evidence that God's providence, after carrying them through such great land battles as Naseby and Worcester, had not deserted the 'good old cause' and its adherents. In Europe, the victory was further proof that the military and naval machine created during and after the Civil War had elevated England to the status of a feared enemy and a desirable ally; and the direct effects of the battle on Spain itself had significant (perhaps even decisive) consequences for at least two land campaigns far from the Canary Islands.

At the time, Santa Cruz was a glorious victory, and a victory somehow made yet more memorable by the death of its perpetrator, Blake, at the very moment his ship entered Plymouth Sound on its return voyage. However, history has looked a little less kindly on the battle. Santa Cruz was not a spectacular fleet action on the high seas, but the destruction of a squadron of 'sitting ducks' at anchor in harbour (albeit a particularly heavily defended one); it was not the stuff of an abiding legend to stand alongside those created by the great victories of the eighteenth century. Above all, even contemporaries quickly felt the nagging doubt that it was not as great a victory as it could have been. Blake's objective had been the holy grail of English and Dutch admirals of the seventeenth century – the capture of the Spanish bullion fleet from the New World. He destroyed the fleet, but the bullion eluded him: he was the robber who had broken into the most secure of banks, only to find the vault empty.

England had been at war with Spain, both officially and unofficially, since 1654, when Cromwell had launched his 'western design' against the Spanish colonies in the Caribbean. From the beginning, the idea of capturing the Spanish *flota* as it transported its bullion back to Castile was a central element of English naval strategy. In addition to seriously impeding Spain's military operations throughout Europe, the capture of the bullion would shore up the republican government's shaky finances, enabling it to pay for the large armies and fleets it needed to project its power abroad and, above all, to defend it from the exiled royalists and their foreign allies.

In March 1656, Robert Blake, the 57-year-old 'general-at-sea' who had triumphed over the Dutch at the battle of the Gabbard two years before, sailed from England with 37 ships to conduct operations off the coast of Spain and in the Mediterranean. On the whole, the following twelve months were frustratingly unsuccessful for Blake: the Spanish refused to engage him, although his rear admiral, Richard Stayner, did capture two large galleons from a returning *flota* in September. In an unprecedented departure from established practice, Blake kept many of his ships on station off the Spanish coast through the winter of 1656/7 waiting for news of the approach of the next *flota* and unintentionally creating a model of blockade tactics for later admirals. The very existence of Blake's blockade forced the Spanish to vary their own tactics

Right: A portrait of Blake as at the time of his victory at Santa Cruz.

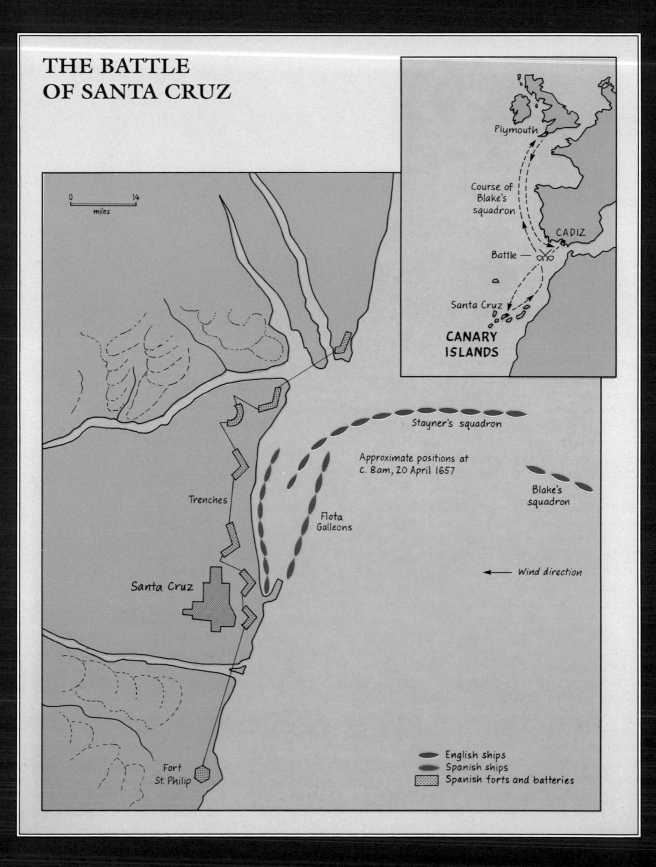

THE BATTLE
OF SANTA CRUZ

0   ¼
miles

Plymouth

Course of
Blake's
squadron

CADIZ

Battle

Santa Cruz

**CANARY
ISLANDS**

Stayner's squadron

Approximate positions at
c. 8am, 20 April 1657

Blake's
squadron

Trenches

Flota
Galleons

Wind direction

Santa Cruz

Fort
St. Philip

English ships
Spanish ships
Spanish forts and batteries

for bringing the *flota* home. Their eleven ships put in to Santa Cruz on the Canary Island of Tenerife, waiting for the English to abandon the blockade or else (as Blake feared, and the Spanish hoped) for an obliging neutral Dutch squadron under Michel de Ruyter to escort the *flota* on the last leg of its voyage. By 12 April 1657, Blake knew for certain where the Spanish were. Without dividing his fleet, and thereby taking the (justified) gamble that the Spanish main fleet would not be able to get out of Cadiz quickly enough in his absence, Blake sailed for the Canaries two days later.

By 18 April the English fleet was off Tenerife, appearing off Santa Cruz on the following day. Tactical disagreements that had plagued the fleet's councils of war throughout the preceding months now came to a head, with Blake and his captains having such a violent disagreement on the 18th that the latter refused to speak to him at all for much of the council on the morning of the 20th. In this rather unpromising atmosphere, the final plan was made. Stayner with twelve ships would enter the bay and attack the moored *flota*, with Blake and the remaining ships staying slightly farther out. Despite the immobility of the enemy, the odds against an English success were considerable. The bay of Santa Cruz was ringed with forts and batteries, some of them recent additions in anticipation of just such an attack, within range of which all the Spanish ships were moored. The *flota*'s formation was in itself a major obstacle, with the larger ships moored to seaward of the smaller ones, their broadsides confronting the English. Moreover, the winds in the bay were unpredictable and often contrary: on 20 April the attacking ships would be carried into the bay on an east wind, but that same wind would make it difficult for the English to withdraw in safety. Despite all these potential dangers, Richard Stayner and the *Speaker* led the line of ships into the harbour of Santa Cruz between 0700 and 0800.

Fortunately for Stayner and Blake, the Spanish had negated some of their own advantages by mooring their ships between the English and many of their own batteries, which could not fire directly on the attacking force as a result. Therefore, Stayner was able to executive relatively unscathed Blake's order for the ships to anchor between the two lines of Spanish vessels, not firing until they had come to their preordained positions. Between 0900 and 1100, the English systematically eliminated resistance from the

inner line of smaller vessels and then turned their attention to the outer line of seven larger galleons. At some point between 1100 and 1200, Blake and the second English line came into the bay, and within the next hour the ships of both the Spanish admiral and vice admiral blew up. Boarding parties from the English vessels fired other ships of the doomed *flota*, which had been lashed together at their moorings, thereby accelerating their fate. By not longer after one that afternoon, the entire Spanish force had been captured or destroyed, and almost all the forts had been abandoned under sustained and accurate fire from the attacking fleet. Blake's victory seemed complete. But it might have been short-lived – he now had to get his ships back to the open sea, despite both contrary winds and Spanish batteries which now (ironically) had a clearer line of fire over the remains of their sunken ships.

At this point, the discipline of the English fleet, which had contributed so much to the victory, threatened to break. Five ships had secured prizes, hoping to tow them out and earn prize money for them, but warping out against the wind would be hard enough even without such added encumbrances. Blake ordered all the prizes to be fired, and, although he had to reiterate the command three times, his reluctant captains eventually complied. Through the rest of the afternoon the fleet struggled to clear the bay, constantly under fire from the re-garrisoned forts. Stayner's ship, the *Speaker*, was in the worst state, with all her masts badly damaged and with holes of up to twenty square feet in her sides; the crew only saved her from sinking by nailing leather hides over them. The *Swiftsure* took the *Speaker* in tow but cut the cable under heavy fire from the shore, leaving Stayner's battered command to face the bombardment alone. The *Speaker* sur-vived until dusk, when the wind changed to blow off-shore, and she limped out of harbour, only just getting to the open sea before all three of her masts

Left: Sir Richard Stayner.

Below: The attack on the Spanish ships at Santa Cruz.

collapsed. The *Plymouth* took her in tow, bringing her safely back to the fleet.

The proportions of the English victory were aston-ishing. Only sixty of Blake's men died, a quarter of them on the *Speaker*, and a further 140 (at most) were wounded. No English ships were lost, despite the pounding some of them had suffered – a tribute, per-haps, to the quality of the republic's shipbuilders. (The *Speaker*, for instance, had been built by Christopher Pett at Woolwich in 1649. Renamed *Mary* after the Restoration, she saw further punishing action in one French and two Dutch wars before perishing on the Goodwins in the 'Great Storm' of 1703.) On the Span-ish side, all sixteen vessels in the harbour of Santa Cruz, including the seven great galleons of the New World *flota*, had been destroyed. Moreover, Blake and Stayn-er had brought off an attack on a heavily defended har-bour despite adverse winds, creating a lesson that both inspired and daunted later commanders assigned simi-lar tasks – including Nelson himself, who was to attack Santa Cruz 139 years later. Not surprisingly, then, a republican government with a religious ideology founded on providentialism took the battle to its heart as nothing short of a miracle. John Weale, an officer in Blake's fleet, said of Santa Cruz that 'it behoveth us to return the Great God of Heaven and Earth thanks for such deliverance as these, and to sing abroad unto his Holy Name'. The official newspaper, *Mercurius Politi-cus*, exalted Blake's triumph in equally ringing terms: 'To the Great Jehovah be ascribed all praise, and thank-ful acknowledgements for so great a mercy vouchsafed to the English nation.' Parliament responded enthusi-astically, setting aside 3 June 1657 as a day of thanks-giving for 'God's marvellous goodness'. But the goodness was not as beneficent as it could have been. The Spanish had landed the bullion from the *flota* well before Blake attacked, hiding it far inland. There would be no windfall to mend the republic's broken finances, and the state's debts continued to mount inexorably.

However, any feeling of disappointment in England was more than outweighed by the disaster that befell Spain, and it is in this regard that the true significance of Blake's victory must be recognised. With no other means of shipping it home (even if any attempt to do so would not have meant running an English gaunt-let), the bullion on which Spain's finances depended remained on Tenerife. The offensive in Portugal, which had been threatening to destroy that state's fledgling independence from Spain, ground to a halt when the army deserted *en masse*, and the government

Left: Blake's *St George* at the Battle of Santa Cruz.

of Philip IV never had such an opportunity again, Spain eventually and reluctantly recognising Portugal's independence in 1667. The Spanish army in Flanders was seriously weakened by the lack of money and was decisively defeated at the battle of the Dunes in 1658 by a French army reinforced by several thousand English troops. In 1659, unable to sustain such an expensive war and in the forlorn hope of being able to concentrate all her resources on reconquering Portugal, Spain came to terms with France at the Peace of the Pyrenees. Although the battle of Santa Cruz was not the only, or even the most important, factor in determining all these events, there is no doubt that it played its part in ensuring that Spain's golden age as a world power was over.

On 10 June 1657, Oliver Cromwell wrote to congratulate Robert Blake on his victory. 'The mercy therein to us and this Commonwealth', he wrote, 'is very signal; both in the loss the enemy received, as also in the preservation of our own ships and men.' The victory, he believed, could be attributed only to the continued 'goodness and loving kindness of the Lord', as had been shown to them throughout the Civil Wars, and therefore they should continue to depend on Him. Cromwell's words suggest at least the possibility that Santa Cruz might have had one further consequence. When news of the triumph arrived in England, the Lord Protector was contemplating the offer of the crown, made to him by Parliament on 31 March. Cromwell debated the pros and cons of the offer for weeks and at several points seemed about to accept, but eventually, on 8 May, he rejected it. When he explained his reasons to Parliament, one of the chief of them was that 'the Providence of God hath laid aside this title of King'. Perhaps, as Cromwell suggested to Blake, Santa Cruz had proved that God had not abandoned His cause after all; and so neither would Oliver Cromwell.

BIBLIOGRAPHY

Firth, Sir C. (ed), 'Richard Stayner's Account of the Battle of Teneriffe' in *The Naval Miscellany*, ii, Navy Records Society, vol 40, 1910. A contemporary account of the battle.
Powell, J. R. (ed), 'Letters of Robert Blake', Navy Records Society, vol 76, 1937.
Powell, J. R. (ed), 'The Journal of John Weale' in *The Naval Miscellany*, iv, Navy Records Society, vol 92, 1952.
Powell, J. R., *Robert Blake, General-at-Sea*, London 1972.

The standard biography, which has been amended but not entirely replaced by M. Baumber, *General-at-Sea: Robert Blake and the Seventeenth Century Revolution in Naval Warfare*, London, 1989.
Capp, B., *Cromwell's Navy: The Fleet and the English Revolution 1648–60*, Oxford, 1989. A concise account of the operations of Blake's fleet and a comprehensive study of the nature of the navy in which he served.

MONCK:
ST. JAMES'S DAY FIGHT, 1666

by Peter Le Fevre

'If a man faint under the burden of such tediousness as usually attendeth upon warlike designments, he is in no way fit for enterprise;'
George Monck, Duke of Albemarle, 1608–70

England declared war on Holland in 1665, partly for economic reasons, partly because of a factional struggle in Charles II's court and partly because of political ideology. The first naval engagement fought after the declaration of war, the battle of Lowestoft in June 1665, was a clear victory for the English. This gave the English fleet control of the sea, and they were quick to capitalise on it by capturing a homeward bound Dutch merchant fleet. Despite some later reverses, 1665 still ended on a high note.

In the following year, 1666, the command of the English fleet was shared by Prince Rupert, the dashing nephew of Charles II, and George Monck, (Duke of Albemarle since 1660), who had been responsible for engineering the restoration of Charles II to the English throne in 1660. Hearing that a French fleet commanded by the Duke of Beaufort was supposed to have been sighted sailing out of the Mediterranean, and believing it was intended to join the Dutch fleet under the command of the Dutch Admiral Michael De Ruyter, Rupert was ordered to sail to the westward to intercept them. Albemarle's scouts spotted the Dutch about 0600 on Friday 1 June 1666. 'Then began the most terrible, obstinate and bloodiest battle that ever was fought on the seas', the hard slogging 'Four Days Battle' of 1–4 June 1666. The English were defeated, losing 10 ships of the line and 6 fireships. The Dutch losses were 4 ships of the line and 5 fireships. The English defeat also led to recriminations, with Albemarle accusing officers of not supporting him and demanding their removal. He ignored criticisms that he should not have fought with inferior numbers.

Over the next few weeks the two sides worked feverishly to get to sea again. The Dutch won the race, De Ruyter leaving port with 59 ships on 25 June followed shortly afterwards by other Dutch ships. Delays caused by head-winds and storms meant, however, that he did not arrive off the English coast until 3 July. The English sailed on 22 July and anchored off Orfordness with the Dutch to the south-east of them. At 1600 on 24 July, the two fleets came in sight of each other.

The next day, 25 July – St. James's Day – the two fleets were 36 miles off Orfordness with the wind at NNE. The English had 89 ships of war, 23 of them new, while the Dutch had 88 ships, including 8 new ships of war. The English van (or White Squadron) was commanded by Sir Thomas Allin; the centre (or Red Squadron) by Rupert and Albemarle in the *Royal Charles*, while the rear (or Blue Squadron) was under the command of Sir Jeremy Smith. The Dutch van was led by the Zealand admiral John Evertsen; De Ruyter commanded the centre; while the rear was under Cornelius Tromp. The Dutch line was badly formed; their rear and van were to windward of their centre and drawn into a half-moon shape, possibly to avoid the English fireships – possibly (so the English thought) to try and weather a large part of the English fleet by the Dutch van or rear.

Jeremy Roch on the *Cambridge* wrote when he saw the Dutch, 'Here was a glorious prospect of 2 fleets, drawn up in such order as perhaps was never observed on the sea before, for here every ship fought single so that valour was not oppressed, nor could cowards well avoid fighting. The English shouted for joy that they had... the opportunity to try it out with the Hogens [the Dutch] on equal terms.'

The battle began about 0930 when the Dutch fired at the leading English ships. Half an hour later the English 'flag of defiance was then spread and we all bore in'. Some of Allin's captains never managed to get into the line and fired over their own ships. Sir

MICHIEL DE RUYTER L. ADMIRAEL GENERAEL etc.

Thomas Teddiman, the vice admiral of the English White in the *Royal Catherine*, was the first ship fired at by the Dutch. The two van squadrons engaged each other so closely that by 1300 the English had disabled two of the Dutch flags so badly that one of them, which had her main topsail yard shot to pieces, bore away accompanied by five Dutch ships intending to render assistance. Evertsen died about the same time, and his death caused his flagship to run into five others. About 1500, the Dutch van bore away and fled back towards their coast followed by Allin's squadron 'so close upon the rear' that the Dutch could only fire their stern guns.

The two centre squadrons meanwhile engaged at 1100. Rupert and Albemarle in the *Royal Charles* made towards De Ruyter in the *Zeven Provincien*. As De Ruyter fired at them, Albemarle ('chewing of tobacco the while') said, 'Now will this fellow come and give me two broadsides, and then he will run'. Soon afterwards the two English admirals fired their first broadsides at De Ruyter and continued firing 'without intermission' as they edged closer and closer

Right: Prince Rupert enjoyed a sea going career first as a corsair during the English Civil War and then as an Admiral after the Restoration.

Left: The Dutch Admiral De Ruyter has been compared to Nelson and ranks as one of the great admirals in history. His leadership marked a new era in fighting at sea.

Left: The 1st Duke of Albermarle, George Monck 1608–1670. Portrait by Sir Peter Lely.

to each other. At last 'we came within half a musket shot or rather more' and fired small shot at each other for over half an hour. The *Royal Charles* was disabled in her yards, masts and rigging and about 1330 was 'forced to give out to repair which held us almost an hour'. At the same time Sir Robert Holmes, the rear admiral of the Red, in the *Henry*, pulled out of the line to replace his fore topmast, which had been shot away. After it was replaced, Holmes was so far away from the main body of the fleet that he joined the Blue Squadron.

The *Royal Charles* completed her repairs and 'bore in again' to De Ruyter. 'One in the ship saying to the Duke, "Sir, methinks De Ruyter hath given us more than two broadsides." "Well," says the Duke, "but you

shall find him run by and by".' The firing produced thick smoke, which enveloped the ships, and one of De Ruyter's fireships took the opportunity to try and burn the English ship. The design was stopped by an English fireship, which was in turn prevented from burning De Ruyter's ship. A sloop, the *Fan Fan* lying under the *Royal Charles*'s stern, made 'very bold sallies' on De Ruyter, 'by the continual firing' of her two small guns. (The *Fan Fan*'s part in De Ruyter's defeat was to inspire a song that included the lines: 'The Mermaids laughed and shouted/and still De Ruyter ran/his honour lost and routed/by the *Fan Fan*).

De Ruyter's main-topmast was shot down at 1500. Rupert called to the captain of the *Triumph* to board the disabled ship, but 'the gale being very small the

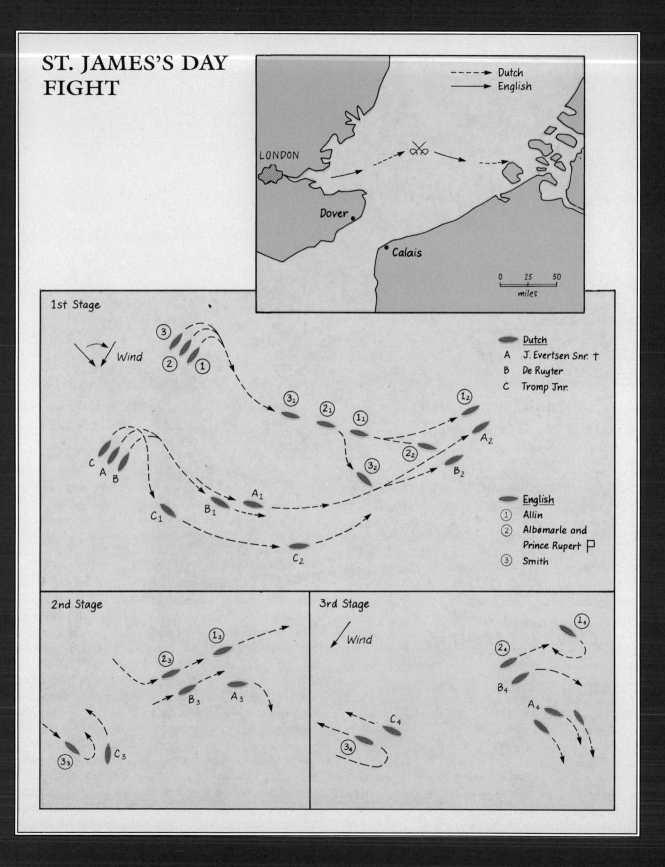

ST. JAMES'S DAY FIGHT

Dutch — — →
English ——→

LONDON

Dover

Calais

0   25   50
miles

1st Stage

Wind

③ ② ①

③₁ ②₁ ①₁ ①₂

③₂ ②₂ A₂

B₂

C A B

C₁ B₁ A₁

C₂

Dutch

A   J. Evertsen Snr. †
B   De Ruyter
C   Tromp Jnr.

English

①   Allin
②   Albemarle and
     Prince Rupert Ⳁ
③   Smith

2nd Stage

①₃

②₃

B₃   A₃

③₃   C₃

3rd Stage

Wind

①₄

②₄

B₄

A₄

C₄

③₄

A Representation of the Battell fought betweene the English Fleet, commanded by his H.ª Prince Rupert, and George Duke of Albemarl...

Above and right: Useful representations of the St. James' Day Fight. An idea of the extended line of ships firing straight at each other is clear from these illustrations and demonstrates visually how naval battles of this period were fought.

Triumph attempted it not'. Then the *Royal Charles* was engaged by De Ruyter's second, Van Gent in the *Gelderland*. When his fore-topmast was shot down he was forced to anchor. Shortly afterwards the Dutch ships began to bear away, ignoring De Ruyter's signal shots. Calling to Admiral Van Ness to come aboard, De Ruyter took him down to his cabin. During their conversation he told Van Ness, 'What is coming to us! I wish I were dead.' Van Ness replied, 'I wish the same for me, but one does not die when one wants to.' Their wish was nearly granted. Shortly after they left the cabin a cannon-ball destroyed the table where the two men had been sitting.

About 1600, De Ruyter gathered his seven remaining ships together and bore away, following his retreating van to the south-east. As the victorious English followed them, De Ruyter 'with great gallantry' endangered his life and ship to help his maimed ships. Seeing an English fireship approaching his disabled second, De Ruyter's boats towed a Dutch fireship, which cut off the similar English vessel. At the same time De Ruyter's second, 'like a hare', anchored, causing the English fireship to pass by. Then the Dutchman cut his anchor and joined the retreat, pursued by the English centre. At 1900 the English Red and White Squadrons joined together.

The Blue Squadron had got into action at midday. Tromp's squadron was slightly stronger than Smith's, whose ships, unlike the Dutch, were strung out at the end of the line. About 1400 the *Resolution* was burnt by a Dutch fireship and the captain and his crew were rescued by another English ship, while Sir John Kempthorne in the *Defiance* narrowly escaped being burnt by an English fireship! The *Loyal London*, Smith's flagship, was disabled and he was forced to have her towed away. Tromp also tacked and followed his prey, both squadrons sailing westerly away from the rest of the fleet. At 1800, Smith and his division were 'all in a smoke intermixted with the Dutch colours'.

The noise of the guns was heard in London all day, while in Bruges the houses and beds were reported to have been shaken by the cannons' thunder. The Dutch casualties were nearly 7,000, while the English losses were estimated to be as low as 300. The Dutch had five flag officers and several captains killed while the English lost only one. The slaughter was appalling:

'You might see the heads of some, the arms, legs or thighs of others shot off, and others... cut off by the

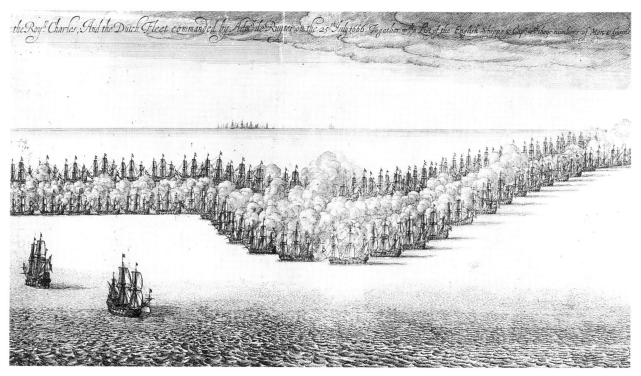

the Roy.ll Charles: And the Dutch Fleet commanded by Adm.ll de Ruyter on the 25.th July 1666. Together w.th the Rest of the English Shipps & Co.gr w.th their numbers of Men & Guns

middle with a chain-shot breathing out their last anguish and pain; some burning in ships fired, and others exposed to the mercy of the liquid Element, some of them sinking, whilst others who have learnt the art of swimming, lift up their heads above water, and implore pity from their very enemies, entreating them to save their lives.'

During the chase on 25 July, Allin captured a Dutch 66-gun ship, the *Snake*, which he burnt as he could not spare the men to bring her in, and continued the pursuit. Vice Admiral Banckert's flagship *Tholen* was boarded by Allin, but Banckert, leaving his officers and men behind, shifted his flag before the English arrived. Like the *Snake*, the ship was burnt.

The English continued their chase on 26 July, but no general action took place. Allin received three painful wounds in his arm and face from splinters when De Ruyter fired at him during the pursuit. The *Fan Fan* harried De Ruyter. Rowing up to the Dutch admiral, the *Fan Fan* 'brought her two little guns on one side' and for nearly an hour fired broadsides at him – 'which was so pleasant a sight when no ship of either side could come near' as there was very little wind. The *Fan Fun*'s behaviour provided amusement for the English, but enraged De Ruyter as he could not depress the *Zeven Provincien*'s guns low enough to fire at the sloop. Before dark the Dutch van and

centre got into Flushing. Tromp was still 30 miles away near the Galloper Sands. A series of mishaps and also confusion on Smith's part prevented the English capturing him, and Tromp joined De Ruyter on 27 July.

There were recriminations after the battle. De Ruyter accused Tromp of dereliction of duty, and in return Tromp accused De Ruyter of trying to shelter behind him and then deserting him. Each refused to serve with the other, and Tromp was dismissed. In England, Holmes blamed Smith for letting Tromp escape and also accused him of cowardice. Albemarle wrote to Charles about Smith, 'to clear a gallant man's reputation... I can assure Your Majesty that he had more men killed and hurt than in any of the fleet.' After investigating the matter, Charles II exonerated Smith.

Sir Robert Holmes rubbed salt into Dutch wounds on 8 August when he burnt the Dutch shipping lying in the Vlie. The English fleet was back in harbour on 15 August and sailed again on 28 August to prevent the Dutch linking up with the French. Despite spying each other, gales forced the two fleets to make for safe harbours.

Rejoicing in England over the victory did not last. Because of a money shortage, and the possibility of peace with the Dutch, the decision was taken not to

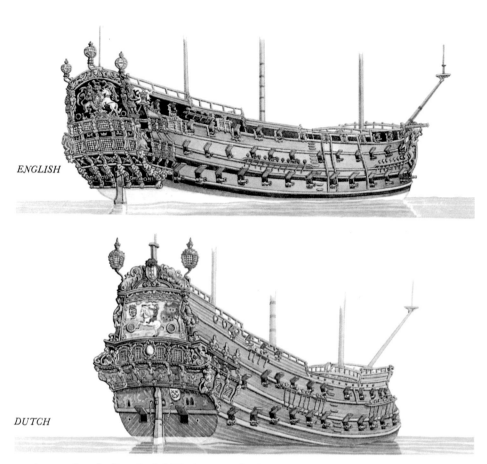

ENGLISH

DUTCH

Left: There was a distinct difference between warships of the rival navies at this time. The English stern (upper illustration) displays a rounded tuck below the gallery when compared to the Dutch ship (lower illustration).

send out a battle fleet in 1667. As a result, De Ruyter and 70 ships sailed up the River Medway on 10 June 1667, storming Sheerness, burning five ships in Chatham two days later and capturing the *Royal Charles*, Albemarle's flagship at the St. James's Day Fight. The Dutch fleet continued in the English Channel until 31 July 1667 when peace was signed at Breda.

BIBLIOGRAPHY

Anderson, R. C. (ed), 'Naval Operations in the Latter Part of the Year 1666' in *The Naval Miscellany*, III, Navy Records Society, 1928. An important account of the battle.

Anderson, R. C. (ed), *The Journal of Sir Thomas Allin, 1660–1678*, 2 vols, Navy Records Society, 1940. Includes a good account of the battle.
Boxer, C. R., *The Anglo-Dutch Wars of the 17th Century 1652–1674*, HMSO/National Maritime Museum, Greenwich, 1974. Excellent brief account of the three wars.
Holmes, Geoffrey, *The Making of a Great Power: Late Stuart and Early Georgian Britain 1660–1722*, 1993. Superb introduction to the period.
Padfield, P., *The Tide of Empires... 1654–1763*, 1982.
Pearsall, A. W. H. (ed), *The Second Dutch War Described in Pictures and Manuscripts of the Time*, HMSO/National Maritime Museum, Greenwich, 1966.

RUSSELL:
LA HOGUE, 1692

by David Aldridge

*'If it please God to send us a little clear weather
I doubt not but we shall destroy their whole fleet.'*
Edward Russell, 1692

On 20 May 1692, Edward Russell, Admiral of the Red, Privy Councillor, and Treasurer of the Navy, wrote as follows to the Earl of Portland, the Dutch-born intimate of William III: 'Cap Barfleur SW distant 7 leagues. Yesterday, about three in the morning, Cap Barfleur bearing SW and by S distant 7 leagues, my scouts made the signal for seeing the enemy the wind westerly, and the French bore down to me, and at II engaged me, but at some distance; they continued fighting till half an hour past 5 in the evening at which time the enemy [were] towed away [by] all their boats, and we after them. T'was calm all day. About 6 there was a fresh engagement to the westward of me which I supposed was the Blue [the other English division of the Allied fleet, the White being the Dutch in the van of Russell's line at the start of the action]. It continued calm all night. I can give no particular account of things but that the French were beaten, and I am now steering away for Conquet Road [the sheltered channel between Ushant and the Brest peninsula], having a fresh gale easterly but extreme foggy; I suppose it is the place they design for. If it please God to send us a little clear weather I doubt not but we shall destroy their whole fleet'.

Thus Russell, the Allied commander-in-chief, described the Barfleur fight between his Anglo-Dutch fleet of more than 90 ships and a French fleet of only 44, under the command of Anne Hilarion de Tourville. In point of ships of over 60 guns the odds were again heavily against the French, 64 to 42. The allies also had 25 fireships at their disposal. These would play a vital role off St Vaast–La Hogue on 23–4 May, when twelve of Tourville's ships, which had been beached for defence, and some 30 transports in the St Vaast harbour, were destroyed. However, at the time Russell wrote, no ships had been lost by either side, though a number had been dismasted and there had been heavy casualties. It was only the day afterwards, 21 May, that Tourville's battle-scarred former flagship *Soleil-Royal*, the pride of the French navy, together with *Triomphant* and *Admirable*, were burnt by English fireships at Cherbourg.

While the evidence in Russell's letter should naturally be respected – and it strikingly confirms the weather conditions, which critically affected the character and course of the battle – the information, or lack of it, that the Admiral conveyed to Portland calls for comment. To start with, the point has to be made that, while the Allied success over the French was undoubted by the time Russell wrote, he made no reference to any contribution the 26 Dutch ships in the van of his battle line might have made to the victory. This is the more extraordinary given Portland's prominence as a Dutch leader and the extent to which, off Beachy Head in July 1690, the Dutch squadron had suffered at Tourville's hands, sufferings which subsequently aroused grave disquiet in London and The Hague about the balance of the Anglo-Dutch naval partnership, and indeed contributed to the court-martialling of the then Allied commander, the Earl of Torrington. Whether or not Russell may be charged with obfuscation in this respect, there is in any case much in distinctness in the prelude to these two battles.

William III had plans to invade France in the early summer of 1692, perhaps through a thrust at St Malo. (It is worth remembering that for part of his exile Charles II had had an admiralty at Roscoff; and it was now known that certain of James II's Irish supporters were at St Malo.) These, however, were hardly more than a month old by the time of Barfleur. Complementarily, Louis XIV's plans to invade Britain through a landing in Torbay, though rather more advanced logistically (cavalry to be embarked at Le Havre, infantry at St Vaast) depended on substantial numbers of transports, and the Brest fleet being reinforced in good time from Rochefort and Toulon. Neither of these essential preliminaries had been achieved by mid-May. Yet Louis XIV, who after Beachy Head concluded that he was '*a présent maître de la Manche*', now chose to believe Jacobite reports of widespread disaffection towards William in the Royal Navy, and to disregard the unpredictability of Channel weather. Giving Tourville a month's notice, the King '*veut absolument*' that on 15 April Tourville should sail from Brest, whether or not he had been reinforced, and make his way to St Vaast–La Hogue. In the event, contrary winds prevented him clearing the Iroise out of Brest before 2 May, and it took Tourville 12 days to beat north-east as far as Plymouth, though he had been off Start Point on 8 May.

By 9 May it was known at Portsmouth, reached by the Anglo-Dutch fleet in favourable easterly winds three days later, that there was a French concentration at La Hogue, on the farther coast of the Cotentin peninsula from the Channel Islands, the French fleet's original supposed objective. Since there was no evidence of concentrations either at St Malo or at Le Havre, the threat posed at La Hogue seemed identifi-

Right: The battle of La Hogue.

able enough to the Allies, and Russell showed sound judgement in not diverting his fleet westward to engage Tourville off Portland but in steering for the Cotentin in the hope of intercepting the French while on passage for La Hogue.

Vauban, the great French military engineer, was confident that St Vaast–La Hogue had the potential for a strong naval base. By constructing locks, he intended making a virtue of the high 20ft tidal rise and fall, so creating basins in which warships could remain afloat and out of range of seaward gunnery at low tide, somewhat on the lines of what he had already carried out at Dunkirk. Unfortunately for the French, all that had been completed by 1692 were

Above: Admiral Edward Russell, hero of the Battle of La Hogue.

the fighting was continuously heavy until flat calm and fog descended at about 1600, by which time parts of the Dutch van under Almonde and the English centre under Shovell had broken the French line. About 1700, with some breeze now from the east and a clearing fog, the French line, which always kept remarkable order, moved westwards. At 1800, the up-Channel flood tide set in, and the French, having anchored, were able to inflict considerable damage on those Allied ships that had not moored and hence passed them eastwards on the tide. By 2200 there was moonlight and fighting had ceased.

The English had tried unsuccessfully to send fire-ships against Tourville's anchored ships, and by the early morning of 20 May, when Russell wrote to Portland, the French fleet was sailing west in thick fog, taking advantage of the ebb tide. The firing away to the west that Russell could hear was not Ashby's Blue division, which was somewhat east of him (Russell's bearing now was probably more N than NE of Cape Barfleur), but the Dutch van under Almonde, which was following Tourville.

During the night, with the wind continuing from the east, both fleets had sailed west on the ebb tide, but the fog Russell was reporting came down again early that morning, allowing the French, some ten miles to the westward, to keep out of sight. To a remarkable extent, Tourville kept his fleet together whereas the Allies, as a result of the pell-mell nature of the battle, were more scattered, making it difficult for commanders to determine their individual positions or to learn where Russell himself was. His letter to Portland shows that his intention was indeed to pursue Tourville all the way to Brest, but this was to be frustrated by weather and tide, and perhaps also by the distraction caused by those French ships that had become detached from the main body towards mid-Channel or towards the east. By noon on 20 May the wind had gone round to the west, and for the next twelve hours the fleets came to anchor within two miles of each other to effect temporary repairs. Both were under sail again by midnight, only to come to anchor again at 0400 on 21 May, with the flood tide and a strengthening westerly wind.

These conditions determined what now ensued: 21 French ships under Pannetier's command weathered Cap de la Hague and chanced the hazardous Race of Alderney to make good their way to St Malo. Some of Ashby's ships had the weather gage to the west and could have intercepted Pannetier before he reached St

two small batteries at Tatihou and St Vaast: beaching ships at high tide was the only way in which, apart from army artillery fire, they could be given fire-cover, for the angle at which a beached ship had to lie meant that only the lowest battery of guns could be brought to bear on an attacker.

The easterly winds that had critically permitted the Anglo-Dutch fleet to make an uneventful junction by 12 May had veered into the SW by daybreak on 18 May, and it was between W and SW when, on the following morning, Tourville's fleet from the west engaged Russell's line. This extended for over two miles on a NE–SW axis some twenty miles off Cape Barfleur. The vigour of Tourville's attack suggests he had hopes of immediate defections to his side among English commanders, but in fact what hanging back there was in the Allied line was owing to part of the Dutch van lying a little to the south of Tourville's, under Nesmond, while to the north the English rear under Ashby took the entire day to get into action with the main body of the French fleet. In the centre,

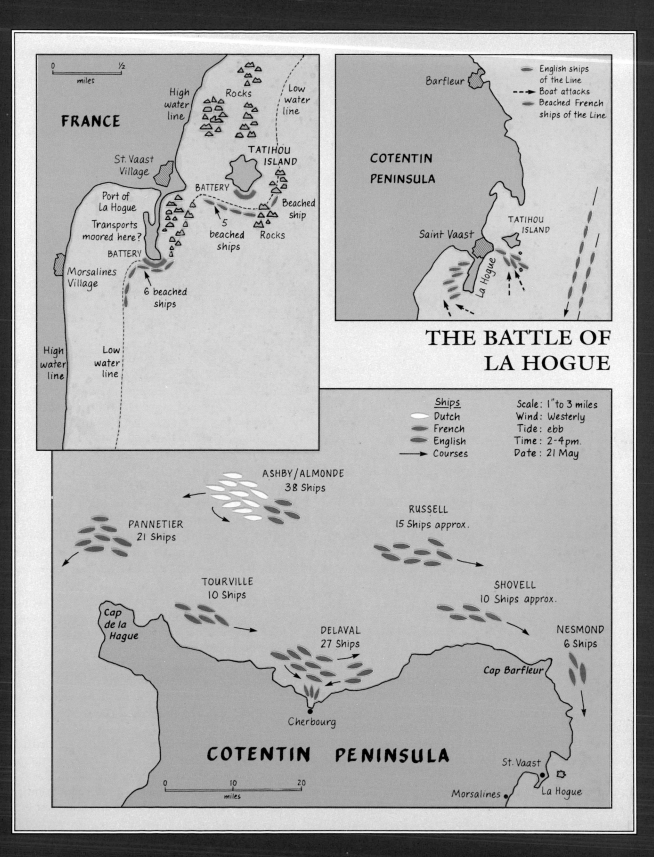

FRANCE

0 — ½
miles

High water line

Rocks

Low water line

St. Vaast Village

TATIHOU ISLAND

BATTERY

Beached ship

Port of La Hogue

Transports moored here?

5 beached ships

Rocks

BATTERY

Morsalines Village

6 beached ships

High water line

Low water line

English ships of the Line
Boat attacks
Beached French ships of the Line

Barfleur

COTENTIN PENINSULA

Saint Vaast

TATIHOU ISLAND

La Hogue

THE BATTLE OF LA HOGUE

Ships
Dutch
French
English
→ Courses

Scale: 1" to 3 miles
Wind: Westerly
Tide: ebb
Time: 2–4 pm.
Date: 21 May

ASHBY/ALMONDE
38 Ships

PANNETIER
21 Ships

RUSSELL
15 Ships approx.

TOURVILLE
10 Ships

Cap de la Hague

DELAVAL
27 Ships

SHOVELL
10 Ships approx.

NESMOND
6 Ships

Cap Barfleur

Cherbourg

COTENTIN PENINSULA

0 — 10 — 20
miles

St. Vaast

Morsalines

La Hogue

Left: The British had made poor use of their opportunities at Barfleur but destroyed the remains of the French Fleet at La Hogue.

Right: James II watched the attempted escape of part of the French fleet into the Creek of St. Vaast where they were pursued by Admiral Rooke and destroyed.

Below right: Fireships were used with great success at La Hogue, but saw little use thereafter. This sectional illustration shows the stowage areas for the explosive and combustible materials.

Malo, a missed chance that might otherwise have ensured a notable British success in which the Dutch would have had a share. Meanwhile, off the north coast of the Cotentin the westerly wind in conjunction with a strong flood tide sent the other French and Allied ships, including those of Tourville and Russell, back towards Barfleur. At some stage Tourville struck his flag in the 96-gun *Ambitieux* (to which ship he had transferred from the ill-fated *Soleil-Royal*) and probably made his way overland to St Vaast–La Hogue. Here, by the late evening of 21 May, twelve French ships were aground in two groups of six, their crews aboard and manning the guns as best as they could.

With the concentration of Russell's Red and Blue divisions (the Dutch White was stood down) off St Vaast–La Hogue by the evening of 22 May the scene was set for the conflagration, commonly called 'La Hogue'. This was witnessed from the shore by James II, who had stationed himself at Morsalines, by Marshal Bellefonds commanding some 24,000 troops, by Bonrepaus, Intendant de la Marine, by Tourville himself, and two of his flag officers, d'Amfreville and Villette. During the night Russell ordered light-draught ships to stand in towards the shore to prevent any French escaping, but the following morning, 23 May, Shovell, who had earlier been wounded, had to be replaced as commander for the attack by Rooke, of the Blue division. His leadership was to prove so distinguished that it gained him a knighthood and a pension. A preliminary bombardment from the English ships, made possible by a favourable tide, was followed up by a fireship and a number of ship's boats which, despite French musketry having an open field of fire, put boarding parties into the six ships beached at Tatihou, now deserted by their crews. Fires were quickly ignited in these ships, *Terrible*, *Ambitieux*, *Magnifique*, *St Philippe*, *Merveilleux* and *Foudroyant*, and although the French commanders were themselves afloat in boats, English activity was little hindered.

By the evening and on a falling tide, the parties were withdrawn in preparation for the morrow's work at St Vaast. Here (24 May) the attack met with stiffer resistance as the batteries were more heavily gunned than at Tatihou and, in addition to the six ships to be fired here, there were the transports in the harbour. The state of the tide permitted fire to be brought to bear on the St Vaast batteries, and the six ships, *Fier*, *Tonnant*, *Gaillard*, *Bourbon*, *St Louis* and *Fort* were duly fired by boarding parties. The heavier English casualties now sustained were partly due to efforts to destroy or tow out the transports. A falling tide in the early afternoon assisted a successful withdrawal with much accomplished. Only the transport craft grounded at the top of the harbour had escaped attention.

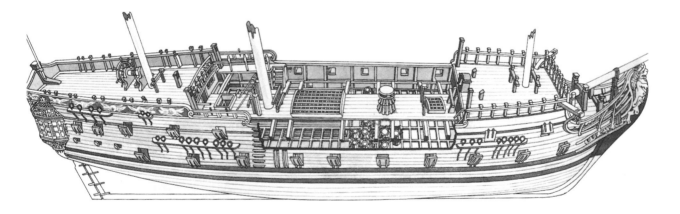

Bellefonds himself had done little to repel the English attack, and turned down James II's suggestion that troops be put aboard the six ships. It had been as much through these well sustained boat operations as through Tourville's remaining ships being forced back to St Malo or Brest that the French invasion threat was lifted.

Barfleur and La Hogue have together been seen as a notable naval victory for England a century after the Armada, hardly to be rivalled until Hawke's action at Quiberon Bay in 1759. While Pannetier, on his perilous passage to St Malo, had no Hawke to contend with, the battles were seen in England as a deliverance, one that was especially marked by Queen Mary's decision to found the Greenwich Naval Hospital. Yet the subsequent war at sea raises doubts about the conventional verdict on the events of May 1692. Within a year, given the momentum behind an already current French capital ship building programme, all fifteen ships lost in the actions had been replaced, and

Above: Adriaen van Diest painted this scene of the end of *La Soliel Royal* at the Battle of La Hogue.

the switch in French naval policy towards *guerre de course* by the mid-1690s appears unrelated to Barfleur and La Hogue. Vauban, though often a lone voice, never lost his belief in the efficacy of a massive strike on the Thames estuary and London from Dunkirk, by means of light-draught warships and galleys. And in 1693, Tourville was able to avenge La Hogue through his interception of the 300 strong Smyrna convoy under Rooke's command off Lagos. This resulted in the expensive loss of more than 80 merchantmen. As for Parliament, the Commons debates of late 1692 and at the time of the Smyrna disaster reveal that Russell's victory had, in itself, contributed nothing towards protecting Britain's merchant fleet from French depredations – 'when all is done, the war cannot be supported unless trade is protected'. The battles were thus but episodes in a longer maritime campaign that, as is usual with such affairs, had many elements.

BIBLIOGRAPHY

Aubrey, Philip, *The Defeat of James Stuart's Armada, 1692*, Leicester, 1979. The only modern treatment available in English.
La Bataille de la Hogue, Association du Tricentennaire, 1692/1992, 1992; no imprint, but with an introduction by A. Zyberg of the University of Caen. An invaluable commentary on the battle.

Battesti, Vaulson, *Thuriférair de Cherbourg ou de L'incidence de la Bataille de La Hogue sur l'evolution due port de Cherbourg*, 1992. A contribution to the proceedings of the Tricentenary conference in June 1992 and without question the most valuable of the sources consulted.

BYNG: PASSARO, 1718

by John B. Hattendorf

*'Naval tactics are based upon conditions the chief caus-
es of which, namely the arms, may change; which in
turn causes necessarily a change... in the disposition
and handling of fleets.'*
Sebastien-François Bigot de Morogues, 1763

Among the famous battles the Royal Navy has fought, the Battle of Cape Passaro is unusual in that it was fought in peacetime. In terms of international politics, it was part of a collective security campaign against Spain, during which Britain, France and Austria maintained the prevailing balance in the international order, forcing Spain to abide by the agreements she had made following the War of the Spanish Succession. From a tactical, naval point of view, Admiral Sir George Byng demonstrated that the Navy of the period was not wedded to a rigid idea in using the line of battle but, on the contrary, used a flexible approach.

The treaties of Utrecht, Rastatt and Baden, ending the War of the Spanish Succession, established an international order for European states that held for more than twenty years. These agreements had created a general international balance of power in terms of complex dynastic successions and territorial divisions. In effect, they created a balance in political control among the major European states, which prevented either the major land powers, France, Spain or Austria, or the maritime powers, the British and the Dutch, from hindering one another's trade and economic development.

While these agreements created the broad basis for European stability, they did not solve all the issues for

Left: George Byng, Viscount Torrington, K.B. An engraving after the painting by Sir Godfrey Kneller.

all countries involved. One of the main concerns was that Spain was not an integral part of the balance in the Mediterranean. Both Spain and Austria were dissatisfied with the settlement and division of control between the two countries in Italy. This was the chief issue leading up to the battle at Cape Passaro. From Britain's perspective, the key problem was to preserve her own commercial interests in the Mediterranean by creating a balance of power in the region. This objective became the basis of Britain's foreign policy in the immediate post-war years, as she worked to balance Spanish and Austrian interests in Italy with those of Savoy between them.

Five years earlier, as part of the Utrecht settlement, the Duke of Savoy had secured from Spain the possession of Sicily as his share of the spoils of war, in return for renouncing his own legitimate claim to the Spanish crown. At the same time, the Austrian Emperor Charles VI obtained the Spanish lands in Lombardy, Sardinia and Naples. The first development beyond this occurred in 1716, when Austria and Britain signed a defensive alliance in which Britain agreed to guarantee Austria's gains through the Utrecht settlement. Next, in a diplomatic revolution in 1716, the former enemies, Britain and France, formed an alliance that served as the first precarious step toward establishing the basis for a kind of collective security in Europe. In the following year, the Dutch Republic reluctantly joined to create a Triple Alliance, and Britain hoped to go further by adding the Austrians to this agreement, creating a Quadruple Alliance.

British diplomats were in the process of negotiation for this objective when a crisis with Spain developed. Spain's King Philip V resented the agreements that had deprived him of the Italian lands he believed to be his own indivisible inheritance. The Queen of Spain, Elizabeth Farnese, was from Parma, while the Spanish prime minister, Cardinal Alberoni, had come from Piacenza, one of Spain's former Italian territories. Both helped to promote thoughts in Spain of regaining the Italian provinces from Austrian control.

In 1717, Philip had organised a fleet and regained the island of Sardinia for Spain. This fleet was the work of Admiral Antonio Gaztañeta y de Iturribálzaga, who had become shipbuilder to the king in 1715 and had begun to build Spain's first new warships of the eighteenth century. Gaztañeta had designed slim, streamlined new warships to protect merchant ships sailing between Spain and America, rather than warships for the line of battle. In their first test, Cardinal Alberoni had directed the fleet to a far different goal – an assault on Austrian-held territory. First, the fleet, with its accompanying troops, had taken Sardinia. The next goal was to be Sicily and other territories on the Italian mainland, thereby upsetting the delicate division of European territories that had brought peace after the War of the Spanish Succession. Thus, Spain's actions were a direct threat to the balance of power.

By the spring of 1718, British, French and Austrian diplomats agreed that the only means to prevent a general war in Europe was to stop Spain. The only naval force that was capable of doing this was the Royal Navy. Based on the agreements reached earlier, in 1713 and 1716, the British government drew up orders to send a fleet to the Mediterranean, but even as they did so, they continued negotiations over the ultimate fate of the Italian territories.

On 20 May 1718, Admiral Sir George Byng sailed from England with a fleet designed to deter Spain's aggression. Delayed by light winds, he did not arrive at Minorca until 1 July. There, he learned that, in retaliation, Spain had laid plans to organise a league of countries against England, in an effort to replace George I with the Stuart pretender. Already, Alberoni had secretly armed an armada of 276 transports and 123 small coasting *tartanas* with 16,000 troops and 8,000 cavalry under the command of the Marquis de Lede, which had already sailed eastward from Barcelona, on 5 June, with a convoy under the command of the architect of the revived Spanish Navy, Admiral Antonio Gaztañeta. Hearing this, Byng sailed for Naples to confer with the Austrian Viceroy, Count Wirich von Daun. Arriving there on 10 July, the Viceroy passed on the latest reports – that the Spaniards had already landed at Palermo on Sicily and that the Savoyard army had been easily forced out of their garrisons, leaving only positions on the northwestern coast holding out.

At Naples, Byng and Daun conferred. Byng assured Daun that if the Spanish would not cease hostilities, he would attack the Spanish fleet. From the best intelligence Byng could obtain, he learned that the Spanish fleet lay in Paradise Road, about a mile north of Messina, where the Spanish Army was besieging the citadel. Local pilots advised that this roadstead would be a difficult place to attack, the Spanish occupying a safe position that was difficult to approach and to manoeuvre about because of strong currents running outside it.

Byng and the fleet left Naples with a land breeze on the night of 14 July. On the following day, news reached Naples that the Quadruple Alliance was signed. Through this agreement, Savoy and Austria joined the Alliance on the basis of a new compromise: Savoy would receive Sardinia from Austria in exchange for Sicily, while Philip V's son, Don Carlos, would eventually obtain rights in Parma and Tuscany. This change was an important one in European politics, but it did not alter the role of Byng's fleet in stopping the Spanish from seizing Sicily. First, Spain would have to accept the compromise – and this was the purpose of Byng's expedition.

Continuing to sail south through the night, Byng arrived off the northern point of the Strait of Messina, where he put ashore his first captain, George Saunders, to try to persuade the commander of the Spanish army, the Marquis de Lede, that he should withdraw his forces from Sicily. Failing in this, Saunders returned to Byng, reporting that the Spanish made every appearance that they were continuing their operations and planning to attack the Kingdom of Naples. With this information, Byng decided to press on through the Strait and to attack the Spanish fleet. Without calling the customary council of war,

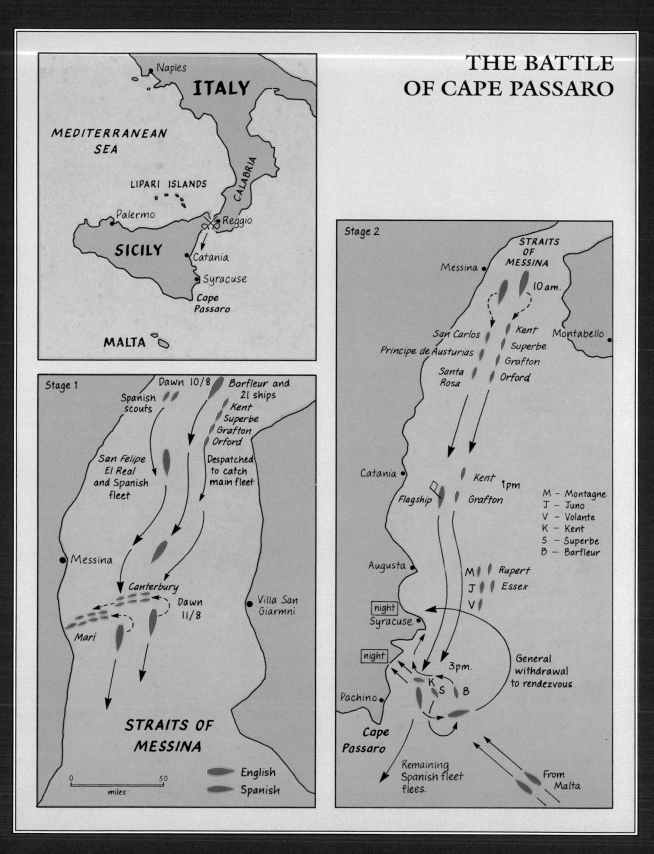

THE BATTLE
OF CAPE PASSARO

Top inset map:

Naples

ITALY

MEDITERRANEAN SEA

LIPARI ISLANDS

CALABRIA

Palermo

Reggio

SICILY

Catania

Syracuse

Cape Passaro

MALTA

Stage 1:

Stage 1

Dawn 10/8

Spanish scouts

Barfleur and 21 ships
Kent
Superbe
Grafton
Orford

San Felipe El Real and Spanish fleet

Despatched to catch main fleet

Messina

Canterbury

Dawn 11/8

Villa San Giarmni

Mari

STRAITS OF MESSINA

0   50
miles

English
Spanish

Stage 2:

Stage 2

STRAITS OF MESSINA

Messina

10 a.m.

San Carlos
Principe de Austurias
Santa Rosa

Kent
Superbe
Grafton
Orford

Montabello

Catania

Kent
Grafton

Flagship

1pm

M – Montagne
J – Juno
V – Volante
K – Kent
S – Superbe
B – Barfleur

Augusta

M   Rupert
J   Essex
V

night
Syracuse

night

3pm.

General withdrawal to rendezvous

Pachino

K S B

Cape Passaro

Remaining Spanish fleet flees.

From Malta

Above: The firing was fast and furious.

he prepared for an engagement, believing, as his son later reported, that 'a commanding officer should only call a Council of War to screen him from what he has no mind to undertake.'

Early in the morning of 30 July, Byng stood in toward Messina, where he sighted two Spanish scouts in the Fare, the narrowest portion of the Strait. As Byng and his fleet appeared in sight, a felucca from the town of Reggio on the Italian mainland came out to him with a report from the Governor of the citadel that observers on the Calabrian shore could see, from the hills, the Spanish fleet lying by. On this report, Byng continued through the Strait after the Spanish scouts, using them to lead him to the main Spanish fleet. Before noon, he sighted the entire Spanish fleet under Gaztañeta, drawn up in a line of battle. The approach of Byng's 21 ships took the Spanish by surprise: they had received no warning of Byng's movements or of the related diplomatic activity in Spain. Gaztañeta moved away from Byng's fleet in fair weather with light north-easterly winds, but maintained his battle line of 21 men of war, a small ship of fourteen guns, two fireships, four bomb vessels and seven galleys.

Demonstrating his tactical flexibility, Byng detached his fastest sailing ships, the *Kent*, (70) Captain Thomas Mathews, *Superbe*, (60) Captain Streynsham Master, *Grafton*, (70) Captain Nicholas Haddock, and *Orford*, (70) Captain Edward Falkingham, to make all the sail they could to get up with the Spanish. Byng ordered whatever ship among them that could lead ahead, nearest the enemy, to carry the lights his flagship would normally carry, so that the fleet did not lose sight of them at night. With little wind during the night, the Spanish galleys proved their usefulness by towing their largest ships through the night.

At break of day the next morning, 31 July, the British fleet was nearly up with the Spaniards. Seeing this, one of the Spanish rear admirals, the Marquis de Mari, took the Spanish rear of six men of war, along with the galleys, fire-ships and bomb-ships, separated from the main fleet and stood in toward the Sicilian shore. Byng ordered the *Canterbury*, (60) Captain George Walton, with five other ships under his command, to pursue the small Spanish ships as they fled. The *Argyle*, (50) Captain Conningsby Norbury, and the *Canterbury* came up within gunshot range of the headmost ship about six in the morning. *Argyle* fired a shot to bring her to, which she ignored, upon which *Argyle* fired another shot. *Canterbury* was somewhat closer to the Spaniard and she fired her stern chaser at *Canterbury*. One of the Spanish then fired a broadside at the *Argyle*, beginning the engagement with the detached squadron. Observing this from a distance, Byng sent orders to them, and to the rest of the fleet, to rendezvous after the action at Syracuse.

At the same time, Byng and the remainder of his fleet drew up toward the main Spanish fleet. With four ships, *Kent*, *Superbe*, *Grafton*, and *Orford*, moving ahead to attack the Spanish van, the remainder would deal with the enemy rear. Despite the fact that the Spaniards retained their battle line formation, Byng apparently ordered his ships to pursue the Spanish in a general chase, with a loose line ahead, allowing some of his ships to approach on one side, and some on the other side, of the Spanish formation, expecting his captains to engage individual ships of similar size. About ten in the morning, when they were coming within gunshot range, Byng ordered the captains of the two ships that were the first to come up with the Spanish van, the *Grafton* and *Orford*, not to return the Spaniards' stern-chaser fire unless they repeatedly fired on the approaching English ships.

When they did, Edward Falkingham in *Orford* returned the fire, attacking and capturing the *Santa Rosa* (56). Shortly thereafter, the *San Carlos* (60) struck, without much opposition, to Thomas Mathews in the *Kent*, while Nicholas Haddock in the *Grafton* attacked Rear Admiral Chacon's flagship, *Principe de Asturias* (70). When the *Captain*, (70) Captain Archibald Hamilton, and the *Bredah*, (70) Captain Barrow Harris, came up, Haddock left them to take the *Asturias*, while he moved ahead to attack a 60-gun ship on his starboard bow that had repeatedly been annoying him during the initial attack on the *Asturias*, firing her stern guns on the *Grafton*.

About 1300, Mathews in the *Kent* and Haddock in the *Grafton* engaged the *San Felipe El Real*, (74) flagship of Admiral Gaztañeta, and two other ships. The running fight between them, about six leagues off Cape Passaro, lasted until about three o'clock in the afternoon, when Mathews suddenly bore down on the *San Felipe* and, passing under her stern, fired a broadside. Meanwhile, Streynsham Master in the *Superbe* bore down upon *San Felipe* and attempted to board the Spanish flagship on the weather quarter. By shifting her helm, the Spanish flagship avoided the *Superbe*'s boarding manoeuvre. Meanwhile, Byng in *Barfleur* (90) was within gunshot range astern, on the Spanish Admiral's weather quarter, and Byng's brother-in-law, Captain Streynsham Master, manoeuvred *Superbe* up under the Spaniard's lee quarter, upon which Admiral Gaztañeta, wounded in both legs, struck his flagship to Master. This was a rare occasion, for Master, a private captain, to take a commander-in-chief prisoner of war.

While this action was taking place, two Spanish 70-gun ships under Rear Admiral Guevara approached the battle area *en route* from Malta. With little chance of successfully relieving Gaztañeta, Guevara, nevertheless came down from windward on Byng, and each fired a broadside. Then, seeing the flag being hauled down in *San Felipe*, Guevara and his two Spanish ships took advantage of the wind, quickly tacked and headed in toward shore. Byng pursued the two until just before nightfall, when, there being little wind, the Spaniards took to their oars and rowed their ships out of reach. Byng then returned to his fleet, arriving two hours after dark.

In the meantime, the *Essex*, (70) Captain Richard Rowzier, took the Spanish *Juno* (36); while the *Montague*, (60) Captain Thomas Beverly, and *Rupert*, (60) Captain Arthur Field, took the *Volante* (44) as it

was on the verge of sinking. Vice Admiral Charles Cornwall in the *Shrewsbury* (80) proceeded to the support of Nicholas Haddock in the *Grafton*, but in light winds the Spanish escaped. Rear Admiral George DeLaval in the *Dorsetshire* (80) along with the *Royal Oak* (70) pursued two more Spanish ships that lay more leewardly than the others, capturing the *Santa Isabel* (60). These Spanish ships were under the command of Rear Admiral George Camocke, a former captain in the Royal Navy who had been dismissed from the service in 1714 for supporting the Stuart cause.

In the action of the main fleet, Byng singled out for particular praise the actions of Thomas Mathews in the *Grafton*. 'Tho' he had not the fortune to take any particular ship, yet was engaged with several,' Byng wrote, 'he behaved himself very much like an officer and a seaman, and bid far for the general good, and for stopping the way of those four ships that he pursued who got away not through his fault, but failure of wind and his own sails and rigging much shattered.' This was more than he would say for some of the others, privately thinking that several of his captains had let some of the Spaniards escape by two or three English ships attacking a single Spanish ship, while failing to follow and attack others of equal force and size.

Heading for the rendezvous at Syracuse, Byng captured another ship of 40 guns as well as some small ships and vessels that had tried to run in under the fortifications on the Sicilian coast for protection. During these operations, he received Walton's famous dispatch reporting that he had taken Rear Admiral the Marquis de Mari with six ships and burned seven others. Often quoted as an example of a short and decisive report, Walton wrote: 'We have taken and destroyed all the Spanish ships and vessels which were upon the coast, the number as in the margin and as for them we have with us, hope we shall get into Syracuse this day.'

At the final tally, Byng's fleet had succeeded in capturing eleven ships and destroying three more of the original 21 Spanish ships. It was a remarkable success by any standard and a major blow to Spain's ambitions, putting an immediate end to her plans for creating a wider European league against England. Nevertheless, it did not immediately solve the situation in Sicily. It would take more time to persuade the Spaniards to withdraw and to relinquish the island to Austria under the terms of the Quadruple Alliance.

Above: Painting by Richard Paton of Byng's victory at Cape Passaro.

While Byng reflected on his success and the operations that would be required in the following months, he warned Admiralty Secretary Josiah Burchett, 'upon the first report of the action, which happened between the Spanish Fleet & ours, it was conceived all their fleet was destroyed...'. But by his latest intelligence after the battle, the Spanish had seventeen ships in the Mediterranean and would soon add at least two more 60-gun ships. Byng advised London to keep at least twenty ships of the line in the Mediterranean, 'until the Spaniards are brought to reason'.

Four months after the battle, on 17 December 1718, England and France declared war on Spain. Their effort to force Spain to agree to the terms of the Quadruple Alliance and to the new partition of Italian lands lasted until June 1720. During this time, Byng remained in command of the Mediterranean Fleet and played a leading role in the diplomacy coordinating and facilitating a complex series of combined operations. For his success, George I elevated him to the peerage in 1721 as Baron Southill and Viscount Torrington. Subsequently he served as First Commissioner of the Admiralty from 1727 until his death in January 1733.

BIBLIOGRAPHY

Public Record Office, ADM 1/377, Byng's original correspondence and reports on the battle.

Cranmer-Byng, J. L., *Pattee Byng's Journal 1718–1720*, Navy Records Society, vol 88, London, 1950. The diary of Sir George Byng's son and confidant.

Hattendorf, Knight, Pearsall, Roger and Till (eds), *British Naval Documents, 1204–1960*, Navy Records Society, vol 131, London, 1993. Contains Byng's account of the battle.

Corbett, T., *An Account of the Expedition of the British Fleet to Sicily in the Years 1718, 1719 and 1720 Under the Command of Sir George Byng, Bart, London 1739*. The standard account.

Harbron, John D., *Trafalgar and the Spanish Navy*, Annapolis, 1988. Pages 17–19 and 29–32 provide a summary of Spanish naval shipbuilding in the period 1715–18.

Hattendorf, J. B., *Naval Force and Peacetime Deterrence: Case Studies from British Naval History* (forthcoming). A detailed study of the diplomacy leading up to the battle; it contains a revised version of his 'Admiral Sir George Byng and the Cape Passaro Incident', first published in 1987 in *Guerres et Paix, 1660-1815*.

Richmond, Sir Herbert W., 'The Expedition to Sicily, 1718, under Sir George Byng' in *Journal of the Royal United Services Institution*, LIII, July–December 1909. Examines in detail the combined operations following the battle.

ANSON: CAPE FINISTERRE, 1747

by Pat Crimmin

'In war opportunity waits for no man,'
Pericles in Thucydides, THE PELOPONNESIAN WAR, 404 BC

If the war fought by Britain between 1739 and 1748 is remembered at all by the general reader, it is for the curiously named War of Jenkin's Ear of 1739 against Spain in the West Indies, which gave Smollett the material for his novel Roderick Random, or for George II at Dettingen in 1743 leading his troops into battle, the last British monarch to do so. The Royal Navy's part in this conflict often appears muted, yet it was critical, both in home defence in 1745 against the Jacobite rebellion and in making a serious challenge to French power in North America and India. It marked the beginning of that series of eighteenth-century conflicts between Britain and her rivals, France and Spain, for overseas trade and colonial empire in which naval power played such a crucial part.

Once war was officially declared between France and Britain in 1744, the French determined to send reinforcements to strengthen their settlements overseas, and the British attempted to prevent them. Yet though the key French naval base and fortress of Louisbourg, on Cape Breton island, commanding the entrance to the St. Lawrence, was taken by a British and colonial force in June 1745, a plan to take Quebec failed. French reinforcements evaded a lax British blockade of French western ports and relieved the city. The true function of a western squadron was still evolving, and it was only when Rear Admiral George Anson was appointed to command that squadron in August 1746 that it began to be reorganised, along lines advocated earlier by Admiral Vernon, as a force to protect British trade, while harrying that of the enemy and cruising as an anti-invasion force. Anson was given more ships than his predecessors, seventeen sail of the line, six 50-gun ships, four frigates and two sloops, forming a squadron capable of protecting British trade passing through that area and of engaging an enemy contesting the entrance to the Channel or trying to escape into the Atlantic. The action of 1747 was to prove the value of such arrangements.

Anson had already become famous through his circumnavigation of the world between September 1740 and June 1744, which had effectively challenged the power of Spain in the Pacific and seemed to recall the glorious and profitable days of Drake and the first Elizabeth. Anson's voyage was notable for the courage and endurance shown by those who took part and for the number of young officers who were trained by him in seamanship and leadership to become famous sea officers in succeeding years, such as Keppel, Howe, Brett, Saumarez, Saunders, Hyde Parker and Denis.

By 1746 the French had achieved initial success in India, capturing Madras under the combined leadership of Dupleix and La Bourdonnais. But reinforcements were necessary if British ships were to be permanently defeated and British factories taken. For these reasons the French government decided in the spring of 1747 to send from Rochefort three warships as an escort to an East India convoy of eighteen merchantmen, carrying reinforcements to India. Although St. Georges, their commander, evaded the small British squadron cruising off the French shore by a successful ruse, he was prevented by gales from clearing the coast and was forced to return to Aix roads. Here he found another squadron and convoy, under the command of Rear Admiral de la Jonquière consisting of five warships and 24 merchant vessels, destined for Canada to retake Cape Breton island. Prudence dictated that the two squadrons should sail together as far as Madeira before going their separate ways, presenting a formidable force against any small British blockading squadron they might meet.

When they finally sailed in late April 1747, the French numbered six warships, the recently built *L'Invincible* (74), commanded by St. Georges, *Le Sérieux* (66), de la Jonquière's flagship, three ships with between 50 and 56 guns each, *La Gloire* (44) plus three East India Company ships fitted as warships and bearing between 20 and 30 guns each. La Jonquière headed south-west for the Spanish coast, passing Cape Ortegal (the name by which this battle is known to the French) and Cape Finisterre, on the north-west Spanish coast, before heading for Madeira. He thus avoided the fourteen British ships reported cruising off Brittany, and by 2 May he was twelve miles north of Cape Finisterre.

It was impossible to keep secret the sailing of such a large force, and the British were already on the lookout for it. Anson had sailed from Spithead on 26 March, leaving orders for those ships not ready to proceed to join him twenty leagues north of the island of Belle Ile. Moving down-Channel to Plymouth, where he was joined by the bulk of his force, he left similar orders for other latecomers. Once off Ushant, he sent two ships to investigate French preparedness at Brest. Though the western squadron was well placed and Anson had done all he could to intercept a French break-out, like Nelson later, he impressed on

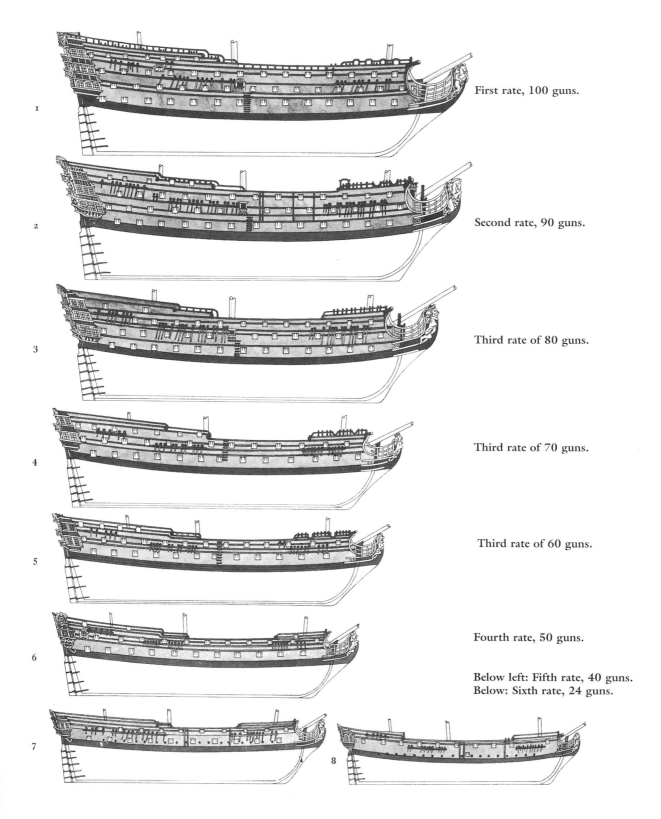

1 First rate, 100 guns.

2 Second rate, 90 guns.

3 Third rate of 80 guns.

4 Third rate of 70 guns.

5 Third rate of 60 guns.

6 Fourth rate, 50 guns.

Below left: Fifth rate, 40 guns.
Below: Sixth rate, 24 guns.

7

8

the Admiralty his need for more frigates to collect intelligence. Gales hampered the ships looking into Brest, and it was not until 9 April that he learned of a sizeable French squadron in the Rochefort area bound, possibly, for Canada which might have sailed. Judging that Brest was probably empty, Anson determined to cruise north of Cape Ortegal, as being the likeliest point of interception. He therefore sent two ships to look into Rochefort, left two at the Belle Ile rendezvous to inform latecomers and reinforcements, and himself moved to the Bay of Biscay, exercising his ships *en route* and working them up into a state of battle readiness. Anson strung his ships out in line abreast a mile apart from each other to form a net which the French would find impossible to avoid. Early in the morning of 3 May, informed by the sloop *Falcon* of a large enemy force, he collected his ships and sailed south-west to intercept them.

Anson outnumbered the French in ships and gun power. He had fourteen sail of the line including his flagship, the *Prince George* of 90 guns, the *Namur* (74), nine ships carrying between 60 and 66 guns each and two 50-gun ships, plus the *Ambuscade* (40), a sloop and a fireship. The French were the first to sight their enemy early the same morning, but by 0830 the British had made contact and began to give chase. La Jonquière was determined to protect his convoy of merchantmen and so put himself between them and what he immediately saw was a much stronger British force than his own. To give his convoy more time to disperse, he therefore attempted the ruse St. Georges had practised six weeks earlier –

Below: Eleven prizes were taken at the action off Finisterre. Shown here are *Gloire* and *Jason* and on the right is the Spanish *Glorioso*, taken at about the same time.

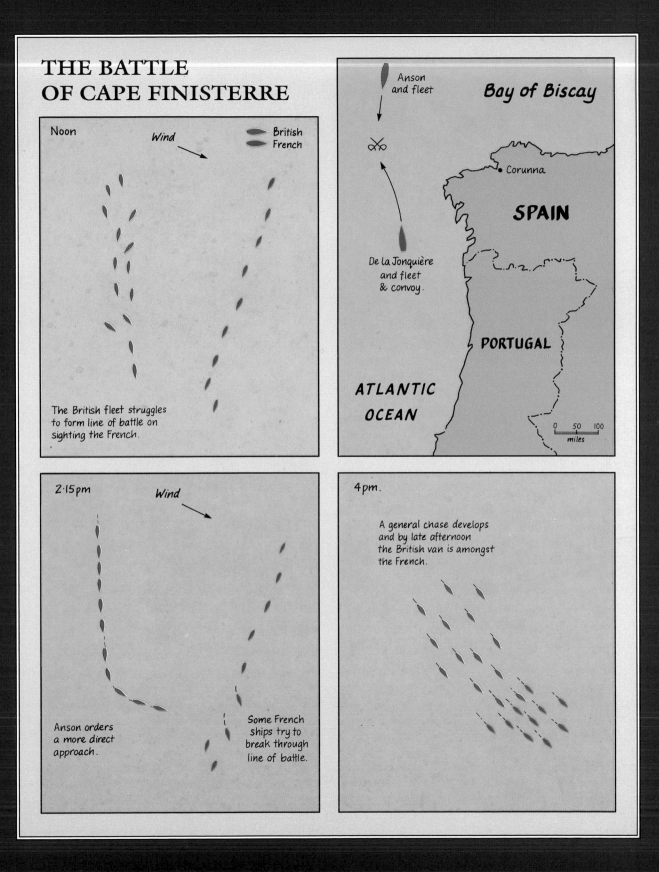

THE BATTLE OF CAPE FINISTERRE

Noon

Wind

⬤ British
⬤ French

The British fleet struggles to form line of battle on sighting the French.

Anson and fleet

Bay of Biscay

• Corunna

SPAIN

De la Jonquière and fleet & convoy.

PORTUGAL

ATLANTIC OCEAN

0   50   100
miles

2·15pm

Wind

Anson orders a more direct approach.

Some French ships try to break through line of battle.

4pm.

A general chase develops and by late afternoon the British van is amongst the French.

Above: Anson's Fleet returning to Portsmouth, from an engraving of 1747.

forming a line of battle with his warships and including three of the East India ships which most closely resembled them in appearance. Thus confronted, Anson formed his own ships, first into line abreast and shortly after into line ahead, Captain Boscawen in *HMS Namur* leading.

At this stage of the encounter the two fleets were more than a mile apart. Anson's second-in-command, Rear Admiral Peter Warren in *HMS Devonshire*, is said to have urged a more pell-mell approach to prevent the convoy escaping; now, perhaps frustrated by the poor pace of the slowest British ships, he bore away in the van in chase as soon as Anson made the signal to sail large, that is with the wind abaft on the rear beam. He was immediately recalled. The perils of individual or uncoordinated attacks on a properly formed enemy line, even if inferior in numbers, were too great and specifically condemned by the *Fighting Instructions*. The defensive and offensive strength of the line of battle lay in its unity and combined firepower, advantages commanders did not lightly throw away .

By early afternoon, when the fleets had drawn closer to each other, Anson signalled his leading ships to head for the centre of the French line. As they bore down, two of the French East Indiamen, with limited firepower, panicked and began to move out of the line, throwing the French fleet into some confusion as St. Georges tried to force them back. La Jonquière, seeing his plans aborted, but having given his convoy more time in their bid to escape, gave the signal for retreat and the French line began to break up as they sailed for the south-west. Seeing this, Anson now promptly abandoned his formal line and ordered a general chase. Captain Denis, commanding *Centurion* (50), was the first to come up with the French rear and began the action about 1600. The *Centurion* was battered for ten hectic minutes between *L'Invincible* and *Le Serieux* until the *Namur* and *Defiance* came to her support and with accurate and effective gunnery engaged the French. Other British ships followed, overwhelming the rearmost French ships and passing on to prevent the van escaping. By 1800, when Anson in the slow-sailing *Prince George* came up, several French ships had surrendered, including *Le Sérieux* and her commander, and *L'Invincible* did so shortly after.

An account of the battle, published in *The Gentleman's Magazine* later that year, canvassed the claims of *Devonshire* and *Bristol* for the active part they had played and deplored the way in which the actions of some meritorious officers had been passed over. *Devonshire*, Warren's flagship, sustained heavy fire from *Le Seriouex* as the two ships fought within pistol shot of each other until the Frenchman struck. Warren then moved on to attack *L'Invincible*, supported by Montagu in *Bristol*. Montagu, known to his colleagues as 'Mad Montagu', is reported to have fended off *Pembroke*, attempting to get between *L'Invincible* and the *Bristol*, shouting, 'Sir, run foul of me and be damned; neither you, nor any other man in the World shall come between me and my enemy!' But while the anonymous author commended the 'pleasant' contest between these ships, he denied that *L'Invincible* had ultimately struck to the *Prince George*, which was then a mile astern, and while commending 'this glorious day' deplored the jealousy of unnamed individuals who allowed the heroism of brave man to be 'buried in oblivion'. The mid-Georgian navy was still very far from being a band of brothers.

Total British prizes after the battle were six men of war, and several East Indiamen. Five merchant ships and three frigates were taken by ships Anson sent in pursuit after the main action was over. Though numerically inferior to the British, Anson considered the French had fought gallantly, doing their duty well and 'had lost their ships with honour; scarce any of them striking their colours till their ships were dismasted'. Anson considered the victory due chiefly to superior British gunnery: 'The fire on our side was much greater and more regular than theirs; and it is evident our shott were better plac'd.' When the *Bristol*'s lieutenant went on board the French *Diamant* (56), after a two-hour engagement, most of the time within pistol shot, he found the rigging shattered, one of the upper deck guns burst and 'the poop and quarter deck like a slaughter house, cover'd over with

blood'. The exercising and training Anson had imposed on his squadron while cruising had brought results.

Captain Denis of the *Centurion* arrived at Portsmouth with this good news on 4 May, to a rapturous welcome. Naval victories had been scarce. This was the first since 1744 and was suitably rewarded. Denis received £500 for bringing the good news, Anson a peerage, considerable prize money and admittance to the inner circle of government. Within a year he had married the daughter of the Lord Chancellor, Lord Hardwicke and in 1751 became First Lord of the Admiralty. Here he proved an administrator of genius, initiating far-reaching reforms in every area of naval administration.

Advances in French naval architecture in the 1730s and 40s were creating the 74-gun ship, the pre-eminent warship of the later eighteenth century. *L'Invincible*, captured at Finisterre and newly built in 1744, was taken into the Royal Navy and used as a pattern for such warships thereafter.

Strategically the victory damaged France's naval strength and weakened her position in North America and India, denying reinforcements at a crucial moment. John Creswell, in his study of British tactics in the eighteenth century, denied that there were any tactical lessons to be learned from the battle, though noting that this was the first time mention was made of a flag signal ordering a general chase. He also argued that the *Fighting Instructions*, whose rigidity is so often criticised for the delay in bringing the British ships to action, were not as unbending as was once thought. Certainly they were capable of interpretation by a commander with the ability, courage and independence to think for himself and seize an opportunity. Anson was such a commander, as an earlier comment of his, in 1744, reveals: 'It has ever been my opinion that a person trusted with command may and ought to exceed his orders and dispense with the common rules of proceeding when extraordinary occasions require it.'

The prestige of both Anson and the Royal Navy gained immeasurably from the victory. For Anson it marked the climax of his fighting career and enabled him more easily to pursue reforming policies and promote those protégés who were also imbued with his ideas and fighting spirit. He showed it was possible to win victories by taking calculated risks and by rigorous training of a unified squadron, a welcome lesson after the reverses, divisions and courts-martial of earlier

Left: A portrait of Admiral Lord Anson, painted c.1845 and presented to Dartmouth in 1918 by the Captain and Commander of the College.

years. He thus made it possible for other commanders to follow his example and achieve decisive victories by abandoning, on occasion, tactics that had stultified development and resulted in inconclusive actions. The longer term effect of this on the Royal Navy could only be beneficial, while in the short term its prestige and national standing was enhanced.

BIBLIOGRAPHY

Barrow, J., *Life of Anson*, London, 1839.

Coad, Jonahan G., *The Royal Dockyards 1690–1850*, Aldershot, 1989.

Marcus, G. J., *The Formative Centuries*, vol 1 of *A Naval History of England*, London, 1961.

Richmond, H. W., *The Navy in the War of 1739–1748*, 3 vols, Cambridge, 1920.

Lavery, Brian, *The Royal Navy's First* Invincible *1744–1758*, Portsmouth, 1988.

Kemp, Peter (ed), *The Oxford Companion to Ships and the Sea*, London, 1976.

HAWKE: QUIBERON BAY, 1759

by Ruddock Mackay

*'You have done your duty in the remonstrance; now obey
my orders, and lay me alongside the French admiral.'*
Sir Edward Hawke, 1759

The Battle of Quiberon Bay was certainly one of the finest and most important victories in the long history of the Royal Navy. On 20 November 1759, Sir Edward Hawke, Knight of the Bath and Admiral of the Blue, rose inspiringly and conclusively to the challenges facing him on a darkening, tempestuous day, amid the rocks and hidden shoals of Quiberon Bay on the coast of Brittany.

In terms of overseas territorial acquisition, the Seven Years War (1756–63) brought British success on a scale unequalled in any other war. Indeed, by 1759 the French were desperate. In Canada and India they were beleaguered. In Europe, they and their Russian and Austrian allies were still held off by Frederick of Prussia, who was supported by Britain and George II's vulnerable Electorate of Hanover. The French therefore decided to attempt an invasion of the British Isles and solve many problems at a blow. It was plausibly assumed that by the autumn westerly gales would drive the Western Squadron (for whose origins, see the previous chapter) off its station. When the wind changed, the French fleet would come out of Brest. Even if observed by the remaining British frigates, the French would have a huge lead in a race for Quiberon Bay. Here, in the labyrinthine Gulf of Morbihan, the French transports would be safely congregated, ready to embark the invasion army quartered at Vannes and Auray.

In ship design and artillery, the French fleet preparing for sea at Brest was probably superior to its British adversary; but in terms of training and experience the advantage certainly lay with the blockading force. The British combined the ability to deliver a quicker rate of fire with higher standards of seamanship – such was the effect of more continuous training over the years and more time spent at sea.

However, the Battle of Quiberon Bay would not have been won – or indeed fought at all – without a British commanding admiral of exceptional calibre. Unshakeable resolution, adaptability to conditions, mature professional and tactical judgement, a very cool head and a fund of moral and physical courage would be required on this critical occasion.

Hawke's tactics at Quiberon Bay cannot be properly appreciated without some account of his previous operational record. In 1744, he commanded the *Berwick* of 70 guns at the Battle of Toulon. On that occasion a large British fleet, indifferently led by Admiral Thomas Mathews, encountered a Franco-Spanish fleet of comparable numbers sailing southwards in a rather irregular line ahead. Mathews was to windward with a light north-easterly breeze. He bungled an attempt to bear down on the enemy. Fear of disciplinary consequences discouraged his captains from using initiative and leaving the line, disordered though it was – with the single exception of Edward Hawke. Hawke ran down until he got to leeward of an advancing Spanish ship; he then engaged her at pistol shot and hammered her into submission. Mathews himself and a number of his captains were later court-martialed for their lack of spirit. Perversely, when Hawke's turn came in 1747 to be considered for flag rank, the Admiralty wished to retire him! He was saved only by the personal intervention of George II and was appointed to the shorebound command at Plymouth.

In the same year, the French mounted a major effort to supply their threatened possessions in the West Indies. A strong escort was to see a large convoy safely on its way from the Bay of Biscay into the Atlantic. However, just when the British expected the French to sail, the vice admiral commanding the Western Squadron came ashore sick at Plymouth and Hawke was the only flag officer immediately available to replace him. The Admiralty reluctantly appointed the junior rear admiral (now aged 42) on an explicitly temporary basis. Hawke, however, prepared to use the most aggressive tactical option offered by the *Fighting Instructions* – the general chase. The relevant signal ordered every captain, without reference to his assigned place in the line of battle, to close on the enemy as quickly as possible, engage the first available enemy ship, and then press ahead to make way for following British ships. No room would be left in any captain's mind for doubt and indecision such as had prevailed at the Battle of Toulon. On 14 October 1747, Hawke intercepted the French to the westward of Brest in the meridian of Cape Finisterre – the action being called on this account the *Second* Battle of Cape Finisterre, Anson having fought the First earlier in the same year, as recounted in the last chapter. Hawke hoisted the chase signal. His squadron responded. Six out of the eight French ships of the line, mostly of superior power, were taken. This was a conclusive blow to French sea power in that war. However, French predominance on land led to a neutral peace in 1748.

While blockading Brest in 1759, Hawke had to envisage a battle between larger fleets than those of

October 1747. As always, he impressed on his captains the primary aim of a very close engagement. The general chase offered the tactical system most likely to achieve this aim. Moreover, considering the poor visibility often liable to restrict communication by flags in European waters, advantage lay in being able to hoist the crucial signal (a white flag with a red cross) well before the action began. Nor would captains really need to see any more signals as the battle developed. The *Fighting Instructions* basically required a formal (and in practice negative) line of battle, but permitted use of the general chase where an enemy was outnumbered or retreating. In case of doubt, Hawke was prone to choose the positive option.

After arriving off Ushant in May 1759, Hawke obtained the Admiralty's acceptance of a continuous close blockade. This entailed unprecedented logistical and health problems – disease then being by far the main cause of death at sea. These difficulties were largely surmounted. In November, however, westerly gales forced the admiral to seek refuge in Torbay, and it was only on the 14th that he was able to head back towards Ushant. By the 16th he knew that the French fleet was out of Brest and far ahead of him. However, both fleets soon encountered contrary winds, sometimes of gale force. Superior British seamanship now gave Hawke a chance to catch up with his adversary.

By the night of the 19th, the wind was setting in westerly. Hawke believed that on the following day he would catch the French to the south of Belle Ile. Indeed, early on the 20th, with a gale coming on at WNW, the French were sighted there in chase of some British frigates. (Alerted just in time, these frigates had escaped from Quiberon Bay by the little-known Teigneuse Passage.) At 0945 Hawke made the signal for a general chase and fired three guns. By this refinement devised by Anson, the seven leading ships formed line ahead as they chased. During the next few hours the British, under a crowd of sail despite the

strengthening gales, closed inexorably on the French. Meanwhile the French commander, the Comte de Conflans, despite his considerable experience, misjudged the speed of the British advance. He invested time in forming line ahead. Then, in the *Soleil Royal* (80), he rather sedately led his three divisions towards the presumed safety of Quiberon Bay. With a 40-knot gale now blowing, he thought it most unlikely that Hawke would risk his fleet in such a constricted arena.

Hawke had 23 ships of the line. It was difficult to tell how many Conflans had. (In fact, he had 21.) As the *Soleil Royal* got round the Cardinals Rocks, Hawke remained determined, despite the gales and hidden hazards, to leave the chase signal flying throughout the battle. He would use the French as pilots.

At 1445 Hawke's leading ships began to engage the French rear division just outside the Cardinals. By

Above: A first rate of 1741 and as used at Quiberon Bay, with improved rigging when compared with the warships employed at La Hogue or Santa Cruz.

now the French van and centre were well into the Bay, sailing close-hauled and aiming, in the teeth of the continuing gales, to tack up towards the Morbihan. Hawke, some distance back in the *Royal George* (100), hoisted a red flag to confirm a general engagement. His captains were already pressing ahead into the action with total commitment.

Soon after 1500, a sudden and significant shift took place in the direction of the wind. As a frigate captain noted in his log, at '17 minutes past 3 a very hard squall came on at North'. The *Chichester* (70) lost a topsail yard and three other British ships ran foul of each other. The French for their part were thrown

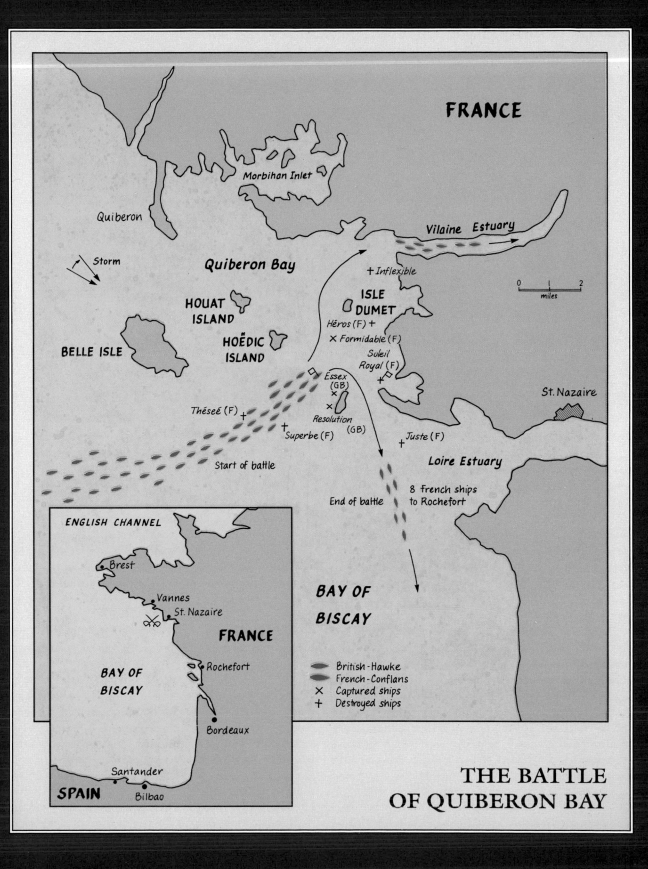

THE BATTLE OF QUIBERON BAY

into great disorder – a spectacle most disconcerting to Conflans. It was soon evident that the gales were now blowing from NW rather than from WNW. The Morbihan was becoming unattainable. Having reached a position perhaps six miles WNW of Dumet Island, Conflans decided on a reversal of course. He would get his unengaged ships back into line and lead them out of Quiberon Bay before dark. However, some ships had trouble in tacking and had to wear, thus falling away to leeward. Nevertheless, still accompanied by a dozen ships, Conflans headed towards the entrance.

Meanwhile, owing to the change of wind the *Royal George* did not negotiate the Cardinals until 1555. But Hawke was soon gratified to learn that the *Soleil Royal* and a number of other French ships were heading back towards him. Conway, the master of the *Royal George*, remarked on the navigational dangers within the Bay. Hawke commended this attention to his duty. 'Let us now', he said, 'see how well you can comply with my orders. I say, lay me alongside the French admiral.'

At about this time the flagship of the French rear division ('pierced like a cullender') struck her flag. This was the *Formidable* (80). Elsewhere the *Thésée*

(74) foundered while embattled with Keppel's *Torbay* (also a 74): despite the hard gales, the captain of the *Thésée* had kept his lower gun-ports open. When the ship rolled well over, she filled and abruptly sank. Keppel, having no other opponent, lowered some boats. Out of more than 600 French sailors, 29 were saved.

By 1630 Hawke was converging on Conflans and his dozen ships. The French fired as they wore towards Dumet Island. The *Royal George* came up with the *Superbe* (70). In characteristic style, Hawke closed right in and an event rare in the days of sail swiftly ensued. At 4.41 the *Superbe* received the *Royal George*'s second broadside and immediately sank. Thus all the routine gun drills coalesced with Hawke's standard method of attack to produce a spectacular result. Hawke now manoeuvred to rake the French flagship but was frustrated by the brave interposition of the *Intrépide* (70). Amid the ensuing excitement two French ships fell aboard the *Soleil*

Royal. With darkness now closing in, Conflans found he had been driven towards le Croisic. He was to leeward of extensive Four Shoal. Knowing that he could not escape from Quiberon Bay that night, he dropped anchor.

Meanwhile, by 1700, Hawke was two or three miles S by W of Dumet Island, and he fired two guns for the fleet to anchor. However, several captains, still in pursuit NE of Dumet, did not hear the signal. For them the general chase remained in effect. Above the howling of the wind, their firing was still heard at Hawke's anchorage for an hour after dark.

The risks accepted that day by Hawke are emphasised by the fact that, at about 2200, the *Resolution* (74), in trying to work up towards the admiral, went aground on the Four Shoal and became a total loss.

Of the French ships chased late that evening to the NE of Dumet, six would find a difficult refuge in the River Vilaine, but a seventh, the *Inflexible* (64), was lost on a sandbank at the entrance. However, nine ships did get out to sea on the night of the 20th. One, the badly shattered *Juste* (70), was wrecked on the Charpentier Rock near St. Nazaire; but eight reached Rochefort, only to be bottled up.

Meanwhile at dawn on the 21st, Conflans found himself anchored almost among the British! The damaged *Héros* (74) was nearby. With the wind blowing hard from NNW, the two French ships cut their cables and ran for the narrow entrance to the little port of le Croisic, where they drove on to the shoals just outside. The *Soleil Royal* was later burnt by the French, the *Héros* by the British. But meantime the pursuing British had lost the *Essex* (64) on the northerly edge of the Four.

In terms of ships of the line taken or destroyed, the French lost seven and the British two: more importantly, as a unified force the Brest fleet had ceased to exist. Hawke wrote in his dispatch: 'When I consider the season of the year, the hard gales on the day of action, a flying enemy, the shortness of the day, and the coast they were on, I can boldly affirm that all that could possibly be done has been done... Had we had but two hours more daylight, the whole had been totally destroyed or taken...' Henceforth the blockade could be based on Quiberon Bay. The Quiberon Peninsula afforded shelter from westerly winds, and the Biscay ports right down to Rochefort and Bordeaux could be even more tightly blockaded than before. In August the Allies on land had won at Minden, while at sea Boscawen had defeated the French Mediterranean fleet off Lagos. Quiberon Bay set the conclusive seal on 'the year of victories'.

As a role-model in the naval service, Hawke has much to commend him. Essentially humane, he depended on leadership by example rather than on the established system of punishment. He was thoroughly master of his profession. While entirely untheatrical, he was clear and forthright in both speech and correspondence. In administration he showed good sense. In every trial by battle, he displayed a calm self-confidence and outstanding moral and physical courage. His use of the general chase left his captains free to act within the bounds of an aggressive doctrine. His conduct of the innovative close blockade of Brest was crowned by the remarkable good health, the fighting spirit, the superb seamanship, and the fearsome gunnery of the fleet which swept into Quiberon Bay on 20 November 1759.

Below: Edward Hawke.

Above: The action at Quiberon Bay. Painted by Nicolas Pocock.

BIBLIOGRAPHY

Marcus, Geoffrey, *Quiberon Bay*, London, 1960. A good account of the campaign and battle.

Mackay, Ruddock F., *Admiral Hawke*, Oxford, 1965.

Mackay, Ruddock F. (ed), *The Hawke Papers*, Navy Records Society, 1990. The Papers include much of the basic material for the campaign of 1759, culminating with Hawke's dispatches of 17 and 24 November. The captains' logs are also important, especially for the battle itself; these, like most of the relevant original documents, are at the Public Record office.

Troude, O., *Batailles Navales de la France*, 4 vols, Paris, 1867. Crucial for the French side of the battle is Conflans' dispatch, which is reproduced in vol 1.

RODNEY: LES SAINTES, 1782

by Ken Breen

'He who seizes on the moment, he is the right man.'
Goethe, 1808

'I have the honour and pleasure to acquaint your Lordship that his Majesty's fleet has given such a beating to that of France as no great fleet ever had before.' So wrote Sir Samuel Hood to the First Lord of the Admiralty, Lord Sandwich, on 13 April 1782. The following month, Charles James Fox rose in the House of Commons to move a vote of thanks for 'the most brilliant victory that this country had seen this century'. Fox's praise had been prompted by dispatches from Sir George Rodney, received in London on 10 May, describing the great victory of his fleet over that of the Count de Grasse on 12 April 1782 at Les Iles des Saintes in the West Indies. The news, when it came, made a stimulating counterpoint to the succession of grim accounts that had been reaching London from the West Indies since January of 1782.

In the final months of 1781, Sir George Rodney had been recuperating in Bath from the stone and gout when he received letters from Sandwich enquiring when he would be able to resume his command in the Leeward Islands. Anxious always to do his duty,

Left: Engraving of a painting by Watson of George Bridges Rodney.

but with a cautious worry about his health, Rodney at once set in train preparations to join his squadron of reinforcements at Plymouth. Gales and heavy seas frustrated his departure until 8 January 1782. Bad weather continued to haunt him. Indeed, it is clear that, in his response to the pressure of the French threat to the islands, Rodney risked his squadron in a way that in less urgent times would have been regarded as imprudent. 'Ushant', he wrote to his wife, 'we weathered in a storm but two leagues (i.e., about 6 miles), the sea mountains high...'

When Rodney reached St. Lucia in mid-February he was depressed by the reports that greeted him. St Eustatius had fallen to de Grasse in November, and Demerary, together with six frigates, had surrendered in early January. St. Christopher, which Hood had judged to be perfectly safe, fell to the French on 12 February, quickly followed by Montserrat. Finally, to add to these losses, when he met Hood on 25 February, Rodney learnt that the ships of Hood's squadron were in 'the greatest want of repair, water, stores and provisions (particularly bread)... likewise of anchors, the whole fleet on their departure from St Christophers having been obliged to leave them behind'.

Two major tasks needed Rodney's immediate attention. The first was to remedy the deficiencies in Hood's squadron. With the local storehouses empty, he immediately put his own ships on reduced rations and transferred victuals of all kinds, but especially bread, to Hood. The second was to decide upon the best deployment of his ships to counter the French threat to the islands. Intelligence from England made it clear that the French intended an attack on Jamaica, and Rodney's plans were made accordingly. To intercept the reinforcements de Grasse was expecting at Martinique, Rodney ordered Hood, his second-in-command, to cruise to windward of Point Salines while Drake, his third, would patrol between Point Salines and St. Lucia. Drake was also to keep a close eye on the French in Fort Royal, sending regular information to Rodney so that any opportunity to attack them could be grasped. Hood was not in the least happy with these dispositions and constantly badgered Rodney to split the fleet by posting ships farther north lest the French slip into Fort Royal around the northern end of the island. Belatedly, Rodney did post three ships of the line to cruise off Marie Galante, but the trap was avoided. By 28 March it was learnt that three French sail of the line with three frigates and six thousand soldiers had managed,

Above: The Count de Grasse.

undetected, to join the main French fleet in Fort Royal. Even so, Rodney was sufficiently confident to write to Sir Peter Parker in Jamaica of his conviction that 'an end is now put to the Enemy's conquests'.

By contrast, Sir Samuel Hood showed his pessimism in a long and complaining letter to Sandwich in which he bemoaned that he had 'really fretted myself ill, for nothing, my Lord, short of a miracle, can now retrieve the affairs of the nation in these seas'. But the pieces for Rodney's great battle were now in place and the 'miracle' was soon to come.

At Fort Royal, Martinique, Count de Grasse had 36 sail of the line and enough soldiers, commanded by the Marquis de Bouille, for the investment of Jamaica. To the south, anchored in Gros Islet Bay, was Sir George Rodney with his 37 ships of the line. British frigates had been set to watch Fort Royal and report immediately on any motion on the part of the French.

After a false start on 5 April, the whole French force left Fort Royal and sailed northward to collect

Left: A painting by Richard Paren of the action at Les Saintes. The close ranges at which the battles of this era were fought is clearly shown.

more troops at Guadeloupe and then continue to Jamaica. Rodney at once weighed and ordered a general chase which continued into the night. Before daylight on 9 April the quarry was caught, but fitful and baffling winds prevented more than a desultory and unformed action. Even so, the engagements were sufficiently fierce to cause considerable damage to the *Royal Oak*, *Montagu* and *Alfred*, while the French *Caton* was so damaged as to be sent to Guadeloupe for repairs. In the early afternoon the French made use of the freshening wind to disengage while the British lay to, repairing the damages sustained in Hood's van division. Next day both fleets worked their way to windward, with the French appearing to Rodney to be cautiously avoiding coming to action.

At daylight on 11 April, the French had gained considerably to windward. The wind was now blowing a gale and Rodney signalled a general chase, which continued all day. By evening the headmost British ships were approaching a straggler damaged in the recent action. To protect her, de Grasse bore down with his whole fleet. This brought him so near that Rodney expressed confidence that he would be able to bring the French to action next day.

The lightening sky of early morning revealed the two fleets a mere four or five leagues distant from each other, in the waters between the northern end of Dominica and Les Saintes. Each was sailing in close order, with the British on a southerly heading as they sought the weather gage. Rodney at once hoisted the signal for the line ahead at two cables lengths asunder, heading NNE. The discipline and skill of the British commanders was evident in the speed and efficiency with which this manoeuvre was carried out. Because

of the damage suffered by Hood's division in the engagement on 9 April, Rodney ordered Rear Admiral Drake to lead with his rear division. Orders were signalled for the cruisers chasing to the north to be recalled and for the reefs to be shaken out of the sails.

The British line was led into battle by Taylor Penny, Captain of the *Marlborough*. He held his close hauled course until, at 0800, 'having fetched near the enemy's centre', he opened fire. Easing the helm to keep parallel with the French, the *Marlborough* sailed and fought her way to the rear of the French line, followed in orderly procession by the remaining ships of Drake's division until, at about 0900, the *Russell*, last in line, ceased firing and hauled her wind, having passed and raked the rearmost ship of the French. Heavy damage had been inflicted on the French, but Drake's division too had suffered damage to masts and spars, and the crews immediately set about repair and replacement. The strong winds of the previous night moderated as the morning advanced and at the same time became more fickle. The impact of this was dramatic. *Formidable*, Rodney's flagship, had come into action at some eight minutes past eight, again towards the centre of the French line. She had deliberately slowed her progress by backing her topsails as she passed de Grasse's *Ville de Paris*, enabling a longer exchange of fire between the two flagships. By now the firing of the guns had reduced visibility to a smoky haze, the light airs being insufficient to clear the smoke away. Even so, as *Formidable* approached the French rear division, it became evident that the orderly progression of the enemy line had been interrupted. The wind was shifting sufficiently far into the south as to prevent the French ships from holding

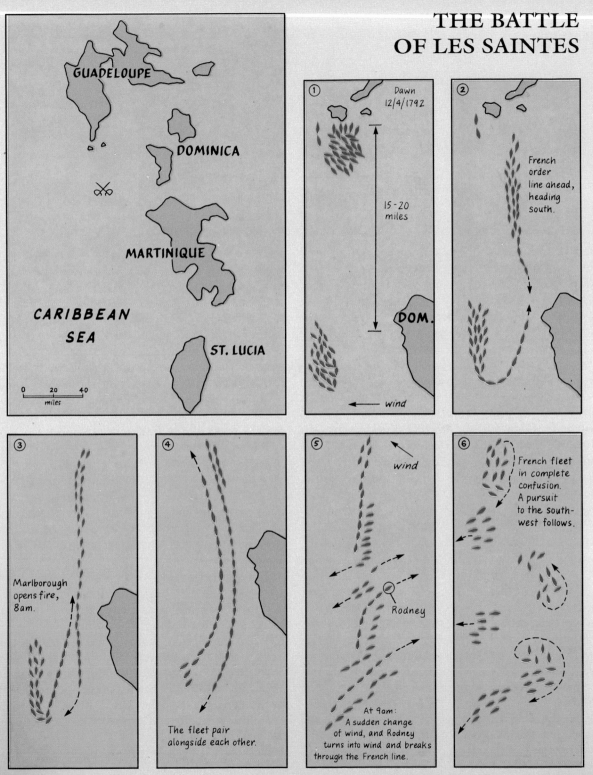

THE BATTLE OF LES SAINTES

GUADELOUPE

DOMINICA

MARTINIQUE

CARIBBEAN SEA

ST. LUCIA

0   20   40
miles

① Dawn 12/4/1792

15-20 miles

DOM.

← wind

② French order line ahead, heading south.

③ Marlborough opens fire, 8am.

④ The fleet pair alongside each other.

⑤ wind

Rodney

At 9am:
A sudden change of wind, and Rodney turns into wind and breaks through the French line.

⑥ French fleet in complete confusion. A pursuit to the south-west follows.

Left: Rodney defeating the Count de Grasse at Les Saintes. The West Indies provided many opportunities for naval distinction during the late eighteenth century.

Right: The Battle of Les Saintes.

their close hauled course. As the new wind reached each ship, so she was forced to bear away.

The first of the ships affected was the *Glorieux*, whose fate was vividly described by Sir Gilbert Blane: 'We passed so near the *Glorieux* that I could see the cannoniers throwing away their sponges and handspikes in order to save themselves below while our guns were served with the utmost animation.' She was swiftly followed by the *Diademe, Destin, Magnanime* and *Reflechi*. The ships astern of the *Formidable*, the *Namur, St. Albans* and *Canada*, continued this animated, destructive fire until, with one last devastating broadside from the *Canada*, the *Glorieux*'s masts tumbled over the side, causing her to roll her lower gun-ports into the sea. Now silent and out of control, she drifted away to leeward.

The log of the *Formidable* is terse in the extreme in its account of the battle. At this point the laconic entry notes, 'stopt our firing having cut through the Enemy's Line. Bore up and raked four of the Enemy's ships which had got foul of each other...' Yet this was the moment which was to give Rodney and his fleet the brilliant victory of Fox's praise. Whose decision it was to alter course is not clear, but the order was given and very shortly the port batteries of the *Formidable*, hitherto silent, were raking the four French ships which had got foul of each other. In this manoeuvre, Rodney was doubtless relieved to see the next in line, the *Namur, St Albans, Canada, Repulse* and *Ajax*, following in his wake. A third break in the French line was made by Commodore Affleck in the *Bedford*, the last ship in the centre division. Having sailed past the leading ships in the French line, he too found that the wind was heading them and causing

them to cross his line of sailing. Maintaining his north-easterly course, he led the ships of the rear division through the line.

These three breaks, helped or perhaps created by the critical early morning wind-shifts, had wrought confusion in the French fleet. By about 0930, de Grasse's ships were falling away towards the south-west in disorganised groups. Many were seriously damaged and the casualties on those ships jammed with troops were frighteningly high. The Marquis de Bouille later wrote that probably no other battle had been so fierce and murderous.

Rodney attempted to collect and redeploy his own ships, which had also lost much of their formation in the course of the battle. Considerable damage aloft needed to be repaired, and for some, such as the *Fame*, shot holes below the waterline had to be stopped. In mid-morning the breeze died almost completely, and the consequent lull was put to good use.

Towards noon the catspaws of wind were becoming a steady breeze and, as the ships gained steerage way, they turned towards the south-west in pursuit of the fleeing enemy. First to become a prize was the *Glorieux*. Dismasted, drifting and full of dead and wounded, she was taken by the *Royal Oak*. All afternoon Rodney conducted the pursuit. At first, he maintained the line of battle but, according to Blane, 'as the signal for the line was now hauled down, every ship annoyed the enemy as their respective commanders judged best'.

Hood and Affleck were both critical of Rodney for not ordering a general chase, which would, they claimed, have given many more prizes. Charles Dou-

flag, despite being hailed by de Grasse to 'stick by him'. The *Ville de Paris* was left isolated and a target, in succession, for the *Canada* and *Barfleur*. Hood presented an evocative cameo when he described the last active moments of the French flagship: 'Observing the *Ville de Paris* to edge towards the *Barfleur*, I concluded the Count de Grasse had a mind to yield to an old friend and therefore met his wishes by going towards him... when I opened such a tremendous fire against him that he could only stand it for about ten minutes and down came his flag...' Immediately upon seeing the surrender of the *Ville de Paris*, Rodney ordered the fleet to bring to on the larboard tack. The action was ended and the victory won.

Until 18 April the British fleet lay becalmed under Guadeloupe. The moment the breeze came, Rodney ordered Hood's squadron 'which had not received in the second action [12 April] near the damage the other two squadrons had,' to sail westward to Point Altavela on the south side of St. Domingo as hard as possible in the hope of intercepting some of the enemy's crippled ships. There they were to await the arrival of the remainder of the fleet. Hood, of the opinion that a chance had already been lost of making prizes of more French ships, set all sail he could in order to be off the Mona Passage at the soonest possible moment. His haste was rewarded for, as daylight strengthened on 19 April, he saw a fleet of five sail heading into the Mona Passage. They were indeed French stragglers, and Hood ordered a general chase.

Between two and three in the afternoon a spirited action started in which the *Ceres* (18), *Aimable* (30), *Caton* (64) and *Jason* (64) were captured, the fifth making off to the west pursued by the *Warrior* and *Prince William*. All four were rated by Hood as very fine ships – the Toulon-built *Caton* and *Jason* being almost new, the *Aimable* a fine coppered frigate and the *Ceres* 'a very elegant coppered ship'. These last captures can justly be counted as part of the fruits of Les Saintes. In all, Rodney's fleet had captured seven ships of the line, including the magnificent 110-gun *Ville de Paris*, a frigate and the sloop *Ceres*.

glas, Rodney's fleet captain, did not accept this, pointing out that the French were given no chance to rally or repair their ships. Hood's claim was supposition. Douglas was reporting events. By 1500 the British ships were up with the French rear and engaging them with great vigour. Already finding it hard to keep up because of damage sustained in the morning encounter, the *César* surrendered at 1530 to the *Centaur* and *Bedford*. At 1630 the *Canada*, which had earlier been fighting the *Ville de Paris*, received the surrender of the *Hector*. About 1800 the *Prince William* and *Belliquex* came up with the *Ardent* and she, too, surrendered after a short exchange of fire. Rodney later noted that the *Ardent* was a particularly valuable prize as she was carrying the French siege train destined for use against Jamaica.

One more French ship was yet to be captured and she was to be, perhaps, the greatest prize of all. As the afternoon wore into evening, de Grasse, in his flagship *Ville de Paris*, continued to try to rally his fleet around the centre – but to no avail. Bougainville, commanding the van, kept sailing westwards under as much canvas as could be carried and was followed by the remaining ships. Even the *Couronne* abandoned the

In less tangible ways, the victory carried even greater rewards. As Rodney immediately wrote to Sandwich, 'I flatter myself I shall soon have an opportunity of congratulating your Lordship upon Jamaica being out of danger.' The great objective of the ministry in sending Rodney to the West Indies earlier in the year had been to protect the islands, especially Jamaica, and this was gloriously achieved. Further-

more, Les Saintes brought to an end the succession of failures that had followed Yorktown and restored, in no small degree, the tarnished British military and naval reputation amongst the European powers. It opened the way to the general peace that followed soon afterwards, with Britain able to negotiate in a position of equality and strength.

Sadly, this bright and glorious success was tarnished by subsequent bickering and criticism. Where Fox, the critic, saw brilliant victory, Hood, the subordinate, saw inadequacy and failure. Though Hood had written to Sandwich about a 'beating as no great Fleet ever had before', he saw no illogicality or disloyalty in adding in the same letter, 'I was most exceedingly disappointed in our commander in chief.' Already critical of the fleet dispositions made by Rodney in the days leading to the battle, Hood now claimed that Rodney should have ordered a general chase during the afternoon of 12 April and continued it during the hours of darkness. Had he done so, he averred, 'it would have enabled him to take almost every ship this day'.

The matter of the breaking the line also proved a fruitful ground for hot debate both at the time and, for historians, ever since. Was it Rodney who saw and seized an opportunity, or was the decision pressed on him by his fleet captain, Sir Charles Douglas? Some would argue that it was unwise for Rodney to have changed course to take him through the French line, already in disarray because of the wind shifts. The argument would claim that the British fleet, maintaining its line, would have inflicted more damage on the French as they were forced, by the wind, to sail

Above: The close of Les Saintes as *Ville de Paris* strikes her colours to *Barfleur*.

towards the British line. The value of these hypotheses cannot now be adequately judged, yet even so, a magnificent victory had been obtained. Honour and courtesy should have kept Hood and his fellow critics silent to allow all in the British fleet to enjoy to the full this moment of triumph. Rodney, by contrast, singled out for the highest praise Samuel Hood, Francis Drake, Edmund Affleck and Charles Douglas for their roles in the battle and ended, 'In short, I want words to express how sensible I am of the Meritorious Conduct of all the Captains, Officers and Men who had a share in this Glorious Victory obtained by their Gallant Exertions.'

BIBLIOGRAPHY

Mackesey, P., *The War for America*, London, 1964. Still unsurpassed in the breadth of coverage and the soundness of its judgements.

Spinney, D., *Rodney*, London, 1969. A very readable biography, soundly based upon Rodney's official and unofficial papers.

Hood, D., *The Admirals Hood*, London, 1942. As yet there is no subsequent volume on Sir Samuel Hood. Dorothy Hood reveals the flaws in the admiral's character.

Mundy, G., *Life and Correspondence of Admiral Lord Rodney*, London, 1830. A subjective view of Rodney by his son-in-law.

Dull, J., *The French Navy and American Independence*, Princeton, 1975. A useful background volume written from the viewpoint of a diplomatic historian.

Sandwich Papers, Navy Records Society, vol IV. A helpful collection of relevant papers judiciously edited.

HOWE: GLORIOUS 1ST JUNE, 1794

by Chris Ware

'Nothing is more difficult than the art of manoeuvre. What is difficult about manoeuvre is to make the devious route the most direct and to turn misfortune to advantage.'
Sun Tzu, 500 BC

This battle in many ways can be seen as the last of the old eighteenth-century engagements; it was also a harbinger of things to come. As the first major fleet action of the Revolutionary War, it has a special significance.

The years 1793–4 were very bad for French agriculture. There was near famine in certain parts of France, which heightened the effects of the chaos that ensued after the Revolution. Although recent French scholarship has played down the effects of this, it is certainly true that it meant the French Directorate had to organise the import of a large quantity of grain. This was to be transported in 117 vessels from Chesapeake Bay and sailed in convoy with a minimal escort, of two 74s, two frigates and a brig under the command of Rear Admiral Vanstabel. The French Fleet at Brest, under Villaret de Joyeuse, was ordered to cover the arrival of the convoy. It was standard practice for both the French and British navies to cover the sailing and arrivals of the different trades throughout the season. A small squadron at Rochefort under Rear Admiral Joseph Marie Neilly, with five 74s, one 80-gun ship of the line and a number of frigates, also had orders to cover the homeward bound convoy.

Villaret did not sail from Brest until 16 May, with the French main fleet of 25 ships of the line plus frigates and corvettes, to swell the escort and covering force. By this point most of the available French Atlantic fleet was out to cover the impending arrival of the convoy, which in itself gives some measure of the seriousness with which the French Directorate viewed the arrival of the ships from the United States of America.

While the grain convoy was being prepared, the British sent frigates off the principal French port to see how prepared the French fleet was to sail. In early May, Lord Howe put to sea with the bulk of the British fleet to cover an outward bound convoy assembling in St. Helens Roads. By the 4th, Howe was off the Lizard, and he detached Rear Admiral Montague with six 74-gun ships of the line and two frigates to cover the British convoy as far as the latitude of Cape Finisterre. Also detached from the British main fleet at this time was Captain Peter Ranier with one 74 and a 64 plus four frigates to carry the convoy further out into the Atlantic. The British fleet was now reduced to 26 ships of the line and seven frigates, one hospital ship and two fireships, approximately the same force as the French convoy escort.

On 17 May the fleets passed close to one another in the fog. By the time it cleared on the 18th they had passed out of sight of one another. On 19 May the French under Nielly captured the British frigate *Castor*. It seemed to Howe that Montague's detachment was in danger. He therefore altered course to make a junction with him. However, the weather and wind forced Howe too far to the south. By 24 May, his fleet was again only a few miles from the French under Nielly: he took two small detached French units, the *Républicaine* (20 guns) and the *Inconnue*. At the same time a 74-gun ship made its escape and rejoined Neilly's squadron.

Howe gave chase but it was not until 0630 on the 28th that the British lookout frigates signalled a fleet to windward. Rear Admiral Pasley was ordered to investigate with his division, which consisted of the *Bellerophon*, *Russell*, *Marlborough* and *Thunderer*. By 0700 the strange sail were seen bearing down on the British under topgallant sails only, i.e., prepared for battle. The French under Vilaret were, however, under orders not to engage the British unless it was the only way to get the convoy through.

The French, consisting of 26 ships of the line and seven frigates, lay to at 1000. The British fleet were ordered to wear and passed to windward of the French. At 1110 a signal was made that the men of the British fleet were to have their dinner. At 1330 the British leading division under Pasley was ordered to 'annoy' the French rear, the French line being more than a little ragged there. At this manoeuvre the French made off, and Admiral Howe ordered a general chase and for ships to engage as they came up with the enemy.

At 1440 one of Palsey's division fired at the French at the range of about a mile – to little effect – and the compliment was returned by the French to the same effect. These opening shots were followed by closer action when several of the British vessels came up with the rearmost of the French, including the *Révolutionnaire* of 110 guns, which was bought to action by the *Bellerophon*. She cannonaded her large antagonist for half an hour before being supported by the *Russell* and *Marlborough*. In the meantime she had sustained sufficient damage aloft to prevent her taking further part in this action, and it was left to the two other British ships to engage the French rear at long range.

Later still, two more British vessels joined the action, *Audacious* and *Leviathan*. The *Audacious* took up where the *Bellerophon* had left off to such an effect that the *Révolutionnaire* was almost completely disabled, but *Audacious* herself did not escape damage. She was very much cut up in her masts and rigging, as were the other units which engaged in this phase of the action. When the British hauled off, the French had sustained a loss of upward of 400 men on the one vessel heavily engaged. The British only lost a few dozen, but they were unable to take possession of the French vessel and the *Audacious* took no further part in the unfolding drama.

On 29 May the fleets manoeuvred to gain the best position to engage, the British trying to gain the weather gage and still chase the French from astern. At 0730 the British opened fire on the rear of the French line again from a distance, and the French returned an equally ineffectual fire. At 0800 the French van manoeuvred to come to support of the rear of their line and at 1000 they opened an ineffectual fire on the British van. Once again it was the British masts and rigging which suffered in this engagement, lessening their ability to manoeuvre in any subsequent action.

On the 29th and 30th the fleets remained within sight of each another. On the night of the 30/31 May the British stood to the westward, and the following morning there was a moderate breeze blowing south by west and a calm sea. By this time Howe had managed to get to windward of the French and at 0716 on 1 June he signalled the fleet should attack the French centre. At 0725 he followed this up with a signal that the fleet should pass through the French line and engage to leeward. At this point the two fleets were approximately four miles apart.

By 0924 the French van had opened a distant fire on the British, the first shot of the main battle, and by

Below: Captain Neville of the Queen's Royal Regiment is shown here mortal- **ly wounded aboard the** *Queen Charlotte.* **(ASKB)**

Above: Admiral of the Fleet Richard Howe. Portrait by John Singleton Copley.

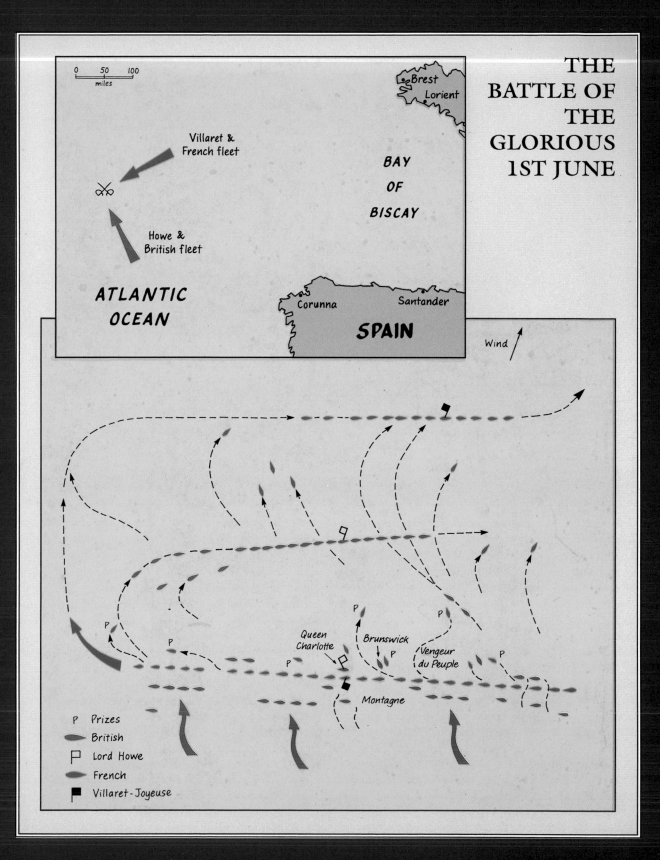

THE BATTLE OF THE GLORIOUS 1ST JUNE

0   50   100
miles

Villaret & French fleet

Howe & British fleet

ATLANTIC OCEAN

Brest
Lorient

BAY OF BISCAY

Corunna   Santander

SPAIN

Wind

Queen Charlotte

Brunswick

Vengeur du Peuple

Montagne

P   Prizes
    British
⊡   Lord Howe
    French
◼   Villaret-Joyeuse

0950 the fire had become general on the French side. The British returned fire at the same time as trying to pass through the French line. However, not all the British ships passed through, and most engaged from the windward side rather than following Howe's orders and engaging to leeward. By the afternoon the action was all but over with the British having 11 ships and the French 12 crippled in the fierce single-ship actions into which the battle had dissolved.

The *Caesar* held off at a length of just over a three cables (600 yards) from the van of the French and took no great part. The *Bellerophon*, which had been heavily engaged in the early actions, attacked the *Eole*. After a brisk action of which the *Bellerophon* had the better, she then came under fire from the *Trajan* as well as the *Eole* and was again damaged in mast and rigging, becoming so unmanageable that she had to signal for a frigate to come to her aid. (In such a general action the frigates of both sides were non-combatants and were used to tow off damaged ships.)

The *Leviathan* engaged the *America* from the windward side and in a sharp action totally disabled her. The *Russell* brought the French *Téméraire* to action but was also engaged by the *Trajan* and *Eole* ahead of her in the French line; she had to be rescued by the *Leviathan*. The next in the British line, the *Royal Sovereign*, engaged the French *Terrible* at long range and was subsequently ordered to engage her more closely. This she did to such effect that the *Terrible* left the line and was raked by the *Royal Sovereign* in the process. The *Terrible* was aided by the *Montagne* and *Jacobin*, which in turn were engaged by the *Valiant*. The *Marlborough* became involved in a sharp action with the *Impetueux* whom she had passed to leeward. The next astern in the French line, *Mucius*, ranged up alongside the *Marlborough* and during the ensuing fierce action all three vessels were dismasted. The *Marlborough* was so unmanageable that she signalled for assistance and was eventually taken in tow by the *Aquilon*. Of her two opponents, the *Impetueux* was taken by the *Russell* and the *Mucius* made good her escape. The *Defence* passed through the French line between the *Mucius* and *Tourville* and was so heavily damaged that she too had to signal for assistance and be taken into tow.

The next three in the British line stayed to windward of their opponents and cannonaded from long range with little effect. The *Invincible* engaged the *Juste*, and forced her to bear up, bringing her under fire from Howe's Flagship, *Queen Charlotte*; she then surrendered. The *Culloden* and *Gibraltar* also engaged from windward, again to very little effect.

Howe's Flagship, the *Queen Charlotte*, steered to cut the French line and came under heavy fire from *Vengeur du Peuple* and *Achille*. She was then engaged by the *Jacobin* and *Montagne*, to leeward and windward of her. After a hot action, the *Jacobin* dropped astern and the *Montagne* made sail and disengaged. The *Queen Charlotte* next fired on the *Juste*, which she dismasted, and which later surrendered.

Left: L'Achille was one of six prizes taken during the Battle of the Glorious First of June.

Below: A 24-pounder carronade, made by the Scots firm of Carron for the Royal Navy from 1779.

The *Brunswick*, being thwarted in her attempts to cut through the line, ran alongside the *Vengeur* and fouled her, the two ships becoming locked together. There commenced a bloody action in which the captain of the *Brunswick*, Havery, was seriously wounded. The *Brunswick* also disabled the French *Achilles*, which was coming to the *Vengeur*'s assistance. The *Vengeur*'s damages were made worse by the *Ramillies*, which came to the *Brunswick*'s aid. *Vengeur du Peuple* had a huge hole torn in her stern, and after three hours in action was left sinking. *Brunswick*, however, was in little better state. She had lost her mizzen mast, while her bowsprit and main mast were heavily damaged, twenty-three guns had been dismounted and she had been on fire three times!

Valiant fought to windward of the *Patriote* and then engaged the *Achille*. The *Orion* had two opponents, the French *Northumberland* and thereafter the *Patriote*. The *Queen* was badly damaged coming into action and brought the *Jemmapes* to action, shooting away her mizzenmast. The *Queen* lost her mainmast in this action and damaged her mizzen. She forced the *Jemmapes* to strike her colours but was unable to take possession of her because of her own condition.

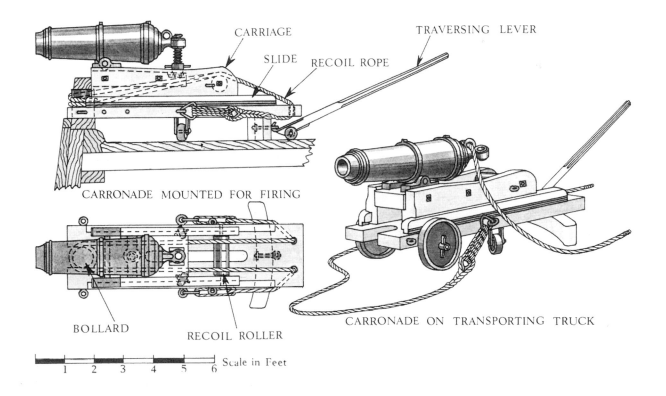

CARRIAGE

TRAVERSING LEVER

SLIDE RECOIL ROPE

CARRONADE MOUNTED FOR FIRING

BOLLARD RECOIL ROLLER

CARRONADE ON TRANSPORTING TRUCK

Scale in Feet
1 2 3 4 5 6

Right: A painting of the Battle of The Glorious First of June by Loutherbourg.

The rear of the British line engaged in a series of short actions with several of the damaged French ships, many of which were trying to make their escape. Several of the British, the *Royal George* in particular, were again badly damaged in masts and rigging during this phase of the action.

The action petered out by 1815 when Villaret drew off to the northward with the remains of his fleet. Admiral Howe had to lay to in order to allow his ships to repair their rigging and masts. It was not until late on 3 June that the British could make sail for Spithead, where they arrived on the 13th. The total losses for the British during the three days in which actions took place between the two fleets was 290 killed and 858 wounded. The French had lost six ships captured and nearly 1,200 killed in just those vessels. Some estimates put their losses of men overall as 8,500 killed, wounded and captured.

The convoy reached France unscathed, but the British had achieved the victory so much desired by the nation. In all the clamour of rejoicing, the missing of the convoy mattered little to a jubilant and grateful public. The French cockerel had had its neck wrung by John Bull and the nation celebrated. The battle had also been a textbook example of the eighteenth-century naval battle, with two fleets manoeuvring for advantage; however, unlike some of its predecessors it came to a bloody conclusion. And while the old enemy had lost none of his courage, there were signs that skill was on the wane.

BIBLIOGRAPHY

James, *Naval History of Great Britain*, 1837.
Clowes, W. L., *Naval History of Great Britain*, vol IV.
Creswell, *Admirals of the Eighteenth Century*, London, 1973.
Laughton G. K., *Logs of Great Sea Fights*, Navy Records Society, 1897

Warner, O., *The First of June*, London, 1963.
Ware, C. J., 'The Royal Navy and Toulon' in *Proceedings of the Anglo French Conference*, Service Historic de la Marine, 1990.

JERVIS:
ST. VINCENT, 1797

by Michael Duffy

Captain of the Fleet:	*There are eight sail of the line, Sir John.*
Lord St. Vincent:	*Very well, Sir.*
Captain of the Fleet:	*There are twenty sail of the line, Sir John.*
Lord St. Vincent:	*Very well, Sir,*
Captain of the Fleet:	*There are twenty-five sail of the line, Sir John.*
Lord St. Vincent:	*Very well, Sir.*
Captain of the Fleet:	*There are twenty-seven sail of the line, Sir John.*
Lord St. Vincent:	*Enough, Sir, no more of that. If there are fifty sail I will go through them.*

Lord St. Vincent, 1797

'A victory is very essential to England at the moment.' There was much truth in this remark of Admiral Sir John Jervis, commander-in-chief of the Mediterranean fleet, as he took his fifteen ships of the line towards where he expected to find a Spanish fleet of some 26 or 27 of the line in the early morning of 14 February 1797.

On 4 October 1796, Spain had joined France and Holland, bringing its 79 ships of the line into the war against the Royal Navy and forcing the Admiralty to order the evacuation of the Mediterranean. Jervis withdrew his fleet to operate from Lisbon, where he could prevent the Spanish fleet combining with the French Brest fleet in order to control the Western Approaches and threaten invasion – as had happened in the previous war in 1779 and 1781. Jervis left a Mediterranean war in which Britain's Austrian ally, repeatedly defeated by Napoleon in Italy, was about to sue for peace. Meanwhile the French Brest fleet had launched an invasion of Ireland, reaching Bantry Bay at Christmas, only to be driven back by the weather. The shock of that was traumatic, so that when a further, though much smaller raiding force landed at Fishguard in February, a panic run on the banks followed, forcing the Bank of England to suspend cash payments. Were the Spanish fleet to link up with the French in the Western Approaches, there was real danger that public demoralisation would bring the war to a disastrous conclusion.

Nor did it seem that the Mediterranean fleet was in any condition to prevent such a catastrophe. In his

Left: Rear Admiral John Jervis, 1735–1823, 1st Earl St. Vincent painted by Sir William Beechey.

Below right: The action of 14 February 1797 as the fleets clash at Cape St. Vincent.

THE BATTLE OF ST. VINCENT

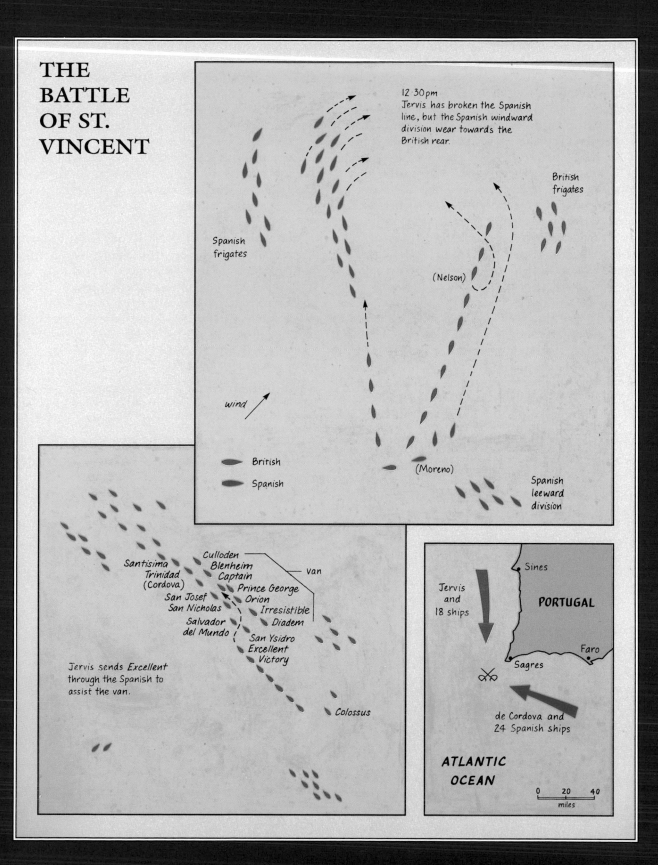

12.30 pm
Jervis has broken the Spanish line, but the Spanish windward division wear towards the British rear.

British frigates

Spanish frigates

(Nelson)

wind

British
Spanish

(Moreno)

Spanish leeward division

Santisima Trinidad (Cordova)
Culloden
Blenheim
Captain
van
San Josef
San Nicholas
Prince George
Orion
Irresistible
Diadem
Salvador del Mundo
San Ysidro
Excellent
Victory
Colossus

Jervis sends *Excellent* through the Spanish to assist the van.

Jervis and 18 ships

Sines

PORTUGAL

Faro

Sagres

de Cordova and 24 Spanish ships

ATLANTIC OCEAN

0   20   40
miles

fifteen months as its commander, Jervis had trained it into a superbly efficient fighting force, but the move to Lisbon inflicted worse casualties than a lost battle – two 74s were wrecked, and a 74, 80 and 98 so damaged from grounding as to be inoperative until repaired, reducing Jervis's fleet by a third. He was joined on 6 February by five of the line from England – 'so good a batch', he wrote, as to make 'a valuable addition to my excellent stock' – bringing his force to two first rates, four second, and nine thirds (including one 64). Yet again, misfortune struck. Shortly after learning that the Spanish fleet had passed Gibraltar, a night collision threatened to force *Culloden* (74) back to port. Her captain, however, was Thomas Troubridge, one of the most outstanding of Jervis's 'excellent stock', and he and his crew epitomised the high fighting morale of this fleet by energetically repairing their damages at sea so as not to miss the expected battle. On 13 February, Jervis was rejoined by his brightest star, Commodore Horatio Nelson, bringing the British Viceroy of Corsica back from the Mediterranean, who reported sailing through the Spanish fleet during the night. Jervis gave the signal to prepare for action and sailed into

the night of 13/14 February with his fleet in close order in expectation of imminent battle. The Spanish fleet was reported to be nearly double his own strength, and a third of his own force had only been with him for a week; nevertheless, as he subsequently wrote, he was 'confident in the skill, valour and discipline of the officers and men I had the happiness to command, and judging that the honour of His Majesty's arms, and the circumstances of the war in these seas, required a considerable degree of enterprise...' he went looking for the victory that was so 'very essential to England'.

The Spanish fleet of 27 of the line had sailed from Cartagena on 1 February. The French were pressing for its passage to Brest, but it was not yet ready and had instead a more limited mission, to escort a troop convoy to Algeciras and a mercury convoy to Cadiz. Admiral Juan de Cordova fulfilled the first part of his mission, dropping off the troop convoy under the care of three of his ships of the line; but he was then

Below: Fought against a larger Spanish Fleet, the Battle of St. Vincent made the reputation of Nelson as well as that of Sir John Jervis.

Above: Lord Collingwood who with Nelson fought the Spanish alone at Cape St. Vincent until the British main fleet closed up. An engraving by C. Turner.

blown into Jervis's path by strong easterly winds, which took him beyond Cadiz to the south-west of Cape St. Vincent, before changing to westerly and enabling him to make his way back towards Spain's main naval base. His scouting frigates spotted some of Jervis's ships on the 13th, but he dismissed this as a merchant convoy. On the morning of the following day, his fleet was sailing ESE in three loose columns, with four mercury-laden *urcas* under separate escort of two ships of the line. He had detached two more of the line to investigate gunfire astern, leaving him seven first rates and fifteen third rates in company.

In hazy weather, he did not see Jervis's approaching fleet until too late. When he did, he made a last-minute attempt both to get his three columns into a line and to gain the weather gage by ordering them to form on the reverse course. This proved to be a double manoeuvre beyond the ability of crews both little exercised in fleet evolutions and under-strength – it was reported after the battle that 'the flagships had not more than sixty or eighty seamen on board, the

remainder of their crews consisting of pressed landsmen, and soldiers of their new levies'. Subsequent cohesion was not helped by the fact that the struggle to form line, pell-mell on the reverse course, left most of the flagships, formerly *leading* their columns, back towards the rear. Seventeen ships hauled their wind on the larboard tack, but many were still three or four abreast rather than in line as the British fleet came up with them. Worse still, the *urca* convoy had shot ahead to the ESE and was unable to get back to the main fleet, causing the three rearmost Spanish ships to stand across the oncoming British line to help protect them. In this chaos and division, the Spanish numerical advantage evaporated.

Jervis, in his flagship *Victory*, had been proceeding with his fleet on a southerly course in two tight columns. When his scouts sighted the first distant sails, he had ordered his leading ships to chase, but when it became clear he was in the presence of the entire Spanish fleet he formed line, while pressing onwards. The evident Spanish disorder must have dispelled any remaining doubts about attacking – the master of Rear Admiral Parker's van flagship, *Prince George*, noted that 'on our closing up so fast with them they attempted to draw upon the larboard tack, I say attempted, because they form'd the evolution so ill, that in viewing them with a seaman's eye, it was sufficient to inspire us with a confidence of success in spite of the superiority of their numbers.' With the haze clearing and the fleets closing, Jervis's flag captain counted their opponents for the admiral: 8, 20, 25, 27... at which Jervis cut him short with a curt, 'Enough, Sir, no more of that: the die is cast, and if there are fifty sail I will go through them.'

Jervis directed his line SSW on the starboard tack towards the gap developing between the *urca* convoy and the rest of the Spanish fleet struggling to form line NNW on the larboard tack to windward. At about 11.30, Troubridge, leading in *Culloden*, opened fire as he passed the windward division. In his way was Vice Admiral Moreno with two first rates and a third bearing towards the exposed convoy. On collision course, Troubridge dismissed his first lieutenant's warning – 'Can't help it, Griffiths, let the weakest fend off.' The Spaniards cleared away and Troubridge swept through the gap with a crashing broadside.

Having broken the enemy line, Jervis had to decide which part to attack – Cordova's seventeen ships to windward or the nine ships to leeward. Throughout the action the British thought that all nine vessels to leeward were ships of the line, not realising that four were large, armed merchantmen carrying mercury needed in the Spanish American mines to amalgamate the silver ores so essential for sustaining the enemy war effort. It is unlikely, however, that Jervis would have changed his decision to tack after the larger windward force. His most immediate and pressing need was to cripple as much as he could of the Spanish main fleet, and he had the chance to do so on nearly even terms – fifteen ships against seventeen – before the Spanish leeward division could tack back against the wind to reinforce them, whereas the leeward force would get quicker support from the windward division. After allowing his van to extend sufficiently beyond the gap, both to tack in safety and to prevent the leeward force rounding the end of his line, at 1208 Jervis signalled to Troubridge to tack. The latter, waiting in readiness for the signal, brought *Culloden* round smartly in pursuit of the Spanish main body.

The first five ships of Jervis's van tacked in succession before Moreno's two first rates sought to disrupt the British manoeuvre, either to ensure none of British line wore after the convoy or because he saw the chance of catching the British ships at a disadvantage while in stays as they tacked. This one aggressive action of the Spanish fleet during the engagement brought down *Colossus*'s fore and fore topsail yards, putting that ship out of the action. *Victory*, following, caught Moreno as he tacked under the flagship's lee and raked him both ahead and astern, but Moreno's second managed to damage two more of the centre, slowing its passage in pursuit of the main body, before they drew off again.

Moreno's intervention and a shift of the wind to south-west caused a gap to develop between the main body and the British van, now in hot pursuit of the Spanish windward division, threatening to lose Jervis the chance of a decisive re-engagement. Looking to bring support more quickly to the van, at 1250 Jervis signalled *Britannia*, leading his rear division, to tack at once to its support, followed by the signal for each rear ship as they came up to take suitable station among the van and engage. Occupied with a fire and clearing

Below: The action of 14 February 1797 as the fleets clash at Cape St. Vincent.

Right: Nelson boarding the *San Josef* at the Battle of St. Vincent.

wreckage from the engagement with the windward force, *Britannia* failed to respond. However, two ships behind him was Nelson, flying his pennant on *Captain* (74), who divined Jervis's intentions. Nelson had also noticed that Cordova's flagship, the giant, four-decked, 136-gun *Santisima Trinidad*, had begun to bear up in the hope of leading the windward division either to attack the last isolated ships of the British line or to work behind them to join his leeward division. Without waiting for *Britannia*'s lead, Nelson on his own initiative wore his ship out of line and set course to head off the Spanish flagship.

At about 1.20 *Culloden* caught up with the rearmost Spanish ships and renewed the action, followed ten minutes later by *Blenheim* in her wake, and almost immediately after by *Captain* farther up the Spanish line, taking on alone the Spanish flagship and its two seconds until the others came to Nelson's relief. Cordova gave up his attempt to wear the British line and hauled to windward again. While *Culloden* and *Blenheim* took over the contest with the Spanish flagship and its consorts, Nelson, still full of fight, fell back into a prolonged action with the *San Josef* (112) and *San Nicholas* (80).

The action thereafter focused on the last six Spanish ships, headed by the *Santisima Trinidad*. As the remaining three ships of Jervis's van, backed by *Diadem* (64) from the rear, joined the attack from the leeward, an eyewitness, John Drinkwater, noted that 'the cannonade became more animated and impressive. The superiority of the British fire over that of the enemy, and its effect on the enemy's hulls and sails, were so evident, that we in the frigate no longer hesitated to pronounce a glorious termination to the contest.' The centre and remaining ships of the British rear had merged and were coming up in line to windward of this contest, and the final decisive move came when Jervis ordered *Excellent* (74), which had tacked from the rear to head this column, to press ahead and pass through the Spanish rear. Commanded by the gunnery expert Collingwood, *Excellent*'s rapid broadsides forced *Salvador Del Mundo* (112) into temporary surrender and he then turned on the sternmost Spanish ship, *San Ysidro* (74), which also struck. The *Salvador* had resumed action but finally struck as *Victory* came up in Collingwood's wake. Collingwood then passed forward to the relief of the now badly damaged *Captain*, and a broadside within ten feet of

San Nicholas shattered that ship and drove it aboard *San Josef*, already partially dismasted by *Captain*. *Excellent* moved on to engage the Spanish flagship, but Nelson, fearful of losing his prize to the other ships now coming up, luffed the damaged *Captain* alongside the *San Nicholas*, boarded and forced its surrender. *San Josef*, unable to disentangle from *San Nicholas* and further damaged by *Prince George*, thereupon surrendered to Nelson also.

The last scenes were played out around the *Santisima Trinidad*, as ship after ship now came up to fire on the giant Spanish flagship, which put up a heroic resistance. At one point it was thought that she too had surrendered, but Moreno brought the leeward division to his admiral's assistance, the two ships detached earlier in the day now returned, and some of the Spanish van also turned back in support, so that Jervis felt it best to end the action. His prizes had to be secured from recapture with a diminished force. *Colossus* had been crippled earlier, and *Culloden*, *Blenheim*, and *Captain* were now too damaged to continue – indeed the latter had still to be disentangled from her captures. Jervis formed line between his prizes and casualties and the enemy, who then bore off with their crippled flagship. The two fleets remained in sight next day, but neither felt strong enough to renew the action. The Spanish then limped back into Cadiz and Jervis into Lagos Bay to repair damages.

Quite apart from the capture of two first rates and two thirds from a superior fleet, the Battle of Cape St Vincent was crucial to regaining the initiative for Britain in the naval war. The shattered and demoralised Spanish fleet played no offensive part in the war for another two years. While a number of Spanish ships had fought bravely, their crews lacked the disciplined gun-drill of the British fleet and had been unable to match the British rate and accuracy of fire, while some officers had shown an incompetence and cowardice that resulted in Cordova's banishment from royal service and an admiral and four captains being stripped of their rank. Jervis, in contrast, was rewarded with the earldom of St. Vincent, and Nelson with the Order of the Bath and promotion to rear admiral.

BIBLIOGRAPHY

Drinkwater-Bethune, J., *A Narrative of the Battle of St. Vincent*, London, 1840. The classic description, by an eye-witness; but to be treated with caution because of the steps taken by Nelson to ensure that his particular contribution dominated Drinkwater's account.

Sturges Jackson, T., *Logs of the Great Sea Fights, 1794–1805*, Navy Records Society, vol XVI, 1899. The official logs of all the individual British ships involved in the battle, recorded in varied but sometimes vivid detail.

Taylor, A. H., 'The Battle of Cape St. Vincent' in *The Mariner's Mirror*, No 40, 1954. A necessary corrective embodying the Spanish view of the battle.

James, W., *A Naval History of Great Britain*, vol II, London, 1837.

Lloyd, C., *Battles of St. Vincent and Camperdown*, London, 1963.

Palmer, M. A. J., 'Sir John's Victory: The Battle of Cape St. Vincent Reconsidered' in *The Mariner's Mirror*, no 77, 1991. Accords the credit that should be given to Jervis for his handling of the action.

NELSON: ABOUKIR, 1798

by Brian Lavery

*'Before this time tomorrow I shall have
gained a Peerage or Westminster Abbey.'*
Nelson before the battle, 1798

At half past two on the afternoon of 1 August 1798, the lookout at the masthead of HMS Zealous spotted the French fleet at anchor in Aboukir Bay. A signal was made to the rest of the ships, and according to Nelson's flag captain, Sir Edward Berry of the Vanguard, 'The utmost joy seemed to animate every breast on board the squadron, at the sight of the enemy.' It was the end of a chase that had begun when Rear Admiral Nelson had entered the Mediterranean in May, resuming a British presence after a gap of more than eighteen months. It had taken him to Sardinia, Elba, Citta Vecchia, Naples, Sicily, Alexandria, and back to Sicily again, before he finally returned to Egypt and success. It had been made especially difficult by the fact that he had neither a base nor an ally in the Mediterranean.

Nor was his fleet a balanced one, on contemporary terms. He had no three-decker as his flagship, for his superior, Admiral the Earl of St. Vincent, had taken care to send him two-deckers of 74 guns, rather than clumsy ships of 98 or 100 guns. Meanwhile the total lack of frigates (separated due to an accident at an early stage of the chase) had made it much harder to find the enemy. On the eve of the battle Nelson wrote, 'No frigates! to which has been, and may again, be attributed the loss of the French fleet.' But he had no reason to complain about his 74s. According to an eminent naval architect of the period, 'The 74 gun ship on the contrary contains the properties of the first rate and the frigate. She will not shrink from an encounter with a first rate, nor abandon the chase of a frigate on account of swiftness.' Apart from thirteen 74s, Nelson had one 50-gun ship, the *Leander*. This type was a product of a poor compromise in past ages, and it was neither a good frigate nor an effective ship of the line (though the *Leander* was to do her best in the latter role). In addition he had the tiny brig *Mutine*, far too small for effective fleet reconnaissance.

The French squadron was commanded by Admiral Brueys. It had thirteen ships of the line, and in that respect it was equal to Nelson's. In gun power it was considerably stronger, for it included a 120-gun three-decker, *L'Orient*, three ships of 80 guns, and nine 74s. Including frigates, it mounted 1,196 guns, compared with Nelson's 1,012. If both fleets had been fully manned, which they were not, Nelson would have had 8,068 men under him, while Brueys would have had 11,230. But this advantage was cancelled out by several factors: the disruptive effect of the Revolution on the French Navy; the excessive caution of French admirals over the last century; the supreme confidence and professionalism of the British seamen; and, of course, the tactical and leadership skills of Nelson.

Brueys had left Toulon in May, at almost the same time as Nelson re-entered the Mediterranean. He had sailed in support of a fleet of more than 100 transports bearing an army commanded by the rising star

Left: The Battle of the Nile from a painting by Loutherbourg.

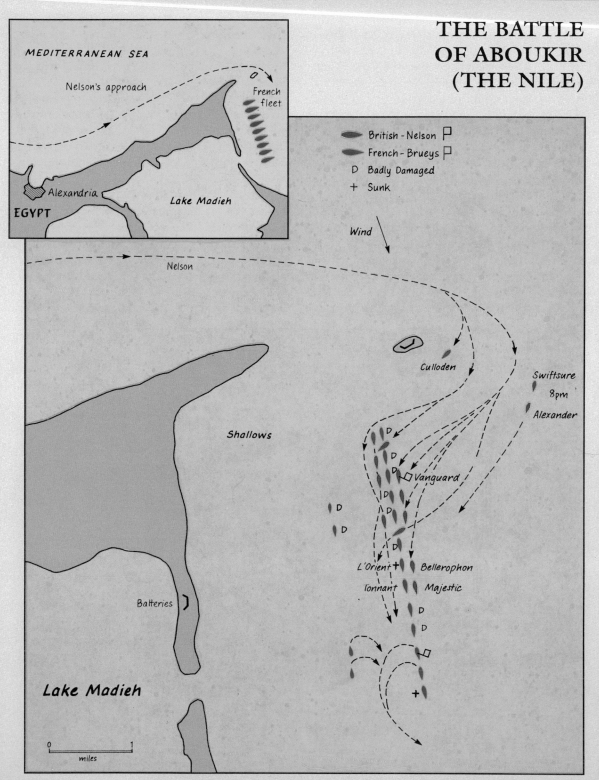

THE BATTLE OF ABOUKIR (THE NILE)

MEDITERRANEAN SEA

Nelson's approach

French fleet

Alexandria

EGYPT

Lake Madieh

British - Nelson
French - Brueys
D Badly Damaged
+ Sunk

Wind

Nelson

Culloden

Swiftsure
8pm
Alexander

Shallows

D

D
D

Vanguard

D

D
D

D

L'Orient +   Bellerophon

Tonnant   Majestic

D
D

Batteries

Lake Madieh

+

0   1
miles

of the French army, the 29-year-old General Bonaparte. Taking advantage of the British absence from the Mediterranean, Bonaparte had seen the chance to strike at Egypt and thus to open up the route to India and the East. The British knew something was afoot – but not the French destination. Bonaparte had evaded Nelson, picked up more troops and ships in Italy, taken Malta from the Knights of St. John, landed in Egypt and defeated the local troops at the Battle of the Pyramids in July.

The French squadron had taken up a seemingly strong position in Aboukir Bay. Perhaps influenced by Hood's tactics at Frigate Bay in 1782, it was anchored in an obtuse angle across the bay. In theory it would be able to deploy full broadsides against an advancing enemy, while the attacker exposed his vulnerable bows during his approach. This worked well with the steady winds of the Caribbean, but in the variable winds of the Mediterranean the direction of the attacker's approach was much less predictable. Furthermore, the

disposition had not been well handled. The ships were at single anchor and thus likely to swing with the wind. There were wide gaps between them, and also a gap between the leading ship and the shoal water to the west. Above all, the French admiral had failed to maintain a reconnaissance screen. Unlike Nelson, he had an adequate number of frigates, but four of them were anchored behind the line of battle, instead of at sea looking for the British squadron. As a result, the French were not ready for the battle; parties from the ships were ashore looking for water and supplies when Nelson appeared.

Nelson's relationship with his captains was one of the keys to his tactical system. Whereas past admirals had controlled their subordinates rigidly, and often had acrimonious disputes with them, Nelson regarded his captains as a 'band of brothers'. He had taken them into his confidence and developed their initiative. According to Captain Berry, 'It had been his practice during the whole of the cruise, whenever the weather

Left: The first of a quartet of views of the Battle of The Nile, painted by W. Anderson. The scene is the British fleet on the evening of 1 August 1798. *Goliath* and *Zealous* bear down to the enemy anchorage.

Left: 10 p.m. on 1 August. The explosion is of the French flagship *L'Orient*.

and circumstances would permit, to have his captains on board the *Vanguard*, where he would fully develop to them his own ideas of the different and best modes of attack, and such plans as he proposed to execute upon falling in with the enemy... With the masterly ideas of their admiral, therefore, on the subject of naval tactics, every one of the captains of his squadron was most thoroughly acquainted.' This was to become important in the approach to battle.

On sighting the enemy, Nelson decided instantly to engage them right away, despite the perceived dangers of a night action. He chose to attack the head of the line, towards the western end of the bay. The squadron formed a rough line of battle, and eventually the *Goliath*, with Captain Thomas Foley in command, took the leading position, while Nelson in the *Vanguard* dropped back to the middle of the line.

Foley was fortunate enough to have the latest French chart in his possession, and he soon spotted the weakness in the French position – the ships, being at single anchor, needed room to swing, and so there would be room for him to pass between the leading French ship, *Le Guerrier*, and the shoal waters to the west. At 6.15 (according to the ship's own log), the *Goliath* passed ahead of the bows of *Le Guerrier*.

It is not certain how much of this manoeuvre was planned by Nelson, and how much on Foley's own initiative; the evidence suggests initiative by Foley, but inspired and guided by what he knew Nelson would have expected. In any case, it completely altered the nature of the battle. The French were placed in some confusion. A witness on board the *Goliath* reported, 'As we passed the *Guerrier*'s bow, I saw her lower deck guns were not run out and there were lumber such as bags and boxes on the upper deck ports which I reported with no small pleasure.'

Foley had intended to anchor abreast *Le Guerrier*, but under fire the manoeuvre was slightly mishandled, and he ended up alongside the second ship, *Le Conquerant*. The second British ship, the *Zealous* under

Right: *Généraux, Guillaume Tell, Justice* and *Diane* attempt to escape, pursued by *Zealous*.

Right: *Tonnant* strikes to the *Theseus* and *Leander*. To the left, *Le Timoleon* burns on the shore.

Captain Hood, also rounded the line and anchored in the position Foley had intended to take. The *Culloden* went aground on the approach, but three more ships, the *Audacious*, *Orion* and *Theseus*, followed the same tactics as the *Goliath* and anchored opposite the third, fourth and fifth ships in the French line. The French frigate *Sérieuse*, on the starboard side of the British ships, was pounded and driven ashore, the first casualty of the battle.

The leading ships were soon heavily engaged in close-range action. According to Hood, 'I commenced such a well directed fire into her bow within pistol shot a little after six that her foremast went by

Above: Portrait of Nelson, architect of British naval supremacy during the Napoleonic Wars.

the board in about seven minutes, just as the sun was closing the horizon... And in ten minutes more her main and mizzen masts went.'

Meanwhile Nelson in the *Vanguard* had arrived at the French line. He decided not to follow the *Goliath* round the line, but to head straight for the starboard side of the third French ship, the *Spartiate*. Five more ships followed this tactic, and the *Bellerophon* found herself alone against the might of the French flagship, the 120-gun *L'Orient*. She suffered heavy casualties and lost two masts, but was eventually supported by the *Swiftsure*. The little *Leander*, under Captain Thompson, adopted yet another approach. Noting that the fifth French ship, the *Peuple Souverain*, was drifting out of position, she took up a position where she could fire on the bows of the 80-gun *Franklin* and the stern of the *Aquilon*, while avoiding the broadsides of both ships. The last ship to reach action, the *Alexander*, broke through the French line astern of *L'Orient*.

Thus the first eight ships in the French line were subjected to concentrated and devastating fire from thirteen British ships. They suffered heavy casualties, as Brueys and most of his captains were killed or wounded. On the British side, Nelson was hit in the forehead and taken below. But by nine o'clock the *Guerrier* and *Conquerant* had surrendered, the *Peuple Souverain* had been driven ashore, and two more ships were virtually defeated.

Then – in a moment that engraved itself on the memories of all present – the French flagship blew up. Engaged by several British ships, she had been on fire for some time before the blaze reached her magazine, around ten o'clock. Berry, standing on the deck of the *Vanguard*, noted 'a most tremendous explosion.' Even in the bowels of the *Goliath*, the seamen were shocked by the explosion. 'The *Goliath* got such a shake, we thought the after part of her had blown up until the boys told us what it was.'

The whole of the French line ahead of *L'Orient* was soon disposed of. The last four ships in their line were so far unaffected by the battle, and had done nothing – they had not moved up to support their comrades, nor had they tried to escape. Exhaustion was taking its toll among the British ships after six hours of action, and gun crews sometimes fell asleep where they stood. But on the instructions of the wounded Nelson, the *Zealous*, *Theseus* and *Goliath* proceeded down the line to tackle the last of the French. The *Mercure* soon surrendered, the *Timoleon* (last in the line) was driven

ashore by the guns of the *Theseus*, while two ships of the line, the *Guillaume Tell* and the *Généreux*, made their escape. Two of the French frigates had already been sunk, while the other two escaped.

It was the most decisive battle of the age of sail. The French had lost eleven ships of the line out of thirteen (and even the two that had escaped were themselves captured in 1800). Six of the French ships had been destroyed, and five captured. Three of these were incorporated in the British navy and the *Franklin*, renamed *Canopus*, served as a model for British 80-gun ships for more than twenty years.

Both sides had suffered heavy casualties. On the British side, 218 men had been killed, including the captain of the *Majestic*, and fifteen other officers; 677 had been wounded, including Nelson himself, and the captains of the *Alexander*, *Orion* and *Bellerophon*. Naturally the French casualties were much heavier. Dead and wounded are difficult to assess in the circumstances, but Nelson reckoned that there were 5,225 men 'taken, drowned, burnt and missing'.

Strategically, the British had won control of the Mediterranean from the French. Bonaparte's army was now isolated in Egypt, and the great general had suffered his first reverse. His campaign, though still pursued with vigour, was ultimately doomed. The French fleet, which could claim a *strategic* victory from the 'Glorious 1st June', could salvage nothing

Above: Sir Edward Berry was Nelson's captain on the *Vanguard*, a gallant seaman.

Below: Nelson in the cockpit of HMS *Vanguard* at the Battle of the Nile.

Left: The Battle of The Nile, the morning after.

Below: A Christmas print of the Battle of The Nile. These patriotic prints were very popular in England at time.

from Aboukir Bay. In the words of two modern French historians, it was 'une defaite absolue, ecrasante et sans appel', with enormous strategic consequences.

Nelson was already a celebrity after his actions at St. Vincent and Teneriffe, but the Nile raised his fame to an unprecedented level. It was his first fleet battle in command, and he was raised to the peerage (technically he was under St. Vincent as commander-in-chief, so he was given only a barony, not an earldom). All the elements of the Nelsonian system were used – the inspiring leadership; the ability to train captains, and to delegate crucial tactical decisions to them in the heat of battle; and the taking of carefully calculated risks in order to make a battle not just decisive but devastating to an enemy. There was no dramatic gesture – no telescope to the blind eye, no memorable signal – but the other parts of the Nelson legend were in place: personal courage, tactical decisiveness and the support of a 'band of brothers'. All this would be reinforced at Copenhagen and Trafalgar, but as a great victory Aboukir Bay was never to be surpassed.

BBLIOGRAPHY

Berry, Sir Edward, *An Authentic Narrative of the Proceedings of His Majesty's Squadron*, London, 1798.
Elliot, Sir George, *Memoir*, London, 1863.

Kennedy, L., *Nelson and his Captains*, London, 1975.
Lloyd, C., *The Nile Campaign*, Newton Abbot, 1973.
Sturges Jackson, T. (ed) *Logs of the Great Sea Fights*, Navy

Records Society, 1900.
Nicol, John, *Life and Adventures*, Edinburgh, 1822.
Nicolas (ed), *Dispatches and Letters of Lord Nelson*, vol III,

London, 1845.
Warner, O., *The Battle of the Nile*, London, 1960

NELSON: COPENHAGEN, 1801

by D. J. Lyon

'A ship's a fool to fight a fort.'
Attrib. Nelson

This was one of the most unusual battles of the age of sail. Fought close inshore, it was as much a conflict between ships and forts as between ships and other ships. The main aim of one side was to attack a city; that of the other was to defend it. Usually only ships of the line took an active part in the fleet actions; this battle involved other, smaller craft as well. Finally, politics and diplomacy were much closer to the events of this battle than is normal in maritime war.

The battle happened because Tsar Paul of Russia was in process of forming an Armed Neutrality of the Baltic powers, playing on their discontent at the often arbitrary and inconsiderate way Britain dealt with neutrals and their trade. Britain, fighting for survival against France, was determined to make the best use of her maritime preponderance as a weapon in that fight. From the British point of view an alliance intended to back up neutral rights at sea by force was a direct threat to her, and something to be nipped in the bud.

Fortunately for Britain, and unfortunately for Denmark, geography made a pre-emptive attack easy and exposed the Danes as both the most obvious and the easiest of victims. Denmark is at the entrance of the Baltic, her capital, Copenhagen, on the shores of the Sound, the usual passage between the North Sea and the Baltic, and exposed to attack from the sea. Furthermore the northern and eastern parts of the Baltic freeze in winter, and ice would prevent the Swedish or the Russian fleets breaking out of their harbours until late spring. Each Baltic navy was exposed to attack in turn and in reverse order of relative power before it could be joined by its allies from further East.

The British prepared a fleet carefully tailored for its intended role in the Baltic. Its most powerful element consisted of its three-decker ships of the line, 98-gun ships whose upper decks gave them the commanding position against smaller and lower ships. However, these would be too deep-draughted to deal with the defences of Copenhagen; for this, two-deckers, 74- or 64-gun ships of the line, plus two smaller fourth rates of 50 guns were allocated. One of these two was a converted East Indiaman of 56 guns, the *Glatton*, with an armament consisting entirely of the short, light guns known as carronades, which normally fired a very heavy shot for their size, but on this occasion were also intended to fire lighter projectiles fitted with incendiary material, known as 'carcasses'. Also with a main armament of carronades were the extraordinary experimental vessels *Dart* and *Arrow*, classed as sloops but bigger and more powerfully armed than any other sloop. Because they were fitted with 'sliding keels' they were also capable of operating in shallow water. This pair were to be attached to the fleet's frigates in the battle. A number of the shallow-draught 'gun-brigs', built for work against the French invasion flotilla, were part of the fleet. The use of fire and special weapons was, however, most obvious with the group of seven specialist shore-bombardment vessels, the 'bombs', with their mortars firing explosive shells at a high trajectory. It is also significant that two fireships accompanied the fleet.

Copenhagen was very vulnerable to bombardment from the sea. A narrow channel separated the city itself from the slender island on which the naval dockyard stood, beyond which ran the difficult channel of the 'King's Deep', itself bounded by the shoal known as the 'Middle Ground'. The normal approach to Copenhagen was from the north, and that was protected by shore batteries and by a new and incomplete

Below: Sir Hyde Parker, Vice-Admiral of the Blue.

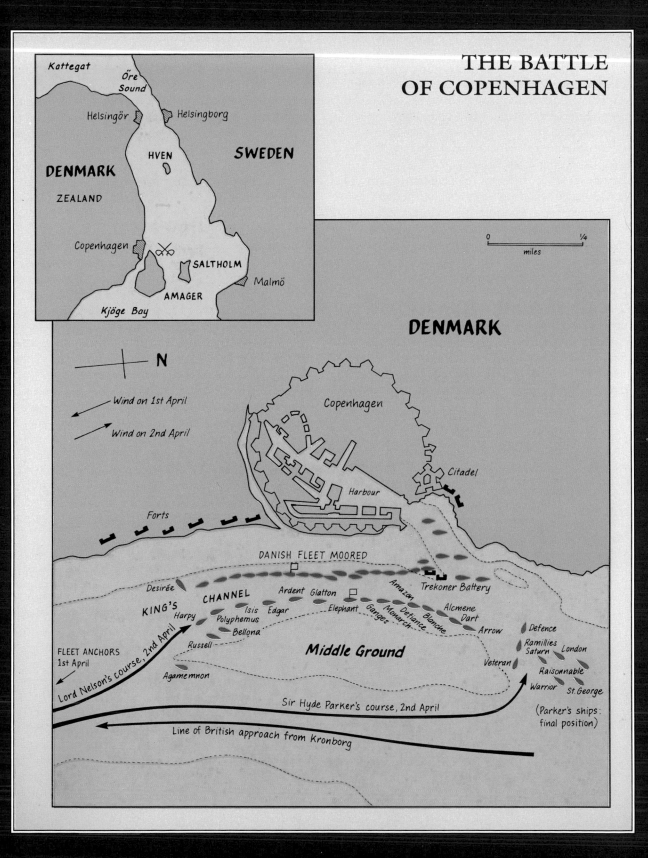

THE BATTLE OF COPENHAGEN

Kattegat

Öre Sound

Helsingör   Helsingborg

DENMARK   HVEN   SWEDEN

ZEALAND

Copenhagen

SALTHOLM

AMAGER

Malmö

Kjöge Bay

DENMARK

0   ¼
miles

N

Wind on 1st April

Wind on 2nd April

Copenhagen

Citadel

Harbour

Forts

DANISH FLEET MOORED

Desirée   Trekoner Battery

CHANNEL   Ardent Glatton   Amazon

KING'S   Isis   Edgar   Elephant   Defiance Blanche   Alcmene Dart

Harpy   Polyphemus   Ganges Monarch   Arrow

Bellona   Defence

Russell   Middle Ground   Ramillies London
    Saturn

Veteran   Raisonnable

FLEET ANCHORS
1st April

Agamemnon   Warrior St.George

Sir Hyde Parker's course, 2nd April

Lord Nelson's course, 2nd April   (Parker's ships:
    final position)

Line of British approach from Kronborg

addition to the Copenhagen defences. This was the Trekroner fort, built on piles in shallow water. Lack of finance had delayed its completion and arming, just as it had prevented the starting of two other similar forts whose fire would have protected the rest of the King's Deep. Instead the Danes had a line of old line of battle ships, converted transports and merchantmen fitted as 'blockships' with minimal masts and sails, or none at all, but with heavy guns. These ships were moored in a line offshore to protect the city. They were supplemented by a number of 'floating batteries', which were basically gun-armed rafts, and by some oared gunboats. To make the city more secure, the Danes removed all the buoys and sea-marks that normally made navigation through the narrow channels and past the shallows relatively safe.

These were the defences confronting the British fleet when it arrived off the city on 30 March 1801, having forced the passage past Cronborg (Elsinore) castle at the narrowest part of the Sound between Denmark and Sweden. That fleet was under the command of the elderly and unenterprising Admiral Sir Hyde Parker, whose second-in-command was the young and active Vice Admiral and Viscount Horatio Nelson, victor of the Nile. Nelson had been assigned the task of neutralising the Danish defences to clear the way for the use of the bomb vessels. Copenhagen was vulnerable to fire as later events would prove, and bombardment was a serious threat to the city and its inhabitants – not to mention the dockyard with its flammable stores of timber, pitch and so on.

At this stage the British Navy was a battle-tested force, at the peak of its effectiveness. Serving under Nelson were numbers of very good officers – his captains included such names as Foley, Rieu, Retalick, Fremantle, and Lawford, not to mention William Bligh of the *Glatton* (and formerly the *Bounty*). This was an excellent team of officers and men. Nelson's peculiar genius lay in using that team to best advantage, in producing a situation where his direct subordinates knew exactly what he would want them to do: all under his command were inspired to do their best. The least satisfactory element here was in the relationship between Nelson and *his* commander.

The Danes lacked the Britons' experience, and professionalism was scarcer in a force consisting mostly of recently gathered landsmen, but their fierce patriotism was not in doubt, and fighting from ships at anchor or from shore batteries made pure seamanship of less importance. Moreover, the Danes had no lack of men, and it was easy to ferry out reinforcements to their battle line. Ships moving under sail were large and somewhat vulnerable targets compared with fortress guns. So the two sides were not unevenly matched.

The British fleet spent some time in reconnoitring, Nelson himself going out at night in a boat to make soundings. On 1 April the plan was ready and the ships moved into position. Nelson had decided to attack from the south, up the channel, rather than directly down upon the formidable Trekroner. Fortunately for him, the wind, which had carried the fleet to the south on that day, changed to exactly the opposite direction by the morning of 2 April and carried his force up upon the Danish line.

Three British ships of the line ran aground on the shoals, two in positions from which they could fire to some effect. As each ship had been assigned a particular part of the Danish defences to deal with, this created an unfortunate gap, which would have meant that the Trekroner fort was left unmasked to do its

Left: The Battle of Copenhagen.

Right: Engraving by Tomkins of a painting by Serres depicting the attack on the Danish fleet and batteries at Copenhagen.

Right: A second view of the attack at Copenhagen. The view of the city to the right indicates the daring of Nelson's attack in closing the enemy coast.

worst to the head of the British line of the nine remaining two-deckers. Captain Rieu, leading the force of frigates and sloops, gallantly stepped into this gap with his smaller and lighter ships. Meanwhile the other British ships moored within a couple of hundred yards of their enemies and a close-range battering match began. The shallow-draught gun-brigs, meant to enfilade the Danish line from the south, were (with one exception) prevented by the strong current from getting into position. The bomb vessels awaited their opportunity.

Hyde Parker, with the heavier ships, watched from the north. After two hours of smoke and noise, his nerve broke, and he hoisted the signal to break off the action. He had not the essential will to victory of Nelson, and he was too far away to see what Nelson could detect – that the Danes were suffering greater damage

than they were inflicting and that their line was crumbling. This was the opportunity for Nelson's famous 'blind eye' gesture; so he ignored the signal. Unfortunately Rieu felt compelled to obey it, and, as he withdrew the frigates from their engagement with the Trekroner, he was cut in two by a shot. However, Nelson was right in his perseverance. The main part of the Danish line was badly shattered, some of the ships were on fire (the *Dannebrog*, flagship of Commodore Fischer, who commanded the main line, was set on fire by the *Glatton*'s 'carcasses' and then blew up) and some had fallen silent or had surrendered. Others were in so parlous a state that they would soon fall victim to British boarding parties. The gaps into which the bomb vessels could move were being created.

This was the psychological moment that Nelson chose to suggest a truce to the Danes, so that the wounded could be rescued from burning and sinking ships. The details of the negotiations need not concern us. What mattered was that the Danes stopped firing. They had inflicted severe damage on the British ships, but all of these were still in action, unlike numbers of the block-ships. The Danes still had ships ready for action off the Dockyard, but these were counter-balanced by Hyde Parker's uncommitted force. Had the British all obeyed Parker's signal, then they might have suffered disaster, as three more of their ships ran aground when moving away from their firing positions and several others had badly damaged rigging. Once the cease-fire was in place, the Danish position disintegrated. The 'bombs' moved into position and their deterrent effect began to work on the Danes. Nelson had saved the British fleet from a disastrously unnecessary withdrawal and then prevented both sides from wasting more blood once the balance had begun to tip towards the British. Given sufficient toughness and endurance by the British high command, this result was likely. The British ships were on average bigger, with thicker and stronger sides, and were therefore better protected, than those of the Danes. Added to the advantages of better training and equipment, these were enough advantages to counter-balance those that the Danes enjoyed in fighting on their home ground, and in being in a position to use fortress guns against ships.

The battle was fiercely fought by the standards of the time. The British casualties were just under 1,000 in killed and wounded, the Danes a little more, though the latter lost more dead (370, with another 160 who died of their wounds later, as against 256

British killed, with an indeterminate number fatally wounded). Ironically, the main reason for fighting the battle had already been removed. Tsar Paul had been assassinated a few days earlier, and with his death the driving force behind the Armed Neutrality was removed. News of it did not reach Copenhagen until the day after the battle. The British fleet proceeded into the Baltic where the Swedish fleet withdrew before it. After some hesitation by Hyde Parker, he was replaced by Nelson who sailed on towards Russia, but no more fighting was needed. The Armed Neutrality was dissolved.

Copenhagen's escape from British bombardment was, alas, only temporary. In 1807, Britain launched another pre-emptive strike, this time to prevent Napoleon taking over the Danish fleet. An army was landed on the island of Zealand. Copenhagen was besieged, bombarded from the land side and suffered appalling devastation by fire before surrendering. The Danish fleet was taken away by the British, and Denmark became Napoleon's most faithful ally, only to suffer more defeat and loss. Her unenviable role was that of a small nation forced by her strategic position into having to make unpalatable decisions between powerful and unsympathetic nations to whom she was equally vulnerable.

BIBLIOGRAPHY

The standard works on Nelson plus:
Dudley Pope, *The Great Gamble*, London 1972. Nelson-worshipping detailed account of the battle.
Arne Felbaeck, *Denmark and the Armed Neutrality 1800–1801*, Copenhagen 1980. Excellent. (This author has written a book on the battle itself, which is, alas, not yet translated from the Danish.)

Left: The bombardment of Copenhagen in 1807.

NELSON: TRAFALGAR, 1805

by Gerald Jordan

'The business of the English Commander in Chief being
first to bring an Enemy's fleet to battle on the most
advantageous terms to himself; and secondly to contin-
ue them there until the Business is decided.'
Admiral Lord Nelson, 1805

At about two minutes before noon on 21 October 1805, in a light southerly breeze off Cape Trafalgar, the French 74-gun man-of-war *Fougueux* fired the first shots of the battle that crushed Napoleonic sea power, confirmed British naval supremacy for a hundred years and immortalised the fame of Vice Admiral Lord Nelson. In a little more than four hours, Nelson's 27 ships of the line annihilated the combined Franco-Spanish fleet of 33 ships of the line. Twenty French and Spanish vessels, including the 136-gun four-decker Santissima Trinidad, the largest ship in the world, were at one time taken as prize or lowered their colours.

Ironically, the battle had been precipitated by Napoleon's orders to Vice Admiral Comte de Villeneuve to break out of Cadiz, enter the Mediterranean and destroy the British naval force that was ferrying troops to join General Lacy's Russians in defence of Naples.

Nelson's triumph at the Battle of Trafalgar was the culmination of his embodiment of tradition, duty and professionalism. The last of a long line of illustrious leaders of the days of sail, Nelson became a legend in his own lifetime. Drake and Hawkins, Blake, Vernon, Anson, Hawke, Rodney, the Hoods and others had developed a tradition of naval supremacy to which Nelson was the heir. But their victories were limited in scope. Truly decisive naval victories were rare in the age of sail. Nelson won three: at the Nile in 1798, at Copenhagen in 1801 (see previous chapters) and at Trafalgar in 1805. At a time when genuinely popular heroes were rare, Nelson's popularity with his captains and men, as with the crowds ashore, could never be doubted. 'Nelson was a man to be loved,' declared Sir Pulteney Malcolm, who as captain of the 74-gun *Donegal* sailed with Nelson during the pursuit of Villeneuve's fleet to the West Indies before Trafalgar. Nelson had that rare capacity to inspire to great heights those who served under him. An impulsive generosity of spirit and a colourful personality with a vibrant sense of theatre, joined with rigorous sea-training, an intuitive grasp of tactics and great physical bravery to produce a leader unique in the annals of naval warfare.

For two years Nelson had been trying to bring the French to battle. In May 1803, Britain had broken the fourteen-month-old Peace of Amiens and reimposed the naval blockade, with Admiral Cornwallis stationed off Brest and Nelson off Toulon. Napoleon began to assemble an army for the invasion of England – but success in this enterprise would depend upon French control of the Channel, if only for a few days. Napoleon, never a sailor, devised a hare-brained scheme to force Britain to so disperse her naval forces that they would be unable to respond when the invasion was launched. With the invasion timed for the late summer of 1805, the French fleets would break out of Brest, Rochefort and Toulon. Joined by their Spanish allies and under the command of Villeneuve, they would raid British shipping and colonies in the West Indies. This would draw the Royal Navy in pursuit. Villeneuve would then sail for the Channel, which he would control while Napoleon's 'Army of England' was ferried to the Kentish shore. The plan could have had a chance of success only if Cornwallis abandoned the Brest blockade and left the Channel defenceless. Such a course was never on the cards.

Part of the plan succeeded. In January 1805 the Rochefort squadron evaded the blockade. At the end of March, Villeneuve's fleet slipped out of Toulon. A week later the Spanish left Cadiz. On 10 April, off Palermo, Nelson heard that Villeneuve had passed

Above: Horatio, Vicount Nelson.

through the Straits of Gibraltar. Three weeks later, at Tetuan, he learned that the Toulon fleet, joined by the Spanish Cadiz fleet under Admiral de Gravina, was on its way to the West Indies. Nelson gave chase but was delayed by misinformation received at Barbados. From then on, however, Napoleon's plan became a shambles. Fearing Nelson's arrival, Villeneuve returned to Europe without attacking any British ships or possessions in the Caribbean. Off Cape Finisterre on 22 July, the Combined Fleet lost two ships in an inconclusive fog-shrouded action with a British squadron under Rear Admiral Sir Robert Calder. Unnerved by the encounter and in fear of entrapment between Cornwallis and Nelson, Villeneuve disregarded his orders to move into the English Channel and turned south to safety. By mid-August, the Combined fleet was bottled up in Cadiz. Napoleon's plan had collapsed. With the land forces of the Third Coalition threatening his armies to the east, the invasion of England was cancelled.

Meanwhile, Nelson took his fleet to Gibraltar to make sure that Villeneuve had not re-entered the Mediterranean. In mid-September he returned to England in his flagship, HMS *Victory*, leaving Vice Admiral Cuthbert Collingwood in command of the fleet and three ships of the line and a frigate to keep watch off Cadiz. After a brief rest at 'Paradise Merton', his house in Surrey, Nelson resumed command of the fleet at the end of the month.

The fleet Nelson took to station just over the horizon from Cadiz had been at sea almost continuously for two years. Even so, it was a well trained and healthy fighting force, ready and eager for battle. Dr. Gillespie, fleet physician, believed the high state of health to be 'unexampled perhaps in any squadron heretofore employed on a foreign station'. This he attributed 'to the attention paid by his lordship to the victualling and purveying for the fleet'. The crews had been honed to a knife edge by constant drills during the long, frustrating weeks at sea. Morale was high. 'Intemperance and skulking', Gillespie wrote, 'were never so little practised in any fleet as in this.'

Nelson's captains, too, were thoroughly versed in what they had to do. The battle plan, which he explained to them over dinner on board *Victory* on 29 and 30 September, hit them 'like an electric shock'. The fleet was to attack the enemy from windward in two columns, one commanded by himself, the other by Collingwood. Breaking their line in two places would confuse the enemy and bring on a 'pell-mell' battle. Success depended heavily upon the aggressive initiative of the captains and the discipline of the crews. 'No Captain can do very wrong', Nelson added to a memorandum formally outlining his plan to his captains on 10 October, 'if he places his ship alongside that of an Enemy.'

Such tactics were not entirely new and they were not reckless, but they were daring and did break the rules. The *Fighting Instructions*, dating back to the seventeenth century, laid down formalised manoeuvres for sea battles, whose objective was not annihilation of the enemy but to achieve strategical advantage and to maintain the 'fleet in being'. Adherence to the line of battle clearly put aggressive admirals at a disadvantage and allowed a defensively minded enemy all too easily to escape. By the end of the eighteenth century, more venturesome British admirals were breaking the enemy's line in an effort to prevent their escape. The previous cases of the Glorious 1st June and Cape St. Vincent have been described already; at Camperdown in October 1797, Duncan with sixteen sail had broken the enemy line in two places and taken

Above: Cuthbert, Lord Collingwood. A friend and the successor of Nelson. Collingwood's peculiar personality prevented him from achieving any of Nelson's popularity, but he worked himself to death for what he thought to be the good of the service.

Above: A portrait by Abbot of Thomas Masterman Hardy, well known for his presence at Nelson's death.

eight of fifteen Dutch warships. A combination of circumstances and determination enabled Nelson to use these tactics to achieve virtual destruction of the enemy's sea power. At the Nile, in 1798, as we have seen, his doubling of the French line had achieved near annihilation of the enemy; at Trafalgar, he was to achieve a similar effect.

Villeneuve was under no illusions about his chances of evading Nelson or of countering Nelson's tactics should the Combined Fleet be forced to do battle. The British frigate *Sirius*, hovering off Cadiz, was a clear warning that Nelson's fleet was nearby. Villeneuve had fought at the Battle of the Nile and knew exactly how Nelson would try to fight the battle. 'The British fleet', he told his captains before the Combined Fleet put to sea, 'will not be formed in a line of battle... according to the usage of former days. Nelson... will seek to break our line, envelop our rear, and overpower with groups of his ships as many of ours as he can isolate or cut off.' But forewarned was not forearmed. The French and Spanish crews were not well trained, had little sea time compared with their opponents; their seamanship was poor, and their

morale was low. Villeneuve had good reason to be reluctant to come to grips with the British.

Villeneuve might have procrastinated longer in Cadiz had he not received word that Vice Admiral Rosily had arrived in Madrid on his way to take over command of the Combined Fleet. As dawn broke on 19 October, *Sirius* hoisted signal number 370 – 'Enemy ships are coming out of port.' Repeated down a chain of frigates to the fleet 48 miles off the coast, the signal was received by Nelson at 0930. He immediately ordered a general chase south-east to place his fleet between Cadiz and Gibraltar. Not until noon the next day did the Combined Fleet clear Cadiz and set course towards the Mediterranean. A southerly wind made it virtually impossible for Villeneuve to evade Nelson's waiting ships. By midnight on 20 October, Captain Blackwood in command of the British frigates could see the lights of both fleets. At daylight on 21 October, about nine miles distant, Nelson 'saw the Enemy's Combined Fleet from East to ESE... made the signal for Order of Sailing, and to Prepare for Battle; the Enemy with their heads to the Southward...'

The first move was Villeneuve's. At 7.30 am, realising that he would never make the Straits of Gibraltar before being brought to battle, and as pessimistic of his chances as Nelson was confident of his, Villeneuve wore the Combined Fleet on to a northerly course towards Cadiz. The manoeuvre threw his unpractised vessels into confusion, and the battle line was not re-formed until ten o'clock, giving the British an extra two and a half hours in which to catch their enemy.

Nelson's two columns, the weather division under Nelson in *Victory* and the leeward division under Collingwood in *Royal Sovereign*, studding-sails set in the light wind, ships cleared for action, slipped at about two knots towards the even slower enemy. At 1100, the British crews were piped to dinner and grog or beer. 'We ate and drank, and were as cheerful as ever we had been over a pot of beer,' remarked Able Seaman John Cash of the *Tonnant*. At about 1115, Nelson's famous signal, 'England expects that every man will do his duty', received a mixed reception around the fleet. Collingwood testily asked: 'What is Nelson signalling about? We all know what we have to do', but expressed 'delight and admiration' when it was read to him. Signal number 16, 'Close Action', was then raised to *Victory*'s topgallant masthead, where it remained until it was shot away. In the Admi-

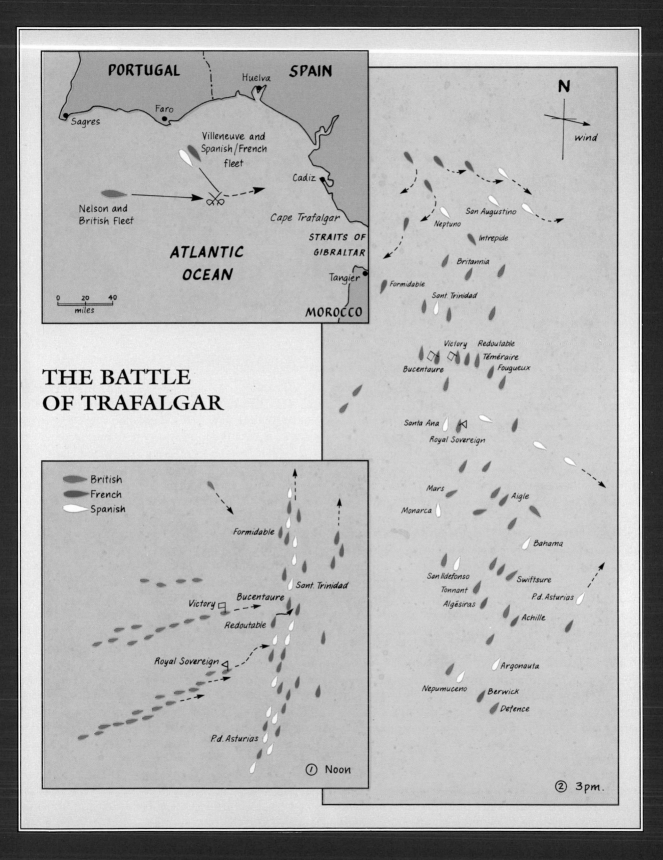

THE BATTLE OF TRAFALGAR

PORTUGAL SPAIN

Huelva

Sagres

Faro

Villeneuve and Spanish / French fleet

Cadiz

Nelson and British Fleet

Cape Trafalgar

ATLANTIC OCEAN

STRAITS OF GIBRALTAR

Tangier

MOROCCO

0 20 40
miles

N

wind

San Augustino

Neptuno

Intrepide

Britannia

Formidable

Sant. Trinidad

Victory   Redoutable

Téméraire

Bucentaure   Fougueux

Santa Ana

Royal Sovereign

Mars   Aigle

Monarca

Bahama

San Ildefonso   Swiftsure

Tonnant   P.d. Asturias

Algésiras

Achille

Argonauta

Nepumuceno   Berwick

Defence

② 3pm.

British
French
Spanish

Formidable

Sant. Trinidad

Victory   Bucentaure

Redoutable

Royal Sovereign

P.d. Asturias

① Noon

ral's cabin on *Victory*, before its sparse furniture was stowed, Nelson prayed that 'the Great God, whom I worship, grant to my Country, and for the benefit of Europe in general, a great and glorious Victory...' and penned a codicil to his will leaving Emma, Lady Hamilton and their 'adopted' daughter, Horatia, 'to my King and Country'. Shortly before noon, Nelson inspected the gun-decks and spoke to his 'noble lads'. Nelson's captains, like Mansfield of the *Minotaur*, had learned well the lesson of inspiration. Addressing the ship's company, Mansfield told them that he trusted 'that this day will prove the most glorious our country ever saw. I shall say nothing to you of courage. Our country never produced a coward.' In sharp contrast, Commodore Churruca, on the Spanish 74-gun *San Juan Nepomuceno*, warned his crew: 'If I see any man shirking I will have him shot on the spot.'

Nelson's plan of penetration exposed the leading ships in each line to raking fire long before they could reply. If the manoeuvre were successful, however, the enemy van would be unable to come to the aid of the centre and rear until it was too late. As it turned out, Nelson's faith in the poor gunnery of the enemy and in the superior ship-handling and good gunnery of his own fleet was justified. His plan worked. As the fleets closed, Collingwood's *Royal Sovereign* drew ahead both of his own column and of Nelson's. *Fougueux*'s opening broadside fell short as the *Royal Sovereign*

moved between her and Vice Admiral de Alava's massive 112-gun *Santa Ana*, the eighteenth ship in the Franco-Spanish line. The *Royal Sovereign*'s opening double-shotted broadsides smashed into *Santa Ana*'s stern and *Fougueux*'s bow. Captain Hargood's *Belleisle*, following Collingwood into action some ten minutes later, came under murderous fire from the *Santa Ana* before engaging the French *Indomptable* at point-blank range. By one o'clock the lee column was in a confused, smoke-shrouded mêlée with seventeen ships of the Combined Fleet. At about 1415, battered and mastless, with de Alava severely wounded, the *Santa Ana* struck her colours to the *Royal Sovereign*.

Nelson himself did not get into action until about 1245 when the *Victory*, closely followed by *Téméraire* and *Neptune*, moved astern of Villeneuve's flagship, the 80-gun *Bucentaure*, crossing the port quarter of the French 74-gun *Redoutable*. *Victory*'s first broadside swept down *Bucentaure*'s stern galleries and gun-decks, causing tremendous damage and loss of life. Engaged on both sides, the *Victory*, too, soon resembled a slaughter-house. Sometime between 1315 and 1335, walking the quarter-deck with Captain Hardy, Nelson was struck in the chest by a musket-ball from a sharpshooter in *Redoutable*'s mizzen-top. Carried below to a painful death, the ball lodged in his spine, Nelson lingered long enough to learn from Hardy

Right: Nelson's chase of the French fleet.

that they had won a brilliant victory, with fourteen or fifteen of the enemy taken. 'That is well, but I bargained for twenty... Thank God I have done my duty.' The *Victory*'s log recorded: 'Partial firing continued until 4.30, when a victory having been reported to the Right Hon. Lord Viscount Nelson, K.B., and Commander-in-Chief, he died of his wound.'

The following day Captain Blackwood, who had watched from the frigate *Euryalus*, wrote of the battle to his wife: 'Almost all seemed as if inspired by the one common sentiment of conquer or die. The Enemy, to do them justice, were not less so. They waited the attack of the British with a coolness I was sorry to witness, and they fought in a way that must do them honour...' Of the 50,000 men present on both sides, some 8,500 had been killed or wounded. The British had taken about 20,000 prisoners. Eighteen of the Combined Fleet's 33 ships had been captured. Four French ships in the van under Rear Admiral Dumanoir escaped to the north only to surrender two weeks later to a British squadron under Sir Richard Strachan. Eleven of the Combined Fleet reached the safety of Cadiz but never ventured out of port again. Of the ships taken by the British, *Achille* blew up, four survived the gales which caught the fleets on 22 October, twelve foundered or ran ashore,

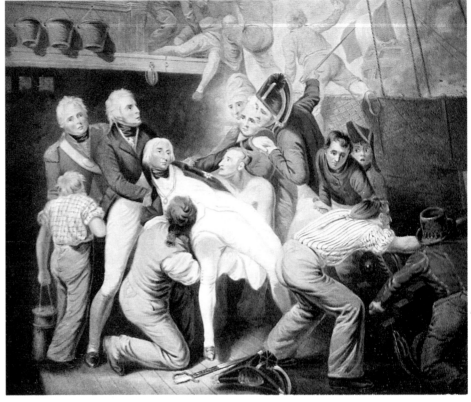

Top left: The Battle of Trafalgar. This view shows the Victory firing its rear lower deck cannon, with the burning wreck of *Santa Ana* to the left.

Bottom left: An alternative view of the battle of Trafalgar, painted by Thomas Luny.

Above: Nelson is mortally wounded by a sharpshooter.

Below: The death of Nelson by E. Armitage.

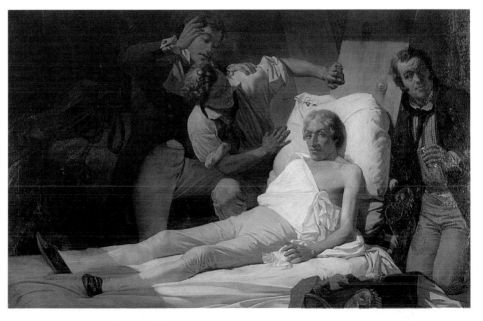

Above: After the Battle of Trafalgar a storm wrecked many of the prizes taken by the British.

and the French *Algésiras* was recaptured by her crew and taken into Cadiz.

One of the last great battles of the sailing navies, Trafalgar was also a foretaste of things to come. Nelson's disregard for the conventions of the *Fighting Instructions* and his willingness to take calculated risks reflected a changing attitude towards warfare and indeed to the political situation in Europe. First Revolutionary France and then Napoleon posed a fundamental threat to the whole system of monarchy. The aim of Britain and her allies was the complete destruction of Napoleonic power and the restoration of the Bourbon monarchy. Nelson's doctrine of total annihilation of the enemy reflected those aims. At the same time, the news of Trafalgar gave the British government and people a much needed boost at a time when Napoleon's troops were marching roughshod over Europe. Perhaps more important in the long run, Trafalgar gave the British their greatest national hero and martyr and confirmed a long tradition of naval supremacy, which affected, for better or worse, the course of British naval affairs for more than a hundred years.

BIBIOGRAPHY

Padfield, P., *Nelson's War*, London, 1976. A fast-paced narrative that makes a splendid introduction to the general topic.
Lavery, B., *Nelson's Navy*, London, 1989. The best single volume look at the ships, men and organisation of the Royal Navy during the period.
Bennett, G., *The Battle of Trafalgar*, London, 1977. A lengthy, readable account of the whole campaign.
Newbolt, Sir Henry, *The Year of Trafalgar*, London, 1905. More detailed, opinionated and nationalistic, and written to commemorate the centenary, this contains a collection of celebratory ballads and poems; still well worth reading.
Keegan, J., *The Price of Admiralty*, London, 1988. A brief but vivid evocation of the battle is provided in the opening chapter, which places Nelson's victory in the context of the technology of the day.
Oman, C., *Nelson*, London, 1947. The most comprehensive of a myriad of Nelson biographies.
Pocock, T., *Nelson*, London, 1988. The most recent biography of the admiral, which deals sketchily with the campaigns but tries with some success to get under the skin of Nelson.

DUCKWORTH: SAN DOMINGO, 1806

by A. B. Sainsbury

'There is nothing so subject to inconstancy of fortune as war.'
Miguel de Cervantes, 1615

The Battle of San Domingo and the events around it typify the life and career of the victor, Vice Admiral Sir John Duckworth, KB (1748–1817), later Admiral, GCB and Baronet. Asked for by Nelson to relieve Northesk as his third in command, he missed Trafalgar, waiting at Plymouth for a suitable flagship (to be the old Superb, which gave him R. G. Keats as his flag captain) and for his band (four fiddlers, absent in the Acasta). Having stopped the Pickle on her way home with Collingwood's Trafalgar dispatch, he was not surprised by orders to watch Cadiz. But, in Collingwood's absence, he was to lift the blockade within two weeks and, having cancelled the chase of a flying foe, was lucky to be presented with another over whom he was to gain the inadvertent, accidental and certainly fortunate victory off San Domingo on 6 February 1806.

He arrived on his station on 15 November, ten days after Sir Richard Strachan had taken four French survivors of Trafalgar. He knew that the Rochefort squadron was still out and undetected, and on hearing that a French force had attacked a convoy off the Salvages assumed it to be Allemand, and abandoned his station in enthusiastic pursuit – but without telling Collingwood, whose approval he had fortunately anticipated. At Cap Verde he decided to give up his pursuit and started back. He did not know that on 13 December a division of the French fleet had got out of Brest, where it had remained during the Trafalgar campaign, and split next day into two detachments, with separate tasks and destinations, under Willaumez and Leissegues. They were reported by the *Arethusa*. So, leaving Cadiz still uncovered, but this time telling his C-in-C of his intentions, Duckworth pursued some ships to the north, believing them to be the Rocheforters – it is to be supposed that he realised eventually that they were not. On Christmas Day, at 30°52" N 20°16" W, he was near enough to signal a chase; but his squadron was strung out, and on questionable grounds he annulled the signal after 36 hours. At 28° 25" N 19° 10" W Duckworth hove to and collected his force. Short of water, it went to Barbados, and on to St. Kitts where it was joined by Rear Admiral Cochrane, commanding the Leeward Islands station and equally ignorant of French whereabouts. It had been a wasted January.

But on 1 February the younger Cochrane arrived in *Kingfisher* (16) and reported French ships in San Domingo Bay. Duckworth set off at once. He 'lost not a moment of time' in getting through the Mona Passage, where on the 5th the *Magicienne* (36) joined, to confirm the intelligence and to report 'an enemy's force of ten sail of the line with as many frigates and corvettes' being in those seas. He continued under easy sail through the night, sending Dunn in the *Acasta* with the *Magicienne* to look into the Bay before dawn. 'At six o'clock the *Acasta*, to our great joy, made the signal for two enemy frigates and between seven or nine sail at anchor; at half past that they were getting under way; the squadron under my command then in close order with all sail set and the *Superb* bearing my flag leading and approaching fast so as to discover before eight o'clock that the enemy was in a compact line under all sail, going before the wind for Cap Nisa to windward of Occa Bay.' Strachan had at once become 'Delighted Sir Dicky' after his November dispatch; alas, Duckworth never became 'Joyous John', while his 'This is glorious', a signal made as he romped into action, is seldom quoted. Keats silently fixed a picture of Nelson to the mainmast, remembering his hero's concern for his ship on their West Indies hunt only months before.

The French slipped their cables at 0730 on the 6th, made sail to the westward and formed a line of battle led by the *Alexandre* (80); Leissegues followed, his flag in the *Imperial* (120), supported by three 74s, *Diomede*, *Jupiter* and *Brave*. *Felicité* and *Comete*, both 40-gun frigates, and a corvette, *Diligente*, formed a parallel line inshore; they were to take no part in the action and were not pursued thereafter.

Duckworth assumed that there were as many other French ships in the vicinity and sought to prevent an enemy junction by making an action certain before nine o'clock. He formed two lines, leading the weather or starboard element in the *Superb* (74), followed by Rear Admiral the Hon. Alexander Cochrane in the *Northumberland* (74, Captain Morrison), *Spencer* (74, Captain the Hon. Robert Stopford) and Nelson's old *Agamemnon* (64, Captain Sir Edward Berry). His second-in-command, Rear Admiral Louis, led the port line to leeward in the *Canopus* (80, Captain Francis Austen, brother of Jane), supported by the *Donegal* (74, Captain Sir Pulteney Malcolm) and the *Atlas* (74, Captain Pym). The two frigates, *Kingfisher* and *Epervier* (14), were to starboard of the squadron.

He telegraphed his intention to concentrate his attack on the French admiral and his seconds; for

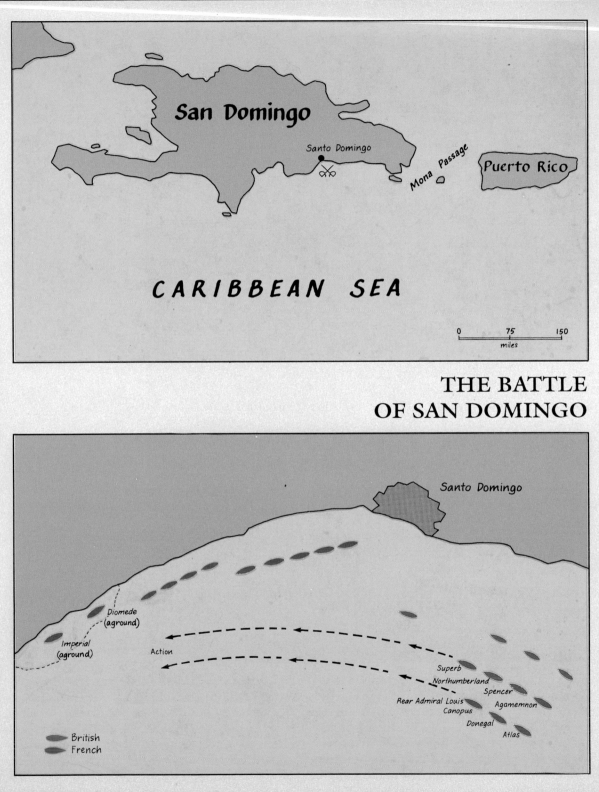

San Domingo

Santo Domingo

Mona Passage

Puerto Rico

CARIBBEAN SEA

0   75   150
miles

THE BATTLE
OF SAN DOMINGO

Santo Domingo

Diomede
(aground)

Imperial
(aground)

Action

Superb
Northumberland
Spencer
Rear Admiral Louis   Agamemnon
Canopus
Donegal
Atlas

British
French

Left: Admiral Sir John Thomas Duckworth.

Right: British gunners plying their deadly trade.

ships to take station for mutual support at 0945 and moments later to engage as closely as possible. A little after ten, *Superb* put three broadsides into the *Alexandre*, which disconcerted her into making off, whereupon Duckworth ordered, 'Engage the enemy more closely.' This was perhaps rodomontade, or for the log, since *Superb* was then hammering the *Imperial*, which was punishing the *Northumberland*. By now the *Alexandre* had tangled with the lee division 'which Louis happily availed himself of', dismasting her. She was then raked by the *Spencer*, which then came round and engaged her on the port tack, thus facing the direction from which she had come. This confused the *Superb* and the *Northumberland* in the heavy smoke, and they fired into her before carrying on, leaving her to accept the surrender of her opponent. The lee division divided, the *Canopus* going for the *Imperial*, and *Donegal* and *Atlas* attacking *Jupiter* and *Brave*. The action became general, only the *Agamemnon* failing to get into action, which was entirely out of character for her captain. The general line of advance was to the westward, at an average of eight knots. *Donegal* forced the *Brave* to strike, then went across the bows of the *Jupiter* as if to rake her, but when her bowsprit came over her port quarter she secured it with a hawser until she had made another conquest. The *Atlas* had perhaps the hardest time. Taking on the much larger *Imperial*, she found her rudder jammed just as the *Diomede* came up to distract her, and then fouled the *Canopus*, carrying away her own bowsprit. The imperturbable Pym worked her off by backing his after sails and returned to deal with the *Diomede*.

The action continued until 1130 when 'the French Admiral, much shattered and completely beaten, hauled direct for the land and, not being a mile off, at twenty minutes before noon, ran on shore', his only surviving mast then coming down; 'the *Diomede* pushed inshore near his Admiral, when all his masts went.' It is not easy to see why the *Superb*, 'being only in 17 fathoms, was forced to haul off to avoid the same evil', or why Duckworth's *Gazette* letter referred to *Diomede* as having struck her colours, 'to comment

on which he left to the world' and which was not the case. A second letter, from Jamaica on the 16th, was necessary to point out that it had been the *Brave* which had struck, thus restoring the honour of Captain Henry of the *Diomede*, whose proffered sword the proud Keats had erroneously and 'disdainfully refused'.

Firing ceased before noon. All five of the enemy line had been taken or destroyed in under two hours. The British ships were not undamaged, but only one had lost a single mast. The Bay was too deep for an anchorage. Cochrane was returned to his command of the Leeward Islands, with the *Agamemnon* in company. Stopford took the *Spencer*, *Donegal* and *Atlas* to Jamaica with the three prizes, and Duckworth, with Louis and the three smaller vessels, followed them once Dunn, in 'a tremendous sea', had taken off the survivors and left the two hulks ashore 'burning gloriously'. There was much glory in the air. But the *Alexandre* was beyond repair, the *Brave* foundered on her way to England, and *Jupiter*, taken into the service as *Maida*, was sold out of it in 1814. As Cochrane wrote to Barham, the enemy had been deprived of five more 'capital ships' – an early use of the adjective in the naval context.

There were some 1,500 French casualties; the British lost 74 dead and 264 wounded, the latter including the son of the late Hugh Seymour whom Duckworth had relieved at Jamaica five years earlier. He was promoted into the *Kingfisher*, whose commander took Duckworth's dispatches to England and was promoted to post captain. The three flag officers and their seven captains were awarded the large gold medal inscribed 'The French squadron captured and destroyed', and the last to be awarded. When the Naval General Service medal was eventually instituted in 1847, 396 survivors of the action claimed the relevant clasp. Cochrane was given the cherished Red Ribbon of the original Order of the Bath the following March, and a baronetcy was conferred upon Louis in April. Duckworth had confidently expected an Irish peerage, though a glance at the terms of the Act of Union would have indicated that his expectation was unrealistic. Being Duckworth, he never ceased to lament being overlooked for San Domingo or for the Dardanelles fiasco of the next year. He was voted the thanks of Parliament but he knew better than many that 'soft words butter no parsnips', and not even an annuity of £1,000 assuaged his disappointment; he wrote 'My dirty annuity' on his copy of the Act. It

Below: Duckworth's action off San Domingo in 1806. Painting Nicholas Pocock.

may have occurred to him that his recent court-martial had been an embarrassment. He had been fortunate to find and beat a second French squadron, for to 'forbear the pursuit of an enemy flying' is traditionally grounds for a court-martial.

BIBLIOGRAPHY

Brenton, P., *The Naval History of Great Britain*, London, 1837. A sound approach to a major history; less impartial is William James's book of the same name, which is overtly hostile and critical.

Marcus, G. J., *The Age of Nelson*, 1971. Part of a naval history of England, generally succinct and reliable.

Jenkins, *A History of the French Navy*, 1973. A somewhat informal and innaccurate study, but provides a source for events from the French side.

The Naval Chronicle, vol 15, 1806. Contains useful letters and notes.

COCHRANE: BASQUE ROADS, 1809

by The Hon. Michael Cochrane

'Whoever is strongest at sea, make him your friend.'
Corcyraeans to the Athenians, 433 BC

Following the defeat of the French in 1805, at Trafalgar, the remnants of the French navy had dispersed between Brest, Lorient and the Basque (or Aix) Roads near Rochefort on the Biscay coast. This still-powerful force posed no great threat to Britain while it remained divided.

However, on 21 February 1809, the British ships blockading Brest were driven off station by a westerly storm, and eight French ships of the line, commanded by Rear Admiral Willaumez, took the opportunity to sail from the harbour. When news of this break-out reached London it caused consternation at the Admiralty, intelligence suggesting that the Willaumez squadron might head for the West Indies to reinforce Martinique, then being besieged by a British force. In fact they did not cross the Atlantic, but sailed south down the French coast, meeting five other French warships which escaped from L'Orient before joining the Rochefort squadron at anchor in the Basque Roads. Here the French breakout ended, as there was a small British force stationed nearby and its commander, Rear Admiral Stopford, was able to hold the French ships at Aix until the remainder of the Channel Squadron arrived, under the command of its C-in-C, Admiral Lord Gambier.

While the Admiralty were relieved that the French were again under blockade, the concentration of such a large proportion of enemy fleet in one place gave cause for concern; after all, Gambier had previously been evaded by a smaller force. Therefore, the C-in-C was instructed to plan for the destruction of the French fleet. The Admiralty suggested the attack might include the use of fire-ships – an earlier proposal from a daring young captain, Lord Cochrane, who had submitted plans for attacking ships at anchor in the Basque Roads. Gambier was unenthusiastic about this idea. He was not a seafaring admiral, having spent most of the previous decade ashore. Moreover, he was a religious zealot, more interested in the distribution of tracts amongst his sailors than in any attack on the French. He replied to the First Lord that a previous attempt to attack a force at the same anchorage had been ineffectual, and described fire-ships as 'a horrible mode of warfare, and the attempt hazardous if not desperate...'.

Frustrated by Lord Gambier's reluctance to attack, Lord Mulgrave sent for the one officer who he considered would not miss an opportunity to fight the French, Captain Lord Cochrane, an officer with an unequalled reputation as a fighting leader, popular with his men for the many prizes he had taken, and now in command of the 38-gun Frigate *Imperieuse*. On 21 March 1809 he had returned to Plymouth following a successful deployment off Catalonia, 'where the good services of His Lordship in aid of the Spaniards and in annoyance of the enemy could not be exceeded'. He knew nothing of the French forces regrouping at the Basque Roads. On reaching London, Cochrane was, unusually for someone so junior, warmly welcomed by the First Lord, who explained the Admiralry's wish to destroy the French at Aix. Lord Mulgrave showed Cochrane the letters from Gambier and asked the young captain to inform the Board how he would neutralise the French fleet.

At this point it became clear to Cochrane why he had been sent for: 'The Channel fleet had been doing worse than nothing. The nation was dissatisfied, and even the existence of the ministry was at stake. They wanted a victory, and the Admiral commanding plainly told them he would not willingly risk a defeat. Other naval officers had been consulted, who had disapproved of the use of fire-ships, and, as last resource, I had been sent for, in the hope that I would undertake the enterprise. If this were successful the fleet would get the credit which would be thus reflected on the ministry; and if it failed the consequence would be the loss of my individual reputation as both ministry and commander-in-chief would lay the blame on me.'

But Cochrane had no fear of failure. He had in mind a terrible new device that he was confident would ensure the destruction of the French fleet – explosive ships. His concept of using these in combination with fire-ships received the unanimous approval of the Board of Admiralty and Cochrane was asked to carry out the attack. Again he expressed his reluctance, 'as being a junior officer it would excite against me a great amount of jealousy. Besides which Lord Gambier might consider it presumptuous on my part to undertake what he had not hesitated to describe as hazardous if not desperate.' Lord Mulgrave insisted that Cochrane go and promised to 'manage it with Lord Gambier that the armour propre of the fleet shall be satisfied'.

The Admiralty wrote to Gambier informing him that twelve fire-ships were being prepared and that the inventor, William Congreve, would attend with some of his new rockets. Cochrane returned to his ship and on 3 April 1809 *Imperieuse* anchored with the British fleet at the Basque Roads. Cochrane immediately reported to Lord Gambier and was sur-

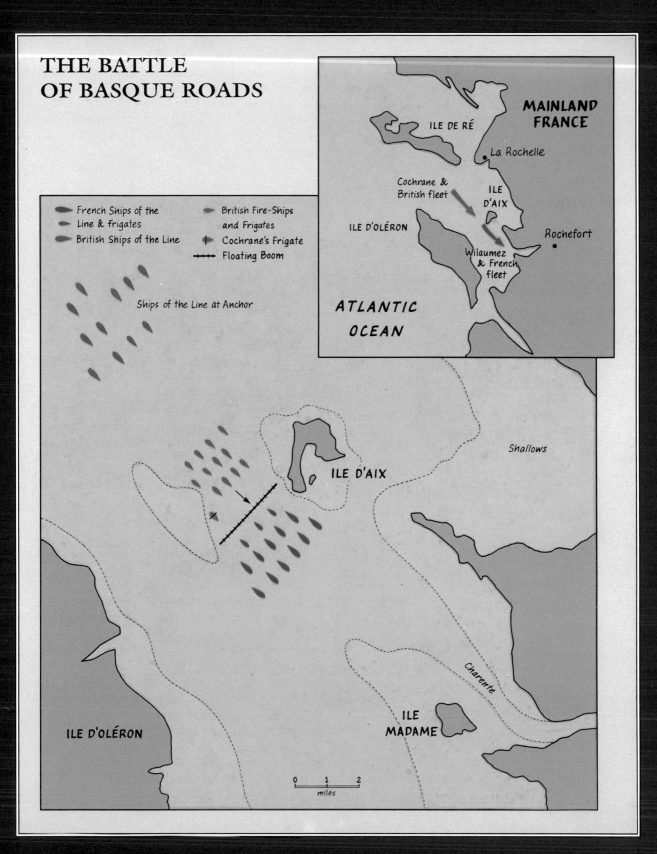

THE BATTLE OF BASQUE ROADS

Legend:
- French Ships of the Line & Frigates
- British Ships of the Line
- British Fire-Ships and Frigates
- Cochrane's Frigate
- Floating Boom

Ships of the Line at Anchor

Inset map:

MAINLAND FRANCE

ILE DE RÉ

La Rochelle

Cochrane & British fleet

ILE D'AIX

Rochefort

ILE D'OLÉRON

Wilaumez & French fleet

ATLANTIC OCEAN

Main map:

ILE D'AIX

Shallows

Charente

ILE D'OLÉRON

ILE MADAME

0   1   2
miles

prised to be received 'with great urbanity'. Whether the C-in-C's civility was due to Lord Mulgrave 'making things all right' with Lord Gambier, or perhaps the result of some other motive, it was soon clear that it was only the Gambier who was happy with the directive that Cochrane was to take charge of the fireships. Every other captain in the squadron was senior to Cochrane, and they were furious at having been passed over in favour of a more junior officer.

Astonished at the low morale he discovered in Gambier's ships, Cochrane returned on board

Left: Captain Lord Cochrane.

Imperieuse and sailed close to the Isle d'Aix so that he could survey both the French fortifications and disposition of the Fleet. It was not only the British who were suffering from poor morale – the French had also experienced problems. As the result of a complaint, Admiral Willaumez had been replaced in command by Vice Admiral Allemand, who seems to have been a better tactician than Willaumez, and he had anchored his ships in two lines to the south of the Isle d'Aix, in a position where mud flats prevented attack from any direction except the north-west, this approach being guarded by a huge floating boom – of which the British knew nothing.

HMS *Imperieuse* anchored a couple of miles south-west of the Isle d'Aix from where Cochrane studied the disposition of the enemy's ships and the dilapidated state of the fortifications. He urged Lord Gambier to expedite the attack by converting some old transport ships which happened to be within the Squadron into fire and explosion vessels. Cochrane personally supervised the conversion of three explosive ships, the hulls of which were strengthened with logs before 1,500 barrels of powder were placed inside them and bound together with hemp. Finally, several hundred shot and 3,000 hand grenades were added before the whole mass was compressed with logs, wedges and sand. The aim of these vessels was to cause 'such an amount of terror, as to induce the enemy to run their ships ashore as the only way to avoid them and save the crews'.

On 10 April, William Congreve arrived in *Beagle*, accompanied by the original twelve fire-ships. Cochrane immediately asked permission to attack that night, but Gambier refused to approve, saying that it was too dangerous for the crews of the fire-ships, who might be captured and then murdered by the enemy. Cochrane felt that this was throwing away 'a most favourable opportunity'. And, sure enough, having detected the arrival of the fire-ships, the French commander lost no time in preparing his defences. He repositioned the two north–south lines of ships of the line so that the frigates lay between them and the boom. The ten ships of the line then struck their topmasts and yards and stowed their sails to reduce the amount of exposed flammable material, leaving only the four Frigates in sailing order. In addition some 70 small boats were stationed close to the boom ready to board and tow away approaching fire-ships. The

Right: His ship crashed through the boom without injury.

French now considered themselves to be impervious to fire-ships or any other form of attack. They had taken all possible precautions, and in any event they had the security of the boom guarding the only approach to their anchorage.

On 11 April, Cochrane at last secured Gambier's approval for the attack, and he decided that they should do so that night, as the day was both dark and stormy and the evening low-water was due at 2036 with a strong flood stream starting a little later. *Imperieuse* again anchored close to the island near the Boyart Shoal, and HM frigates *Aigle*, *Unicorn* and *Pallas* anchored nearby ready to help retrieve the crews of the fire-ships. Lord Cochrane and three volunteers set off in the largest explosive vessel, followed by another, while the third remained secured to the stern of *Imperieuse*, the infernal flotilla being completed by the twenty fire-ships.

It was such a foul night that Cochrane was unable to see the enemy and thus had to navigate blind. On reaching the estimated position of the French, he directed his crew to take to the boat while he lit the fuze. They had not long left the floating bomb, when, after the elapse of only half the intended fifteen-minute delay, the vessel blew up, lighting up the sky with a lurid, red glare. While rowing the three miles back to *Imperieuse*, Cochrane and his gallant crew had the satisfaction of seeing the second explosive vessel blow up and then two fire-ships pass through the newly created gaps in the boom, causing such alarm amongst the French that the enemy ships of the line began shooting at the spot where the explosions had occurred – and thus firing on their own advance frigates.

However, all was not well with the fire-ships. Only four of about twenty reached the enemy, and none did any material damage. But the French believed that they were all explosive vessels, so that the entire French squadron became gripped with terror and, while continuing to fire on each other, almost all of them slipped their anchors to escape this new and dreadful weapon. It is difficult to imagine the panic that there must have been on board the French ships – under way at night without sails and thus unable actually to make way, in a strong wind and a tideway, while under fire from their own side.

At dawn on 12 April, Cochrane saw the extent of the havoc caused by his raid: all but two of the French ships were aground. He was elated. He had more than kept his promise to the Admiralty to disable the enemy; now the Channel Squadron had only to sail in at will and destroy the French ships, some of which were lying on their bilges and consequently incapable of resisting attack. At 0548 Cochrane signalled to Gambier's flagship on the horizon with the news, 'Half the fleet can destroy the enemy... seven on shore.' This was acknowledged with the answer pennant. *Imperieuse*'s crew watched to see the fleet close for the inevitable attack. Nothing seemed to happen, so at 0640 Cochrane signalled again, this time reporting, 'Eleven on shore.' This signal was again acknowledged, but still no apparent activity was seen.

By now Cochrane was uneasy. Low water was due at 0859, and the tide would begin to flood soon after. This would allow the British ships to float in on the rising tide, attack the enemy while they were still aground then sail out on the falling tide. Speed was of the essence, for the high water due at 1509 would allow some, if not all of the French ships to float freely again – thus losing the British all the previous night's hard-won advantage. Thus at 0740 *Imperieuse* signalled to the commander-in-chief, 'Only two afloat.' Still there was no action. Cochrane was by now at a loss for the reason. Seeing the vastly superior British fleet motionless, Cochrane made the signal, 'The frigates alone can destroy the enemy,' which was true – if impertinent. Cochrane was astonished to see only the red and white Answer Pennant fluttering in reply. More signals followed to the flagship, each more frantic than the last – and yet Lord Gambier did nothing.

As a consequence of this inactivity by the C-in-C, Cochrane moved his own ship closer inshore so that if any signal were received from Gambier he would have less distance to sail before engaging the enemy, who were by now furiously attempting to haul themselves off the shore. As the tide turned, Cochrane signalled, 'Enemy preparing to haul off,' but still nothing happened until eventually, almost two hours later, at 1100, Cochrane was relieved to see the British fleet get under way – only to anchor again some three and a half miles west of Aix and five or six miles from the French ships.

This was too much for Cochrane. Now sure that the C-in-C had no intention of attacking the French, he decided to force the issue. In a remarkable feat of seamanship, he allowed his ship to drift stern first towards the enemy. He moved very slowly, not out of fear of alerting the French but to prevent his movements being seen by Gambier, who would surely have recalled him. Cochrane's aim was to so embroil himself with the French that the British squadron would *have* to come to his rescue. Hoisting sail at 1340 to pursue a French ship that had managed to get free, Cochrane signalled, 'Enemy superior to chasing ship but inferior to Fleet.' With this report seemingly ignored, at 1345 he reported, 'In want of assistance.' This was certainly true, as by now *Imperieuse* was right in the midst of the French fleet, simultaneously engaging three ships of the line.

This at last provoked Lord Gambier into action. Two ships of the line and seven frigates were sent to give assistance to the lonely *Imperieuse*. On seeing the approaching reinforcements, the French ship *Calcutta* immediately surrendered to Cochrane. As they came up, the British ships began to engage the enemy, and at 1730 the French ships *Aquilon* and *Ville De Varsovie* also struck. While this was going on, a number of smaller French ships were set alight by their

Right: An 1809 impression of the action at Basque Roads in that year. Cochrane's ship *Imperieuse* is seen at right, with the captain himself centre stage in an open boat with cutlass raised.

crews: one, *Tonnerre*, subsequently exploded. That night, the remains of the French fleet that had managed to re-float themselves moved further east into the mouth of the River Charente, where they were under the protection of Fort Fouras.

At dawn the following morning, Cochrane was stunned to be awakened with the news that Gambier had hoisted the Recall Signal, despite the fact, obvious to him, that there was still work to be done. However, he was not alone in finding this latest message incredible: the signal log of Gambier's flagship shows that the C-in-C was signalled by the captain of the *Valiant*, 'No doubt five more may be destroyed tonight.' And the reply? A reiteration of the Recall! Cochrane hailed the captains of the recalled ships, beseeching them to remain with him, for with their help he intended to destroy Allemagne's flagship, *Ocean*. None, however, would disobey their commander-in-chief.

Cochrane determined to attack the enemy again, and *Imperieuse* had begun to clear her decks for further action when a gig brought a letter from Lord Gambier to Cochrane. This praised his work as admirable but directed him to rejoin the fleet.... but also contained a postscript informing Cochrane that he should continue to attack! Cochrane decided that this letter was indecisive and so chose to remain in the French anchorage. It was not long before further boats brought more letters from Gambier, the final

one ordering *Imperieuse* to return to the fleet, where Cochrane was to report to him. On reaching Gambier's cabin, Lord Cochrane again begged his commander-in-chief to continue the attack. But Admiral Gambier had heard enough: the battle was finished, and he directed Captain Cochrane to return to England with the dispatches. It seems likely that Gambier knew he had failed to press home the attack, as his parting words to Cochrane were, 'If you throw blame on what has been done, it will appear like arrogantly claiming all the merit to yourself.'

On 21 April, *Imperieuse* anchored at Spithead. Cochrane was treated as a hero and the King created him a Knight of the Bath. Nevertheless, Cochrane was unhappy, knowing that so much more could have been done, and soon there were murmurs about a larger victory having been missed. *The Times* editorial on 25 April asked, 'Why then if seven might be destroyed were there only four?' The final straw came when Cochrane informed Lord Mulgrave that as Member of Parliament for Westminster he would vote against the House of Commons motion of thanks to Lord Gambier. Cochrane refused a series of offers from Mulgrave, each of a more adventurous command, intended as a bribe to remove him from Parliament on the appointed day.

Eventually Gambier sought to be court-martialled so that he could clear his name. The ensuing trial was a farce, and evidence that would harm the C-in-C was withheld; Cochrane was not permitted to question Lord Gambier, and the official French chart was redrawn, moving shoals by more than a mile. Needless to say, Gambier was acquitted and the vote of thanks was passed by Parliament despite the opposition of Cochrane and 38 others.

Cochrane had committed professional suicide. After being refused permission to rejoin *Imperieuse*, he returned to his political work with renewed vigour, missing no opportunity to expose the Navy's maladministration and corruption. Eventually, inevitably, the Establishment won: he was implicated in a Stock Exchange fraud and convicted after a dubious trial; he was struck off the Navy List, expelled from Parliament (although promptly re-elected) and removed from the Order of the Bath.

His seagoing career was far from over, however. He travelled abroad, working as a mercenary admiral whose extraordinary daring was instrumental in the liberation of Chile, Peru and Brazil; he also commanded the Greek Navy. In 1831, after succeeding to the earldom of Dundonald, he was received at Court with great acclamation and reinstated in the Navy as a rear admiral. His honours were restored by a special royal warrant awarding Cochrane the enhanced dignity of a GCB, and he was appointed commander-in-chief of the North America Station. Subsequently he continued to be promoted, ending his career as Admiral of the Red. He died in 1860 and was buried in Westminster Abbey.

Some may say that this reinstatement happily completed his rehabilitation. The author believes that it was only when the Battle of Basque Roads was commemorated in Cochrane's name, inside Aston Webb's splendid Gunroom at Dartmouth, that the Royal Navy admitted Lord Cochrane was, and always had been, right.

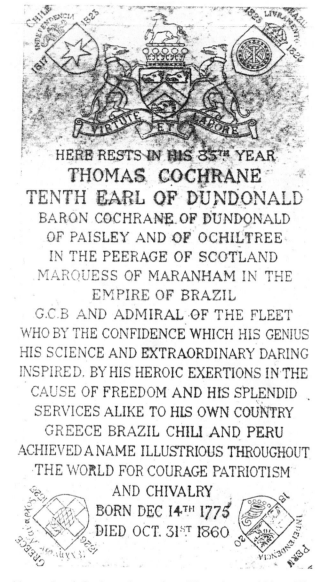

Above: Lord Cochrane's tomb at Westminster Abbey. The epitaph is attributed to Queen Victoria.

BIBLIOGRAPHY

Dundonald, Lord, *Autobiography of a Seaman*, 1860.
Twitchett, E. G., *Life of a Seaman: 10th Earl of Dundonald*, 1931.

Lloyd, C., *Lord Cochrane: Seaman, Radical, Liberator*, 1947.
Tute, Warren, *Cochrane: Life of Admiral Earl of Dundonald*, 1965.

Grimble, I., *The Sea Wolf*, 1978.
Thomas, Donald, *Cochrane: Britannia's Last Sea King*, 1978.

Cochrane, A., *The Fighting Cochranes: A Scottish Clan over 600 Years of Naval and Military History*, 1983.

STOPFORD: ACRE, 1840

by Andrew Lambert

'Every country that has towns within cannon shot of deep water will remember the operations of the British Fleet... whenever such country has any differences with us.'
Lord Palmerston, 1840

The origins of the Syrian campaign lie in the history of Egypt after the Napoleonic invasion, and in the weakness of the Ottoman Empire. In 1805, Mehemet Ali, an Albanian officer, became Viceroy of Egypt and attempted to create a modern, independent state there. While serving his master, the Sultan, Mehemet lost his fleet at Navarino in 1827 and much of his army in Greece the following year. However, he rebuilt both forces, and in 1831 moved into Turkish Syria. The following year, his son, Ibrahim Pasha, defeated the Turkish army at Koniya and conquered the province.

The Sultan could do little but accept the *fait accompli*. France supported Mehemet, as a potential ally; Britain, while committed to Turkey, had no forces to spare in 1832–3. In desperation, the Sultan accepted a temporary Russian occupation of Constantinople. The British Foreign Secretary, Lord Palmerston, based his subsequent policy on the need to reduce Russian influence in Turkey. To this end, he tried to prevent further clashes between Egypt and Turkey, giving Turkey time to modernise. He was also interested in the overland route to India through northern Syria and the River Euphrates.

While the great powers looked on, the Sultan waited to attack Mehemet, and Mehemet in his turn to declare himself independent of Turkey. Finally, in 1838, Mehemet made his declaration, and the Sultan prepared for war. At Nezib in June 1839, Ibrahim once more routed the Turkish army. The Sultan died before news of the disaster could reach Constantinople; but worse was to follow – the fleet deserted to Alexandria, to join the formidable Egyptian force in a combined squadron of fifteen ships of the line, more than double the size of the British Mediterranean Fleet.

Palmerston realised that the situation required the rapid eviction of Egyptian forces from Syria before the other powers could intervene. For this he had to rely on the Mediterranean Fleet under Vice Admiral Sir Robert Stopford, and any Turkish forces that could be found. Initially he hoped for French support against Russia but quickly discovered that, although Russia favoured his policy, France was vehemently opposed, coming close to the point of war. The situation was complicated by the French fleet, which was larger and better manned than that of the British.

Stopford's fleet was composed in the main of relatively elderly ships. His flagship, the 100-gun three-decker *Princess Charlotte*, was a copy of the *Victory*, others were wartime 74-gun ships, and only the 84-gun *Powerful* and *Thunderer* were modern units – but they carried weak peacetime complements. Only later in the crisis, and too late for active service, did more powerful ships arrive.

Stopford, then 72 years of age, had seen much hard service in the French wars, combining experience with professional competence and reserve. Unfortunately, he was out of sympathy with the government, and in particular with Palmerston, on two key issues. His caution and anxiety to follow orders irritated the Foreign Secretary, who looked for some initiative; furthermore, as a Tory serving under a Whig ministry, he could not be trusted with politically sensitive information.

His second-in-command, the energetic and resourceful Commodore Charles Napier (1786–

Left: Acre in more tranquil times.

154

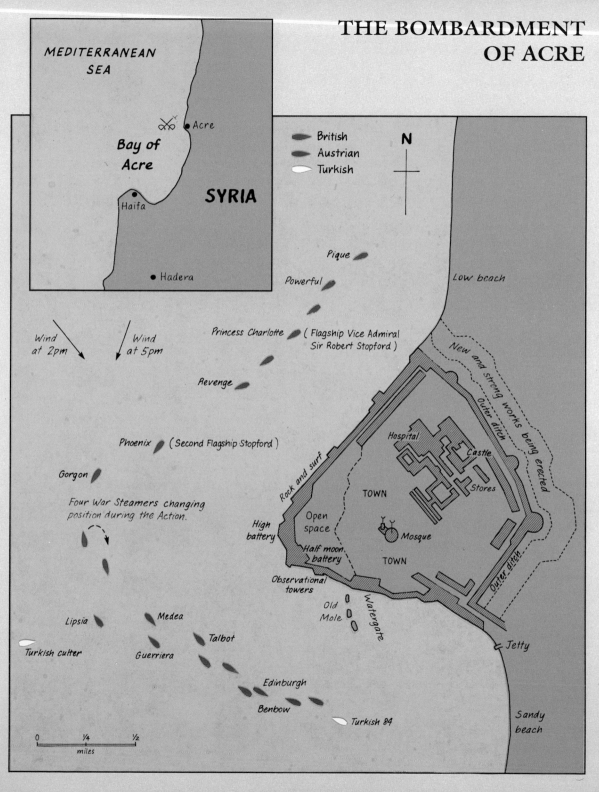

THE BOMBARDMENT OF ACRE

MEDITERRANEAN SEA

Bay of Acre

• Acre

SYRIA

Haifa

• Hadera

British
Austrian
Turkish

N

Pique

Powerful

Low beach

Princess Charlotte (Flagship Vice Admiral Sir Robert Stopford)

Wind at 2pm

Wind at 5pm

Revenge

New and strong works being erected

Outer ditch

Phoenix (Second Flagship Stopford)

Gorgon

Hospital

Castle

Stores

Four War Steamers changing position during the Action.

Rock and surf

TOWN

High battery

Open space

Mosque

Half moon battery

TOWN

Observational towers

Outer ditch

Lipsia

Medea

Old Mole

Watergate

Turkish cutter

Guerriera

Talbot

Jetty

Edinburgh

Benbow

Turkish 84

Sandy beach

0   ¼   ½
miles

1860) was altogether different. His advanced liberal politics and experience of amphibious and coastal operations in the Napoleonic conflict and the War of 1812 made him ideal for the task in hand. He was also in regular private correspondence with the First Lord of the Admiralty, Lord Minto, and with Palmerston, who held him in high regard after his service in the Portuguese Civil War of 1833, which had solved a major diplomatic problem without British intervention. The remaining officers of the squadron were a mixture of Whigs and Tories, many of the latter being Stopford's relatives, including two sons and three nephews.

In April 1840, Stopford was instructed to protect Constantinople from an Egyptian attack. Two months later a minor revolt broke out in Beirut, which was quickly suppressed. In July, Britain, Russia, Austria and Prussia signed a treaty to protect Turkey, the omission of France from this reflecting her unwillingness to coerce Mehemet. Stopford was instructed to cut the sea communications between Egypt and Syria, the only route for men and stores, and to support the insurrection with arms and Turkish troops. All this would be carried out short of war, which left the control of operations with the Foreign Secretary – had war been declared, control would have passed to the Secretary of State for War, Lord John Russell, who lacked Palmerston's ability and did not share his aims.

Palmerston hoped the Egyptians could leave Syria without violence, using overwhelming force to deter resistance. The role of France remained critical, for if she intervened the Syrian campaign would become irrelevant. However, the French had problems fitting out their fleet; and, as the summer wore on, it became

clear that they had lost the race to mobilise. Without a fleet, the aggressive diplomacy of Thiers lacked real weight, and the King of France replaced him with a conservative, pacific ministry in mid-October. But if Palmerston and Minto were certain France would not act, many of their colleagues, and Stopford, were less sanguine.

To avoid complications with France, Palmerston was anxious to move quickly. The pace of the campaign would be dictated by two overriding considerations: seasonal gales would hit the eastern Mediterranean in November and December; and if operations had not been completed by then, France would have had time to mobilise fully. Stopford hesitated to blockade Alexandria or seize Egyptian shipping, earning a strongly worded condemnation from Palmerston, and ensuring that Napier, directed by private letters, would be the chosen vehicle for the conduct of the campaign.

In August, Stopford sent Napier to operate off Beirut, where he attempted to raise a revolt, with little success, and then proceeded to Alexandria, where he met Mehemet Ali and left a squadron to observe the Turco-Egyptian fleet. This squadron remained on station throughout the campaign: effectively, since only one ship at a time could leave Alexandria harbour, they were imprisoning the Turco-Egyptian fleet. In September Stopford was joined by a small squadron of Austrian ships, a few Turkish warships commanded by Captain Baldwin Walker, RN, then

Below: A representation of the action against the gun batteries at Acre. Stopford's flagship *Princess Charlotte* is the largest ship seen.

seconded to the Ottoman fleet, and 5,000 Turkish soldiers. The troops, with Napier in command, landed north of Beirut to arm the local insurgents. Meanwhile the fleet quickly cleared the Egyptians from the smaller forts along the coast. Napier and Walker led a small force that bombarded and stormed Sidon on 26 September, a small-scale demonstration of the plan developed to capture Acre. Ashore again, Napier's army of British and Austrian marines, rocket troops and Turkish soldiers went into battle with Ibrahim Pasha at Boharsef in the mountains of Lebanon on 10 October, gaining one of the Royal Navy's most interesting victories. The defeat of the hitherto invincible Ibrahim by the despised Turks influenced the subsequent collapse of Egyptian morale. In combination with naval pressure, Boharsef forced Ibrahim to evacuate Beirut, leaving Acre as the last Egyptian strongpoint on the Syrian coast. Once more Stopford hesitated to attack, but orders arrived at the end of October.

On 29 October, Stopford and the senior military officer, Sir Charles Smith, agreed a plan of action. The White Mountain pass north of Acre would be occupied by 2,000 Turkish troops, while another 3,000 would embark with the fleet to storm the fortress. Stopford and the senior captains discussed Acre aboard the *Princess Charlotte* on the 30th and, despite Stopford's reservations about the French fleet, agreed to attack.

The combined fleet arrived off Acre late on 2 November, where the shoals had been surveyed by Captain Boxer, *Pique*, and Captain Codrington, *Talbot*. Their work had been facilitated by the Muslim festival of Ramadan, which required the faithful to fast throughout the hours of daylight – as darkness fell, the Egyptians were too busy eating to notice the surveying parties. In addition, the Polish officer who advised them mistook the surveying buoys for moorings, and instructed the gunners to lay their pieces on them. Codrington described the position as follows: 'The walls of Acre are built on a rocky shelf, partly some feet above, and partly level with the water's edge, and surrounded by a prolongation of that shelf on a ledge in the water. The walls rose up nearly perpendicularly; to a height, I think, of between thirty and forty feet... it was an irregular line of battery..., mostly (I speak now of the southern face) of open batteries; they were armed with long guns, 18 pounders and 24 pounders... I think I saw 32 pounders... They were almost all very efficient guns, and had been but

recently cast. The supply of ammunition... was dangerously superabundant; for on going round the batteries *next* day, I saw to the left of each gun, round shot, double headed shot, *live* shell in abundance, and *heaps of full cartridges*.'

At 1730 the captains assembled in Stopford's cabin and elected to tow the fleet into action the following morning, although the shortage of steam ships would require each steamer to make two journeys. The fleet would engage the two sea faces of Acre, the larger ships of the line and the modern frigate *Pique* on the western face, where their heavy guns would be most effective; the smaller ships, which were armed for short-range action, to the south, close to the walls. Walker's flagship, a 74-gun ship, was placed directly opposite the small water gate, supported by the 74s *Edinburgh* and *Hastings*. Their role was to batter a practical breach in the wall through which the troops could storm the city.

The plan was based on the capture of Sidon. Napier requested the post of honour for the *Powerful*, but it was decided that two of the smaller line of battle ships would be more effective than one large one in the restricted space available. The role of Napier's western division, apart from enfilading fire on to the southern walls, was to be entirely diversionary.

Early on 3 November the plan of attack was changed. The fleets would now sail into action, while the steamers kept under way, firing shells into the city. Stopford shifted his flag into the *Phoenix* to control the action, and the fleet got under way at 1100. In view of the light onshore breeze, Napier, in the *Powerful*, elected to lead his division to the north before running down for the western face of the fortress from 1300. At 1430 the *Powerful* anchored by the head and stern 800–900 yards out before opening fire. She continued firing until 1745, receiving considerable damage aloft but few hits in the hull. The gunners ashore had elevated their pieces to hit the navigational marks, while the squadron anchored considerably closer to the walls than they had expected. The error was fatal. Smoke drifting in on the breeze and the rapidity and precision of British fire gave the Egyptians no opportunity to correct their error. It had been intended that Napier's squadron would anchor in succession from the north, each ship passing on the disengaged side of those already in action and occupying the entire western face of the fortress down to the juncture of its two seaward faces. In the event, when the *Powerful* came to, however, her squadron

anchored astern, leaving a large gap at the head of the line. Both Napier and Stopford signalled the *Revenge*, Captain Waldegrave, to fill the position. Furious at being kept in reserve for the attack, Waldegrave moved ahead of the *Powerful*, anchoring at 1530. This incident led to a major dispute between Napier and Stopford, which came close to a court-martial. By the time Stopford signalled the cease fire, at 1750, only one or two guns on the sea face were still firing, and they were quickly silenced by the *Princess Charlotte*. This side of the attack had exceeded even the most sanguine of expectations, but it did not, of itself, lead to the fall of the city.

The southern attack also went in on the sea breeze. The smaller ships had very little in the way of instructions: they were to support the ships of the line, knocking out the guns as they prepared the way for an assault. The ships anchored 500–600 yards out shortly before 1400. At this range the carronades of the older ships were still effective. Once again the Egyptian guns were aiming too high, and once again they had no chance to rectify their error. Midshipman Montagu Burrows recorded: 'The very first broadsides were murderous, and the smoke soon enveloped the whole of them, as there was very little wind. It is also

Above: The bombardment of St. Jean d'Acre by British and Allied squadrons. *Powerful*, centre, was launched at Chatham in 1826 and weighed 2,296 tons; the heaviest guns she was armed with were 32-pounders.

an historical fact that for guns of that period, in wooden ships, something like perfection had been attained. Officers and men had been thoroughly trained under the newest system; and all matters connected with gunnery worked with the regularity of clocks.'

Aboard Burrows' ship, the *Edinburgh*, four men were killed and seven wounded when a single shot struck an upper deck carronade, the only shot to strike the ship as opposed to the rigging. Gradually the Egyptian guns were disabled by direct hits and by the destruction of the stone walls killing the crews – save only for one obstinate piece behind sandbags, which continued to fire at the *Talbot* until the end and remained undamaged the following morning. The gap between the western and southern lines was filled by the steamers, which kept under way, firing shells from their upper deck pivot-guns.

At 1620 there was a flash of light in the south-eastern section of the city, followed by a catastrophic detonation and shock wave. A shell, variously attributed to the steamer *Gorgon* or the *Benbow*, had penetrated the main magazine. In the explosion 1,100 men, more than one quarter of the garrison, were killed. Many were deafened, some for up to three weeks. All firing ceased, ashore and afloat, for a few minutes, and when the shore batteries did resume their fire was weak and quickly fell away to almost nothing. This allowed the naval gunners to concentrate on those pieces that were still firing. The drill of HMS *Excellent*, instilled into a peacetime fleet by trained seamen gunners and professional officers, proved irresistible. By 1700 the southern division had ceased firing. Montagu Burrows, later an *Excellent* man, commented: 'Many of the guns were dismounted and shattered by our shot, gun-carriages in shivers, embrasures driven in. Great credit is therefore due to the defence. It is questionable whether any troops would have done better in standing to their guns, though doubtless many would have fired better while there.'

Stopford signalled the western division to cease fire at 1750, but some ships had already done so for lack of targets. Later the heavy ships of the western division moved into deep water, some under tow, having been badly cut up aloft. Preparations were made to assault the city the following day, but during the night the Egyptians evacuated the city. Informed of this, Walker quietly sent his troops ashore, followed by British marines. By daybreak Acre was in Allied hands. The fleet suffered only 18 killed and 41 wounded, which, together with the loss of a few spars, some rope and the expenditure of more than 48,000 rounds, made this one of the cheapest of the Royal Navy's major victories (although there would be further casualties ashore when another magazine detonated).

After Acre, Stopford sent Napier to command the blockade of Alexandria. Privately informed by Palmerston of the terms he required, Napier quickly settled the crisis with Mehemet Ali. They signed a convention on 25 November; in return for hereditary rule in Egypt, Mehemet would evacuate Syria and restore the Turkish fleet. In fact, Napier had no authority to sign the convention, and was in breach of his duty to Stopford in acting alone, but Palmerston approved the measure. Once Turkey awarded the hereditary *pashalic*, the crisis was settled. Reduced to a proper subordination, Egypt ceased to be a problem until the 1880s, and then it would be her weakness, not her ambition, that involved the great powers.

Acre is rightly considered to be one of the great battles of the Royal Navy – in view of the complete-

ness of the victory, the immediacy of the results and the skilful handling of the campaign. It upheld the integrity of an ally, disciplined a rebellious and troublesome vassal, disabused France of her dreams of maritime equality and replaced Russian influence at Constantinople with the Four-, later Five-Power Straits Convention of 1841. The triumph belonged to Palmerston, and to the fleet. Palmerston himself was in no doubt of the value of the battle, it was 'an event of immense political importance as regards the interests of England not only in connection with the Turkish Question, but in relation to every other question which we may have to discuss with other powers. Every country that has towns within cannon shot of deep water will remember the operations of the British Fleet on the Coast of Syria in September, October and November 1840, whenever such country has any differences with us.'

BIBLIOGRAPHY

Bartlett, C., *Great Britain and Seapower 1815–1853*, Oxford, 1963. The standard account of British naval policy and operations during the period.

Bourchier, Lady, *Letters of Sir Henry Codrington*, London, 1880. A major eye-witness account by an intelligent and experienced officer.

Bourne, K., *Palmerston*, London, 1982. The most recent, and the most satisfactory, account of British diplomatic and war fighting policy.

Hattendorf, J., 'The Bombardment of Acre, 1840' in *Les Empires en Guerre at Paix 1793–1860*, Paris, 1990. The most recent major article to deal with Acre.

Lambert, A. D., *The Last Sailing Battlefleet: Maintaining Naval Mastery 1815–1850*, London, 1991. An in-depth examination of the strategy, tactics and shipbuilding effort of the Royal Navy. This book places Acre in the context of the revolution in gunnery and ship design that occurred between 1815 and 1850.

Marsot, A., *Egypt in the Reign of Muhammad Ali*, Cambridge, 1984 An Egyptian perspective.

Pearsall, A., 'The Bombardment of Acre, November 3, 1840' in *Sefunium* (The Maritime Museum, Haifa), 1967–8. A first-rate account of the battle by an outstanding naval historian.

STURDEE: FALKLAND ISLANDS, 1914

by Jon Sumida

'Take, sink, burn or destroy the enemy fleet.'
Lord St. Vincent, 1798.

On 8 December 1914, in an engagement that was the climax of a campaign that had begun on the outbreak of the First World War, most of the German East Asiatic Squadron was destroyed off the Falkland Islands by a greatly superior British force. From August to October, the German squadron, which consisted of two large armoured cruisers and three light cruisers under the command of Vice Admiral Maximilian Graf von Spee, had travelled from the western Pacific to the coast of Chile. On 1 November, they were intercepted off the Chilean port of Coronel by a British squadron, which consisted of two large armoured cruisers, a light cruiser and an auxiliary cruiser, under the command of Rear Admiral Sir Christopher Cradock. The German big ships enjoyed large advantages in armament and the quality of their gun crews, and there were three German light cruisers to the one British, which was only weakly augmented by the auxiliary cruiser, a hastily converted ocean liner. The encounter thus ended in a decisive victory for von Spee, whose ships sank both British large cruisers, compelling the two inferior units to flee.

On receipt of the news on 4 December of the German victory at Coronel, the Admiralty reacted swiftly. Powerful Allied naval forces had been pursuing von Spee's squadron from the east and barred his way to the north. Admiral Sir John Fisher, who had become First Sea Lord just a few days earlier, in addition ordered the detachment of three battlecruisers from the Grand Fleet to reinforce British cruiser squadrons in the west and South Atlantic. Two of the battlecruisers were placed under the command of Vice Admiral Sir Doveton Sturdee, who departed Britain for the South Atlantic on 11 November. On 26 November, Sturdee met Rear Admiral A. P. Stoddart's squadron, which consisted of three armoured cruisers (after one had been sent to the north to reinforce British forces in the Caribbean), two light cruisers and an auxiliary cruiser, at the Abrolhos Rocks anchorage off the coast of Brazil. The combined squadron, led by Sturdee, moved southwards towards the Falklands on 28 November, proceeding at medium rather than high speed in order to conserve fuel. A slight delay occasioned by a minor mishap meant that it did not reach Port Stanley in the Falklands until the evening of 7 December, which was some four days later than the Admiralty had estimated.

Sturdee's less than rapid transit was balanced, however, by the slow progress of von Spee. For much of November, the Germans dithered in Chilean ports, coaling and considering their options. The German commander concluded that a retreat to the safety of home waters was impossible, but that his squadron might be able to inflict serious damage on the considerable concentration of British shipping in the South Atlantic before running out of ammunition or being destroyed by the Royal Navy. With this intention, von Spee left the Chilean port of St. Quentin on 26 November, but his warships were delayed by bad weather and did not round Cape Horn until 1 December. The following day von Spee captured a British merchant vessel loaded with coal and stopped for four days to fuel his ships. During this time he consulted his captains and was persuaded to attack the British base at the Falkland Islands in order to destroy the wireless station there and further replenish his coal supplies. On 7 December the East Asiatic Squadron weighed anchor and steamed towards the Falklands.

Below: Vice Admiral Doveton Sturdee seen aboard the battleship *Hercules* in 1915.

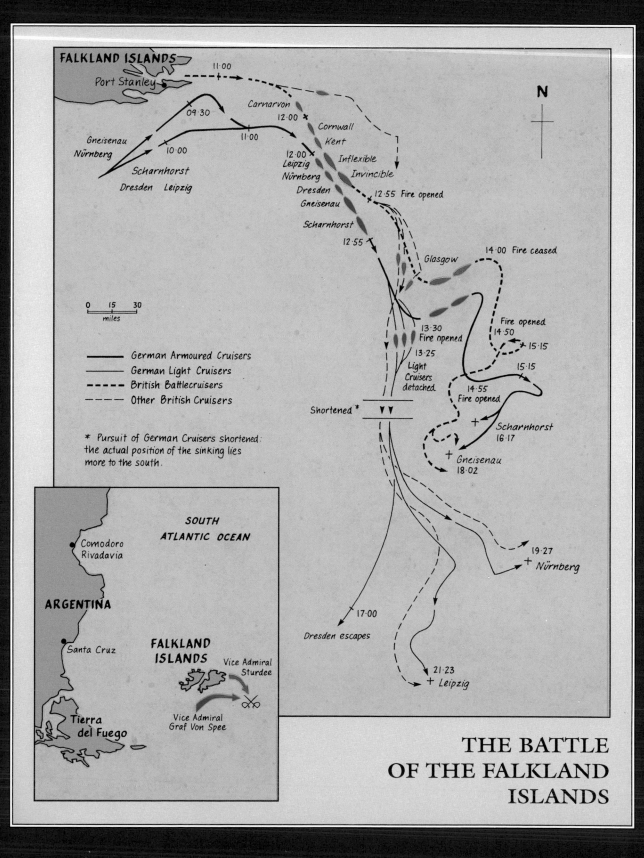

THE BATTLE
OF THE FALKLAND
ISLANDS

Left: *Inflexible* and *Cornwall* are seen here raising steam in Port William, prior to getting under way.

At 0750 on the morning of 8 December, British look-outs on a hill next to Port Stanley observed the approach of two unidentified warships from the south. This was reported to *Canopus*, an old battleship that had been lightly grounded in the harbour, which in turn relayed the alarm to Sturdee. His command was at that moment not prepared for battle: several ships had yet to coal, two had partially dismantled their engines for repairs, and only one, the armoured cruiser *Kent*, was ready for steaming at short notice. The two German vessels were the armoured cruiser *Gneisenau* and the light cruiser *Nürnberg*, which came under fire from the big guns of *Canopus* at 0920. These shots landed close enough to cause the Germans to turn away, but on sighting *Kent* emerging from Port Stanley they resumed their advance. Almost immediately afterwards, however, von Spee signalled his scouts to decline action and follow the armoured cruiser *Scharnhorst*, the flagship, and the light cruisers *Dresden* and *Leipzig* in a full-speed retreat to the east. The German reconnaissance had not discovered the presence of the British battle-

cruisers, so von Spee initially had good reason to believe that his squadron was fast enough to escape, given his long start.

By 1000, some two hours after the sighting of the enemy, the battlecruisers *Invincible* and *Inflexible*, armoured cruisers *Carnarvon* and *Cornwall*, and light cruiser *Glasgow* had raised steam and begun moving out of Port Stanley to join *Kent*. Observing the German squadron in the distance, Sturdee, in his flagship *Invincible*, began the chase, knowing that he had a superiority in speed sufficient to run down his quarry well before nightfall. The light cruiser *Bristol* was unable to get under way until 1100, and not long afterwards Sturdee ordered her to take the auxiliary cruiser *Macedonia* in company and sink several approaching German colliers, which were misidentified as troopships transporting an invading army. The British main force, in the meanwhile, carried on their pursuit at 18 knots, a pace that was well below the maximum of which the battlecruisers were capable but which allowed the slower armoured cruisers to keep sta-

Left: A photograph taken from *Carnarvon* of *Invincible* chasing von Spee's squadron.

Right: *Invincible* making 22 knots during the chase. Note the considerable funnel smoke.

tion or catch up. This was still fast enough for the British ships to draw closer to the fleeing Germans, who had recognised the battlecruisers and thus their extreme peril by 1100, but whose worn engines prevented them from steaming at their nominal top speeds.

At 1220, Sturdee began increasing speed and after thirty minutes had reached 25 knots, which quickly brought the battle cruisers within range of *Leipzig*, the rearmost German ship. *Inflexible* opened fire at 1300 followed by *Invincible* at a range of about 16,000 yards. No hits were scored, but von Spee realised that it would only be a matter of time before his entire squadron was brought under punishing fire. At 1320 he therefore ordered the light cruisers to leave the line and scatter to the south, while he turned his armoured cruisers north-eastwards to engage the British battlecruisers. Sturdee had previously issued orders dealing with the situation that had now arisen. While the battlecruisers followed the two German armoured cruisers, *Cornwall*, *Kent* and *Glasgow* broke away to pursue the German light cruisers. *Carnarvon*, the slowest of the British cruisers, was at this point lagging ten miles behind and would later join in support of the battlecruisers.

The main engagement between the British battlecruisers and the German armoured cruisers may be divided into four phases. In the first, from 1320 to 1405, the range was from 13,000 to 16,000 yards, and the courses of the opposing ships ran roughly parallel. The fire on both sides was slow, the Germans husbanding their ammunition (half of which had been consumed at Coronel), while the fire of the battlecruisers was hampered by their own smoke, which was blown across their lines of sight by the wind. During this period, *Invincible* and the German armoured cruisers were hit several times, but the damage on both sides was not serious. Fire ceased at 1405 when the range opened to above 16,000 yards. In the second phase, from 1405 to 1445, Sturdee turned towards the Germans to renew the action. While this manoeuvre was in progress, however, smoke completely blocked the British view of their quarry, who during the interval turned to the south, increasing the range rapidly.

Right: Photographed from *Kent* – the battlecruisers during the chase.

Left: *Inflexible* opening fire with her 'A' turret on the *Leipzig*.

The British battlecruisers renewed the chase and by 1445 had caught up again, which brought on the decisive third and fourth phases of the battle.

From 1445 to 1530, the two sides engaged at ranges that varied from 15,000 to 10,000 yards. Firing while on parallel courses was several times interrupted by turns that shortened or widened the range or that were intended to secure better visibility. Ranges were often low enough to enable the Germans to use their secondary batteries. Both sides scored a number of hits. The British, however, suffered little, while the Germans were punished so severely that Sturdee was able to close in for the kill. In the fourth and final phase, which lasted from 1530 to 1730, the range fell to 12,000 yards and less, and *Inflexible*, by steaming clear of smoke interference from the flagship, improved her gunnery. The two battlecruisers concentrated fire on *Scharnhorst*, assisted briefly by *Carnarvon*, which had caught up shortly after 1600. The German flagship sank at 1617. The three British warships then engaged *Gneisenau*. Courses were parallel but opposite, and the range between 10,000 and 12,000 yards. The second German armoured cruiser sank at 1730.

By this time, two of the three German light cruisers had been brought to bay in separate actions. *Dresden*, the one survivor, was fast enough to make good her escape (temporarily, as it turned out – she would be scuttled four months later in Chilean waters after being trapped by British cruisers). *Leipzig*, the slowest of the trio, was engaged by *Glasgow* in a running fight beginning at 1450 at 12,000 yards, the range falling after an hour of shooting to 9,000 yards. At 1617, *Cornwall* joined the fray. From 1703 to 1806 the two

Left: *Inflexible* picking up survivors from *Gneisenau*.

British warships bombarded *Leipzig* at ranges of 8,000 to over 10,000 yards, causing severe damage. From 1806 to 1930, *Leipzig* was attacked at distances below 8,000 yards but beyond the effective range of torpedoes (5,000–6,000 yards), and was reduced to a wreck. She sank at about 2030. *Nürnberg*'s fate was similar. Chased by *Kent*, the German cruiser opened fire at 1400 at 12,000 yards and scored several hits. *Kent*'s heavier but shorter-ranged guns were not effective until 1709. From then until 1735 *Kent* used her superior speed to carry on the fight at ranges of 7,000 down to as low as 3,000 yards. At such distances hitting was frequent, and *Nürnberg* sank at 1926.

German casualties were extremely heavy. Von Spee was killed together with the entire crew of *Scharnhorst*. *Leipzig* and *Nürnberg* lost 90 per cent of their men. Only a quarter of *Gneisenau*'s complement survived. Of the 2,086 sailors who had manned the four sunken warships, 1,871 were lost, while 215 were rescued. British casualties, in contrast, were slight. *Inflexible* and *Glasgow* each had one man killed, *Kent* lost four, and there were several wounded. *Invincible* was hit 22 times, *Inflexible* three times, *Glasgow* twice, *Cornwall* eighteen times, and *Kent* 38 times, but material damage was inconsequential. In the main action, the two British battlecruisers fired 1,174 12in projectiles, or two-thirds of the total with which they began, over the course of four hours. Of these, 74, or six per cent, were estimated to have hit their target. *Carnarvon*, which participated for little more than an hour, fired only twelve per cent of her shells. *Cornwall* fired 40 per cent and *Glasgow* 45 per cent of their magazines against *Leipzig* over five hours, while *Kent* expended a quarter of her shells against *Nürnberg* during some two hours of shooting.

At the Battle of the Falklands, the German squadron was outnumbered, outgunned and outpaced by their British opponents. In addition, the weather was clear and the seas calm until the early evening, which facilitated both pursuit and, once the fighting began, good shooting. Finally, because contact was made at the beginning of the day, the British had ample time to finish their work before the Germans could exploit the onset of nightfall to evade contact and destruction. The outcome of the several engagements, therefore, was practically a foregone conclusion. On the other hand, the extended period of time and enormous quantity of ammunition required to dispatch the German warships once the

Above: The man who invented the battlecruiser concept, Admiral Fisher.

battle had been joined requires further tactical and technical explanation.

In firing against *Scharnhorst*, *Gneisenau*, and *Leipzig*, the long period of the fighting and the high expenditure of projectiles were functions of the tactics chosen by the British. These were, in the case of the battlecruisers, to fight at the longer ranges that favoured their heavier calibre guns and that were too great to enable the Germans to use torpedoes. At such distances, the proportion of hits to shots fired was bound to be very low, given the shortcomings of British gunnery equipment (lack of directors and inefficient fire-control computers). Shorter ranges at which the rate of hitting could be much higher were not sought until the fighting power of the German ships had been greatly reduced. *Cornwall* and *Glasgow* were somewhat out-ranged by *Leipzig*'s smaller but higher velocity guns, but like their larger consorts kept their distance once the German cruiser was within reach of their armament until she had suffered such

Above: Shell damage to *Kent* inflicted by the *Nürnberg*.

Kent's relatively speedy victory and economical ammunition consumption, however, were purchased at the price of receiving more hits and suffering higher casualties than in the other British warships.

The Battle of the Falkland Islands was a significant victory. The destruction of the German East Asiatic Squadron eliminated a serious threat to British and Allied merchant shipping, which in turn liberated large naval forces that had been involved in the pursuit for other purposes. On the moral side, the mortifying defeat of Coronel was avenged, and faith in the Admiralty thus restored. And the success of the battlecruisers seemed to justify the wisdom of combining high speed and heavy gun power – the hallmarks of their design – which encouraged the Admiralty to order the construction of additional fast, powerful, but lightly protected capital ships. Within three years, however, much had changed: the reputation of the battlecruiser as a viable type had been destroyed with the sinking of *Invincible* and two other British battlecruisers at Jutland; Britain's vital lines of maritime supply seemed critically vulnerable to German submarines; the resources of the Royal Navy were tightly stretched; and confidence in the Admiralty's judgement was at an all-time low. *Sic transit gloria mundi.*

damage from the larger shells that closure was considered reasonably safe. *Kent* fought a relatively short-range action because she did not close on *Nürnberg* until late afternoon and thus did not have the time to reduce her opponent by degrees before darkness.

BIBLIOGRAPHY

Bennett, Geoffrey, *Coronel and the Falklands*, New York, 1962.
Corbett, Sir Julian S., *Naval Operations*, vol I (To the Battle of the Falklands, December 1914), London, 1920.
Marder, Arthur J., *From the Dreadnought to Scapa Flow*, vol II (The War Years: to the Eve of Jutland), London, 1965.

Pollen, Arthur, *The Navy in Battle*, London, 1918.
Sumida, J. T., *In Defence of Naval Supremacy: Finance, Technology and British Naval Policy, 1889–1914*, Boston, 1989, and London, 1993.
Tarrant, V. E., *Battlecruiser Invincible: The History of the First Battlecruiser, 1909–1916*, London and Annapolis, 1986.

JELLICOE:
JUTLAND, 1916

G. A. Gordon

'There seems to be something wrong with our bloody ships today, Chatfield.'
Sir David Beatty on seeing HMS *Queen Mary* blow up at Jutland, 1916

Britain's declaration of war in 1914 presented the German High Sea Fleet with a fundamental dilemma. Intended as a deterrent to Britain, it had patently failed to deter. Was it now to fight the British Grand Fleet and probably be destroyed, or was it to rot uselessly in harbour? A compromise was reached: it would try to reduce the Grand Fleet's superiority by catching and sinking isolated ships or squadrons, as opportunity allowed, while evading a full fleet action for the time being. This was easier said than done, but U-boats and mines would also, it was hoped, have their part to play in the attrition process.

For its part, the Grand Fleet's task might have seemed clear enough – sink the High Sea Fleet – but to its commander-in-chief, Sir John Jellicoe, it was not that simple. He was the first British admiral since the time of the Spanish Armada to have the country's entire front-line naval strength entrusted to his command, and he was burdened with the knowledge that a disaster to his fleet might soon be followed by the invasion or starvation of Great Britain. He also feared new and untried forms of warfare, such as U-boats and floating mines, which he expected a retreating German fleet to use against him.

The leaders of both sides therefore qualified their desire for battle with terms and conditions that had little common ground. A full fleet encounter could only take place if one side caught the other seriously wrong-footed, and for this reason nearly two years elapsed before the battle fleets met. The Grand Fleet made many forays from its northern base at Scapa Flow in the Orkneys, partly for training, partly in vain hope of meeting the enemy. The High Sea Fleet seldom left its moorings in the Jade estuary. The few actions that took place in the early months of the war involved, at most, their respective (and subordinate) battlecruiser forces: the Battle Cruiser Fleet (BCF) under Vice Admiral Sir David Beatty, and the First Scouting Group (1st SG) under Rear Admiral Franz Hipper.

The spring of 1916 brought promise of change. The High Sea Fleet got a new commander-in-chief, Vice Admiral Reinhard Scheer, who was frustrated by the months of inactivity, and British hopes rose for a more aggressive policy on the part of the Germans - without which there would be little chance of the fleets ever meeting. Their answer came at the end of April, when Hipper's battlecruisers (1st SG) bombarded Lowestoft and Great Yarmouth. The attack

Above: Admiral Jellicoe had no clear idea of the whereabouts of the German Battle Fleet.

caused political pressure in Britain for part of the Grand Fleet to be moved south from Scapa Flow, at least to the BCF's base in the Firth of Forth, the better to intercept or deter further raids – the division of the Grand Fleet, which Scheer had hoped for. This pressure was, in principle, resisted, but the battlecruisers were badly in need of gunnery training (impracticable in the Firth of Forth) and so a squadron of four *Queen Elizabeth* class fast battleships, the 5th Battle Squadron (5th BS) under Rear Admiral Hugh Evan-Thomas in *Barham*, were accordingly detached from the Battle Fleet in the third week of May and sent down to Rosyth to join Beatty's BCF, while a much weaker battlecruiser squadron (3rd BCS), under Sir Horace Hood, went to the north to get some overdue gunnery practice. This was something of an experiment, for Beatty was known to have an independent and jealous attitude to his command, and the Battle Cruiser Fleet by no means always conformed to Grand Fleet practices.

There was planned a provocative sweep towards the Skagerrak (the strait between Norway and Denmark) at the beginning of June, during which the Battle

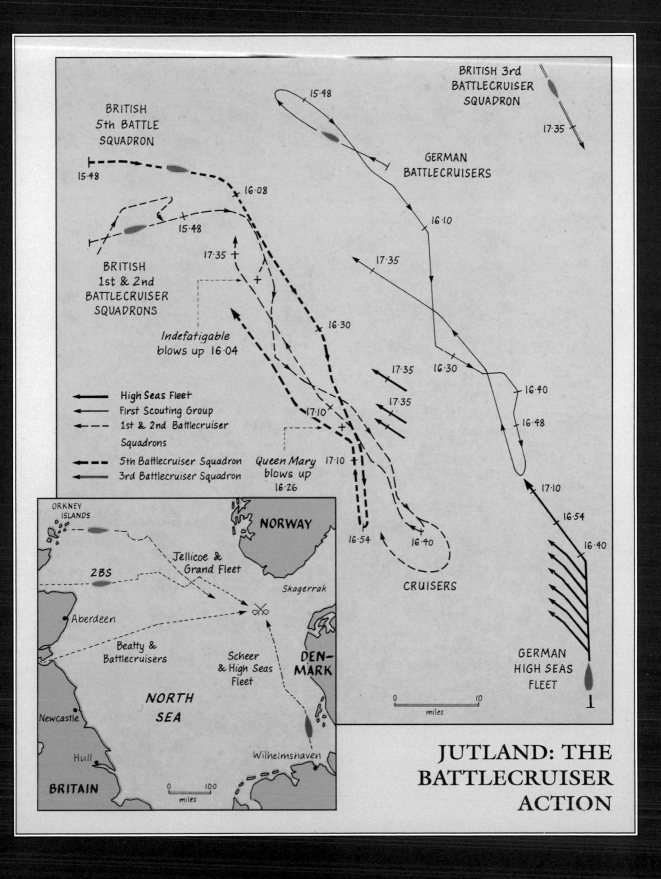

BRITISH 3rd
BATTLECRUISER
SQUADRON

15.48

17.35

BRITISH
5th BATTLE
SQUADRON

GERMAN
BATTLECRUISERS

15.48

16.08

16.10

15.48

17.35

BRITISH
1st & 2nd
BATTLECRUISER
SQUADRONS

17.35

16.30

Indefatigable
blows up 16·04

17.35

16.30

17.35

16.30

16.40

High Seas Fleet
First Scouting Group
1st & 2nd Battlecruiser
Squadrons
5th Battlecruiser Squadron
3rd Battlecruiser Squadron

17.10

16.48

Queen Mary
blows up
16·26

17.10

17.10

16.54

16.54

16.40

16.40

CRUISERS

ORKNEY
ISLANDS

NORWAY

2BS

Jellicoe &
Grand Fleet

Skagerrak

Aberdeen

Beatty &
Battlecruisers

Scheer &
High Seas
Fleet

DEN-
MARK

GERMAN
HIGH SEAS
FLEET

Newcastle

NORTH
SEA

0   10
miles

Hull

Wilhelmshaven

BRITAIN

0   100
miles

JUTLAND: THE
BATTLECRUISER
ACTION

Above: Sir John Fisher, photographed when a vice admiral. His ruling 'Hit first, hit hard and hit any-where' was almost to have tragic consequences at Jutland.

Fleet and the BCF would meet, and the two exchanged squadrons would revert to their normal places. This foray was anticipated, however, by intelligence on the afternoon of Tuesday 30 of May that the German High Sea Fleet was preparing to put to sea. As soon as dusk hid their movements from the prying eyes of U-boats, therefore, Jellicoe and Beatty led their respective forces out of harbour.

Beatty, in his flagship *Lion*, had under his command no fewer than 50 warships, of which his six battle-cruisers and four 'visiting' battleships formed the core. He seems not to have taken seriously the possibility of meeting the enemy. His casual attitude was not just due to a foolish signal at midday from the Admiralty, suggesting that Scheer was still in harbour. It is evident both in his failure to issue Battle Cruiser Fleet Standing Orders to Evan-Thomas (without which the rear admiral could hardly know how Beatty's leadership methods differed in practice from Jellicoe's) and in the way he deployed Evan-Thomas's fast battleships, five miles to the NW of the BCF, from dawn on the 31st. This must have been to assist the forthcoming junction

with Jellicoe's Battle Fleet, upon which the BCF would lead the whole Grand Fleet south-eastwards towards the Horns Reef area, with Evan-Thomas's squadron mid-way between the two British groups. It was certainly not designed to help Evan-Thomas take part in a pursuit of a retreating Hipper.

Thus doubly handicapped, Beatty's forces, impressive on paper, met Hipper's battlecruisers. It happened at the end of the eastward 'leg' of Beatty's planned track, just as he was turning his heavy ships northwards. Hipper was some 35 miles to the east. In the middle was a neutral tramp steamer. Hipper's westernmost screening destroyers signalled her to stop. Beatty's easternmost light cruiser, *Galatea*, spotted her blowing off steam and closed to investigate.

Exactly when *Galatea*'s 1440 (GMT) 'Enemy in sight' signal reached Beatty's hands is not known. As the flagship was on British Summer Time for internal routines, senior officers had probably left *Lion*'s bridge to have tea after witnessing the turn to the north. At any rate, twelve minutes elapsed before Beatty made a flag signal for his heavy groups to turn SSE (to cut the enemy off from his Horns Reef sanctuary) and, without waiting for acknowledgements, wheeled his ships round in that direction. Five miles away to the NNW, *Barham*'s officer of the watch could not make out *Lion*'s flags, mistook them for an expected zig-zagging signal, and turned the 5th BS two points farther west. By the time the *Queen Elizabeths* had received a belated searchlight order from *Lion* and turned SSE, they were ten miles astern of Beatty.

Meanwhile Hipper had gone to the support of his light forces, and at 1520 the five German battlecruisers loomed in the haze to the north-east of the BCF. Hipper came round to a course of SE, as Beatty had expected, and a race ensued in that direction as the adversaries converged. At 1548 both sides opened fire. The Germans shot better with their 11- and 12-inch guns than the British did with their 12- and 13.5-inch weapons, and the BCF was soon receiving hits. Evan-Thomas's battleships, meanwhile, were trying to catch up by cutting corners; but it was twenty minutes before *Barham*'s sighting shots crept up to the hindmost German battlecruiser, *Von der Tann*. Before Evan-Thomas's flagship could distract *Von der Tann*, the latter delivered a knock-out blow to *Indefatigable*, Beatty's hindmost battlecruiser – reeling out of line, she then blew apart, killing all but two of her 900 men.

Four minutes later the 5th BS got into range, and the Germans themselves began to experience accurate bombardment. Their shooting at Beatty's ships lessened. Presently, however, Beatty pressed closer, and there occurred his second, and most serious, loss of the day. Because of a confusion of conning orders, *Lion* briefly left the line to starboard, thus allowing two of the largest German ships, *Derfflinger* and *Seydlitz*, to concentrate their fire on HMS *Queen Mary*. At 1626 this most powerful battlecruiser, whose shooting had earned the admiration of the enemy, fell under a hail of shells. Owing, presumably, to flash relaying into one of her main magazines, she exploded, rolled over and sank with the loss of all but twenty of her crew of 1,200. Beatty's force had suffered cruelly, but Evan-Thomas's battleships were gaining on Hipper and scoring hit after 15in hit on the hindmost German battlecruisers. Then, with the action speeding southwards, and with destroyers busy scrapping in no man's land, the dynamics of the situation suddenly changed.

The German High Sea Fleet, recently emerged from the Horns Reef swept channel, had been 50 miles south of Hipper when battle was first joined, and Scheer had been hurrying north to support his subordinate. At about 1635 the BCF's most advanced light cruisers, under Commodore William Goodenough, sighted a forest of masts and funnels against the dark south-easterly overcast. Beatty waited until he could see them for himself, and then, at 1640, smartly turned his force round to the north as a few long-range shells from the leading enemy battleships fell around him. The first part of his task – to locate the enemy battle fleet – was done, albeit at horrible cost. The second part – to draw Scheer northwards on to Jellicoe's battle fleet – now commenced.

Evan-Thomas turned up astern of the BCF. Again, his turn was some minutes late, owing to another misunderstanding between *Lion* and *Barham*, and the squadron came under sustained bombardment from Scheer's battle fleet. To the High Sea Fleet the British were nicely silhouetted against the clear western horizon, and the Germans had every reason to hope that one of the *Queen Elizabeths* would soon be crippled and harvested; indeed *Malaya* suffered badly. For some time Evan-Thomas's ships were engaging both Hipper's 1st SG *and* the High Sea Fleet, but whenever visibility permitted they gave a good account of themselves.

Meanwhile, away to the north Jellicoe had received Beatty's enemy reports and had released Rear Admiral Hood, who had been occupying Evan-Thomas's usual place in advance of the Battle Fleet, to push ahead at 25½ knots with his three battlecruisers, while he himself hurried the main part of the Grand Fleet southwards at its maximum speed of twenty knots. The fleet was in its cruising formation of six columns of four ships. Before engaging the High Sea Fleet, the C-in-C would have to deploy it into a single battle line in a way that would enable all its heavy guns to bear on the enemy. This would be done by causing five of the six columns to turn into line astern of one or other of the wing columns. The question of *which* wing column would depend on the distance, bearing and course of the enemy, and for two hours Jellicoe – unable to send wireless signals for fear of disclosing his position – was on tenterhooks for precise information as to the enemy's position. The details reaching him from the BCF were sparse and inconsistent.

At 1735, when Beatty estimated Jellicoe's arrival on the scene to be imminent, he prepared to close in once more on the 1st Scouting Group, which was leading Scheer's fleet by some five miles. His intention was to push Hipper off course to the east and prevent him from giving Scheer early warning of Jellicoe's approach. At this point Hipper's light cruisers (2nd Scouting Group) suddenly came up against a cruiser, followed by three capital ships and four destroyers in the haze to the east. They were Hood's 3rd Battle Cruiser Squadron. Because of a discrepancy in reckoning between the BF and the BCF, Hood had aimed too far east and might have missed altogether if the cruiser *Chester* had not stumbled into Hipper's four cruisers at quite short range. *Chester* was the victim of a vicious squall of shellfire that all but disabled her before she could gain the protection of Hood's three *Invincibles* which, fresh from ten days' gunnery training at Scapa Flow, gave her assailants short shrift and battered *Wiesbaden* to pieces. Hipper supposed that these new intruders were battleships, loosed his destroyers for a mass torpedo attack, which was largely parried by a spirited response from Hood's four destroyers (for which Commander Loftus Jones of *Shark* won a posthumous VC), and fell back towards Scheer's battle fleet.

Helped therefore by Hood's surprise intervention, Beatty succeeded in depriving the High Sea Fleet of its advanced scouts at exactly the right moment. Scheer blundered on, following close behind Hipper, now on a north-easterly course.

At 1805, with the head of Scheer's line only some fifteen miles off, the British C-in-C himself caught sight of the BCF on the Battle Fleet's starboard bow, firing furiously at an enemy (Hipper's 1st SG) out of sight. Jellicoe was disconcerted to find his subordinate so far north and west, and his searchlight enquiry about the enemy battle fleet received only a semi-coherent answer. But he had no time left. He had to deploy his fleet. At 1815, with only the sound of gun-fire and Beatty's course to go by, he selected the port column to lead the battle line, and made the Royal Navy's most important tactical decision of the twentieth century. Slowly the Grand Fleet's 24 battleships uncoiled themselves from their cruising formation. The method of deployment was such that, while the Battle Fleet would take about 25 minutes to form a *straight* line, it would be in a single line, albeit with an 80° bend working its way along it, in five. The bend did not matter as it presented a concave angle to the enemy, with all guns able to bear on the killing ground between the fleets. This was the horrifying panorama that confronted Hipper out of the haze at 1822.

Exactly what was going on was less clear to Jellicoe,

Below: Admiral Chatfield.

whose battle line defined the northern and eastern boundaries of the arena, than it was to Hipper, near the centre. Gun smoke from dozens of heavy guns and emissions from hundreds of funnels hid most of the High Sea Fleet from the British, and besides, the Grand Fleet still had some sorting out to do. Beatty and Evan-Thomas, some five miles apart by now, had to decide what to do with themselves, and four armoured cruisers, under Rear Admiral Robert Arbuthnot, had to get from the left flank (which was now forming the lead) to the rear of the battle line. Beatty was still engaging Hipper, and by the time Jellicoe's deployment direction was clear to him he was probably committed to his easterly charge across the front of the deploying Battle Fleet – a course that led him to his preferred position in the van of the line. But in crossing the concave front of the fleet his coal smoke added to the curtain of smog between the fleets; and he almost collided with Arbuthnot, who was coming the other way, having chosen to take the only route he considered a sportsman could take. Arbuthnot's large but obsolescent ships had no business in the arena between the battle fleets, and they presented easy targets. It was suicidal, and his flagship, *Defence*, was blown apart with the loss of all 900 men, while *Black Prince* and *Warrior* were severely mauled. Only *Duke of Edinburgh* escaped in one piece.

Meanwhile Evan-Thomas was wheeling the 5th BS to port to fall in astern of the starboard-hand (rear-most) battle squadron, thus severing himself from Beatty's command. During this manoeuvre the steering gear of the third of his four fast battleships, *Warspite*, jammed and she circled helplessly in full range of Scheer's leading ships until the problem was fixed. She sustained many hits and heavy casualties, but she distracted the German gunners from *Warrior* and may have saved her from *Defence*'s terrible fate. *Warspite*, *Black Prince* and *Warrior* all limped away.

With the arena clear of extraneous British forces, the Grand Fleet set to its work of execution on those German battleships which were emerging into view through the murk. Its opportunity lasted barely fifteen minutes of spasmodic shooting through thickening clouds of smoke, and while carnage was wrought in several German ships, conditions could hardly have been worse for systematic gunnery. Hipper, having been forced farther round, towards the south-east, was being engaged by Beatty, who had been joined ahead by Hood's 3rd BCS. During this fierce exchange, the BCF suffered its third and final disaster

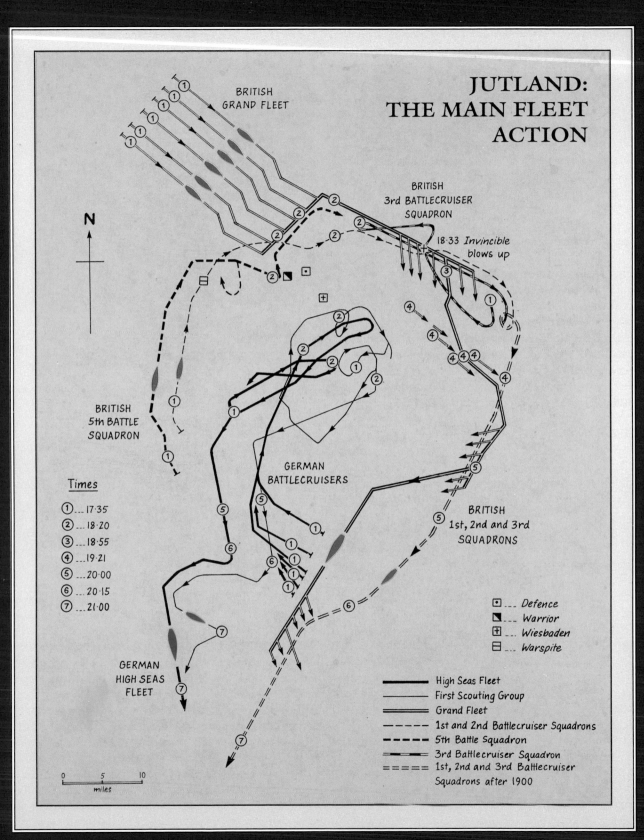

JUTLAND: THE MAIN FLEET ACTION

BRITISH GRAND FLEET

BRITISH 3rd BATTLECRUISER SQUADRON

18.33 Invincible blows up

N

BRITISH 5th BATTLE SQUADRON

GERMAN BATTLECRUISERS

BRITISH 1st, 2nd and 3rd SQUADRONS

Times

① ... 17·35
② ... 18·20
③ ... 18·55
④ ... 19·21
⑤ ... 20·00
⑥ ... 20·15
⑦ ... 21·00

GERMAN HIGH SEAS FLEET

⊡ ... Defence
◪ ... Warrior
⊞ ... Wiesbaden
⊟ ... Warspite

High Seas Fleet
First Scouting Group
Grand Fleet
1st and 2nd Battlecruiser Squadrons
5th Battle Squadron
3rd Battlecruiser Squadron
1st, 2nd and 3rd Battlecruiser
Squadrons after 1900

0   5   10
miles

when Hood's flagship, *Invincible*, received a hit that ignited her amidships magazine and blew her in two. Six men out of more than 1,000 survived, and *Invincible*'s two ends stood up on the shallow sea bed like tombstones as the Battle Fleet swept past.

Meanwhile, Scheer was facing the prospect of certain annihilation. He played one of the only two cards he had left up his sleeve: he ordered a *Gefechstkehrtwendung*, or an emergency turn-away, with each ship putting its helm over when the one astern had begun to turn. It was brilliantly executed, and in a few minutes the High Sea Fleet had disappeared from view. Jellicoe's battle orders had not allowed for such a defensive manoeuvre, and in the dismal visibility it was unclear what had happened. At 1842 an uneasy silence fell over the battlefield.

Scheer had been led by the nose and hopelessly outmanoeuvred, and in spite of spectacular local successes, his desperate need was to escape from this nightmare and get home. It has never been fully explained why, just twenty minutes after his escape, he turned round again. He claimed afterwards that he was seeking to renew the battle, but common sense and evidence from officers around him throw this into doubt. *Possibly* he was hoping to 'cross the T' of the rear of the British line, but more likely he judged Jellicoe to be farther south and hoped to pass unmolested towards the Horns Reef. In fact he barged once more into the British line and had his own T crossed for the second time. At 1910 his battered squadrons re-entered the maelstrom of violence.

This time a *Gefechstkehrtwendung* alone would not be enough, and he played his only remaining card: a mass attack by his torpedo-boats and a so-called 'suicide' charge by Hipper's battlecruisers while the rest of his fleet reversed course for the third time. Some of Hipper's ships were scarcely in a condition to float, let alone charge, and the attack was not pressed home. But the destroyers triggered long-held fears in Jellicoe's safety-conscious mind, and he responded as laid down in his battle orders by turning the fleet away – an action that defeated the torpedo threat but also helped Scheer's disengagement and effectively ended the action.

After escaping destruction for the second time, Scheer settled on a southerly course at 15–16 knots while he recovered his composure and considered what to do. He had at all costs to avoid a further fleet encounter, yet the Grand Fleet blocked his route home. Fortunately for him, visibility was clamping

Above: HMS *Birmingham* coming under heavy fire at Jutland.

down and dusk was approaching.

For his part, Jellicoe, although perplexed by the High Sea Fleet's disappearance, knew more or less where it must be and also meandered southwards, at seventeen knots. Many times he had walked his dividers across the chart from Scapa and wondered how, if he sailed after dark, could he find enough daylight hours to finish a battle near the Horns Reef the following evening. He never found the solution.

There was one further, if local, capital-ship exchange which, if exploited resolutely, might have disrupted and diminished Scheer's battered fleet. At 2023, Beatty, some miles ahead and to the south-west of Jellicoe, sighted and fired at Hipper's battlecruisers trying to regain their place at the head of the reversed German line. The 1st Scouting Group, in no condition to engage an enemy it could scarcely see, received fresh damage and quickly turned away. Then Beatty discovered a squadron of pre-dreadnoughts – which Scheer should not have brought to sea and which were meant to be in the rear, but were now in the van – of the High Sea Fleet. They too turned away after suffering hits, and Beatty invited the nearest (the leading) division of the Battle Fleet to join him in a pur-

Above: HMS *Royal Oak* and HMS *Hercules* in close line astern during the battle.

suit, hoping that this would turn the whole of the Grand Fleet to the south-west. Vice Admiral Jerram declined to act without orders from Jellicoe, and Rear Admiral Leveson of the division next astern insisted on following the ship ahead. Nobody came to Beatty's support, and presently contact was lost. (If Evan-Thomas's battleships had still been with him and under his command, the evening might have ended differently.)

Jellicoe was right not to seek close action after darkness had fallen. Poor visibility, from any cause, can only subvert the numerical advantage of the superior fleet, and the British were not trained for night fighting. Besides, his strategic position – between Scheer and Germany – was satisfactory, and he hoped to bring his enemy to battle at daybreak. The problem was that Scheer had available to him three routes home, one of which lay to the south and one far to the south-west, and Jellicoe had to be ready to block whichever he chose. This is where Jellicoe's subordinates failed him most seriously, for few reports reached him during the night about the High Sea

Fleet – everyone assuming that he, and he alone, could see the whole picture.

Scheer resolved to break his way through south-eastwards, towards the Horns Reef channel, and he found himself crossing astern among the light forces marshalled in the rear of the Grand Fleet. Spasms of violence erupted in the night. With mistaken identities, point-blank gunfire, torpedoes and collisions in the blinding glare of searchlights, hundreds of men on both sides met sudden deaths as the High Sea Fleet trampled its way through. The straggling armoured cruiser *Black Prince*, crippled during Arbuthnot's futile charge across the arena, was sunk by gunfire; the German pre-dreadnought *Pommern* was blown up by torpedo; a number of other German battleships received minor damage; two of Goodenough's light cruisers were mauled, and several destroyers on each side were sunk. Nobody was in control.

And nobody thought to tell Jellicoe what was happening. Goodenough, perhaps, was too busy; but in the 5th BS, only three or four miles distant, men stood on their turret tops to watch the fireworks; *Malaya* even trained her guns on a German dreadnought silhouetted by searchlights. Everyone left it to someone else to inform the C-in-C, so nobody did.

Right: The Battle of Jutland by Wyllie.

Left: The German Battle-
cruiser *Seydlitz* was the victim of heavy shell damage
and a torpedo hit during
one of the destroyer attacks.
She was lucky to survive the
battle.

And the Admiralty, having decrypted Scheer's signals which pointed to the Horns Reef, filed them as not urgent. By the time dawn broke it was too late. There was nothing for the Grand Fleet to see except patches of wreckage and floating bodies, and nothing for it to do but count the cost and begin the long haul back home.

The British lost more ships than the Germans, and because British losses of major ships were sudden and spectacular they are bound to make a disproportionate impression in a narrative of the battle. Total losses for the British were three battlecruisers, three armoured cruisers and nine destroyers. Total German losses were one old battleship, one battlecruiser (Hipper's flagship *Lutzow*, abandoned on the way home), four light cruisers and five destroyers. On the basis of these figures the Germans claimed victory. Several surviving German ships, however, got home with indescribable carnage inside them and were out of commission for weeks and months of repair. Apart from *Marlborough* (torpedoed) none of the British survivors were critically damaged. *Lion* was soon back in service, less one of her turrets, and even *Warspite*'s damage was more apparent than real. A few hours after reaching harbour, Jellicoe was able to report that he had 24 dreadnoughts ready for sea. Scheer could only muster ten. His battlecruiser force had almost, for the time being, ceased to exist. Had such a numerical upset occurred the other way around, the Germans would have wrested control of the British coastline.

The German Navy was lionised by the German press and public. But naval personnel knew they had been very lucky to escape annihilation. Scheer was willing to risk one more attempt to trap a detached portion of the Grand Fleet, which he did in August, but he already realised that Germany's naval efforts should be channelled into submarine warfare. The rank and file had conducted themselves with skill and endurance beyond praise; but, especially after the August affair ended with another narrow escape, they could not pretend to themselves that they were anything but fugitives from British superiority. This was not what they had understood by the boasts of *Der Tag*. In the long run, morale suffered, especially when the best and most ambitious young officers volunteered for U-boats and were transferred away from the big ships. At the end of this road lay mutiny.

For the British, whose heritage was Nelson and Trafalgar, Jutland was a bitter pill. But the battle strengthened rather than weakened their dominance over the High Sea Fleet – the more so with the Grand Fleet's burning anger and determination to wipe out the enemy next time. Whether another meeting would have been a wipe-out can never be known: even Beatty, who replaced Jellicoe in November 1916, would have needed several hours of daylight and good visibility to complete the job. But many lessons were learnt. Lessons which, assuredly, should have been thought through before the fleets met, but lessons which were put to good effect not just by Beatty but by the Royal Navy in another war twenty-five years later.

BIBLIOGRAPHY

Fawcett and Hooper, *The Fighting at Jutland*, London 1921.
Harper, Captain J., *Record of the Battle of Jutland*, London.
Marder, Arthur J., *From the Dreadnought to Scapa Flow*, London 1961–70.
Costello, John, and Terry Hughes, *Jutland 1916*, London 1976

HARWOOD: RIVER PLATE, 1939

by Eric Grove

*'Strenuous, unrelaxing pursuit is therefore
as imperative after a battle as is courage during it.'*
Rear Admiral Alfred T. Mahan, 1911

The Battle of the River Plate was the Royal Navy's first victory in the Second World War. In many ways the engagement paralleled victory in the Falklands a quarter of a century before: the most troublesome detached portion of the German surface fleet was found and destroyed in South American waters. That this German unit was named after the squadron commander who had lost his life in the earlier battle added to the sense of déjà vu. That the Royal Navy owed its success in 1939 not to the employment of superior firepower but to tactical skill and aggressive determination showed how much times had changed from the assured material supremacy of earlier years.

The *Admiral Graf Spee* was one of the three *Panzerschiffe* ('Armoured Ships') built in the early 1930s to squeeze the ultimate capability out of the maximum size of warship allowed to Germany under the Treaty of Versailles. Known as 'Pocket Battleships' they broke the Versailles 10,000 ton displacement limit by an extra twenty per cent, but the need plausibly to appear to be within the limit imposed serious constraints on a warship that was designed for long-range commerce raiding. The ships' designers got round the limitations of size in various ways. Diesel engines provided light weight, relatively high speed (26 knots) and a ready response to sudden threats, but at a price in reliability. The main armament of six 11in guns was heavy for a ship of this size, but it had to be disposed in two triple turrets, which precluded the engagement of more than one target at a time, for all six guns were needed to provide a salvo large enough for effective fire control. The level of armour protection, 3.2 inches on the belt with a 1.8-inch armoured deck, gave only marginal protection against 8in shells. In theory the *Panzerschiffe* could fight anything they could not avoid – except five Anglo-French fast capital ships they would be unlucky to come across by chance. In practice they would have to be very careful to avoid opposition if they were to avoid the fiery fate of the surface raiders of the previous conflict.

As relations with Britain and Germany deteriorated in August 1939, two *Panzerschiffe* were sent to sea to take up waiting positions: *Deutschland* was deployed into the North Atlantic and *Admiral Graf Spee* to the South Atlantic. When Hitler belatedly authorised these ships to begin operations on 26 September, more than three weeks after the outbreak of war, the C-in-C of the German Navy, Admiral Erich Raeder, made it clear than enemy naval forces were to be studiously avoided. No one knew more about the weaknesses of German raiders operating in an environment controlled by their enemies than Raeder. He had been the historian of German raider operations in 1914–18 and saw that their weakness had been the natural desire of their captains to engage Allied warships. This exposed them to damage and to the concentration of superior force against them, with consistently disastrous results. Hence Raeder made clear to the commanding officers

Left: The much vaunted 'Pocket Battleship' *Admiral Graf Spee*. With a relatively heavy armament and a good turn of speed, she made a splendid commerce raider.

Right: Commodore Harwood's flagship, the light cruiser HMS *Ajax*. She weighed 6,840 tons and mounted a main armament of eight 6-inch guns.

of his pocket battleships that under no circumstances were they to seek engagement with warships of any kind. Convoys therefore would have to be avoided and attention focused on individual merchantmen.

The introduction of ocean convoys in the North Atlantic – a fortuitous result of a mistaken U-boat attack on the Atlantic liner *Athenia* – deprived *Deutschland* of many targets, and she eventually returned to Germany with little to show for her patrol. *Graf Spee* was more lucky. South of Sierra Leone virtually all ships still sailed independently, easy pickings for the German warship. Moreover, her captain, Hans Langsdorff, was an able and wily seaman who had a real flair for latter-day privateering. He sank his first ship off Brazil at the end of September and in the following few weeks moved into the Indian Ocean and back, sinking or capturing four more merchantmen and causing considerable disruption to Allied trade in the southern hemisphere.

A number of hunting groups were formed to track down the mystery ship, among them Force 'G', made up of four cruisers under Commodore Henry Harwood, whose beat was the south-east coast of South America. In the huge, open ocean, trying to find the raider was well nigh impossible. Yet a number of remarkable strokes of luck were to play into Harwood's hands. The first was that Langsdorff decided to disobey his strict orders. In the last week of November, *Graf Spee* rendezvoused with her designated auxiliary, *Altmark*, to refuel and to attend to

her troublesome engines, which were in dire need of overhaul. Langsdorff assembled his officers and told them that *Graf Spee*'s engines were in too serious a state to be attended to properly at sea and that she would have to return home. It was unlikely that another heavy German unit would be in these waters for some time, so it was necessary for *Graf Spee* to make her mark. The best way of doing this was to win a significant victory over the Royal Navy, as the ship's namesake had done at Coronel. In future, therefore, if enemy warships appeared he would commit himself fully and accept the risk of limited damage.

The next ship Langsdorff attacked, the cargo liner *Doric Star* on 2 December, was able to get off a message before being taken, as was the next, *Tairoa*, sunk on the following day. Langsdorff may have been looking for trouble. He refuelled for the last time from *Altmark* on 6 December and transferred all but his officer and radio-operator prisoners to the auxiliary. The following day he sighted another prize, the *Streonshalh*, which gave herself up with confidential papers that showed the Plate estuary might offer a lucrative target. A small convoy including a naval auxiliary was apparently due to leave Montevideo on 10 December. This and its light escort, perhaps a small cruiser and a couple of destroyers, was exactly the weak naval target Langsdorff was seeking.

Now came the second stroke of luck for Harwood. Acting on nothing more than instinct, he decided on 9 December to make for the Plate also and concen-

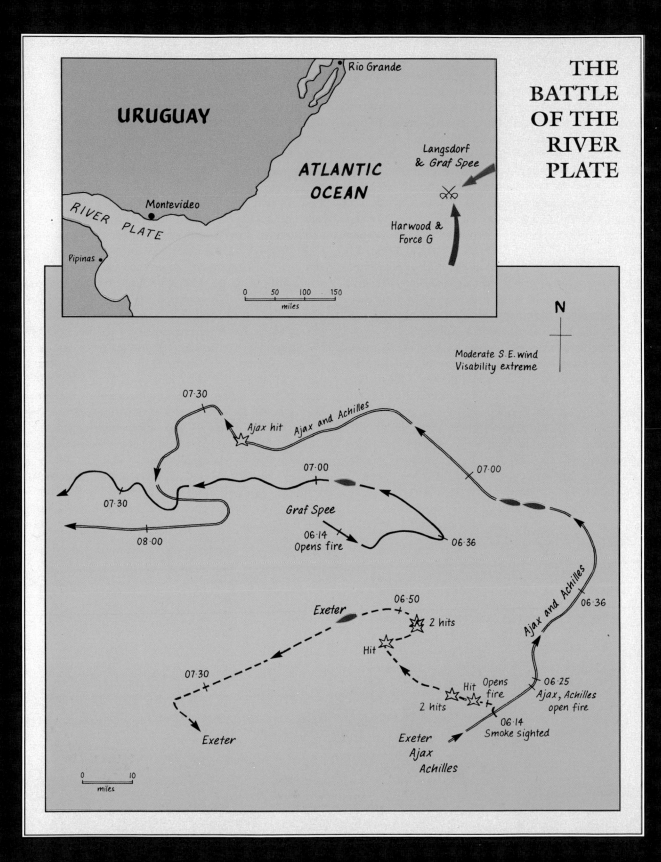

THE BATTLE OF THE RIVER PLATE

Rio Grande

URUGUAY

ATLANTIC OCEAN

Langsdorf & Graf Spee

Harwood & Force G

Montevideo

RIVER PLATE

Pipinas

0   50   100   150
miles

N

Moderate S.E. wind
Visability extreme

07.30

Ajax hit   Ajax and Achilles

07.30

08.00

07.00   07.00

Graf Spee

06.14
Opens fire

06.36

Ajax and Achilles

06.36

Exeter

06.50

2 hits

Hit

07.30

Exeter

Ajax and Achilles

06.25
Ajax, Achilles
open fire

Hit   Opens fire

2 hits

06.14
Smoke sighted

Exeter
Ajax
Achilles

0   10
miles

trate available forces there. He felt that Langsdorff would be attracted to this busy area to find more targets. He had little evidence for this – Langsdorff's last victim had not made any distress calls and the other two had been taken off Africa, but it was inspired guesswork. A third stroke of good luck for Harwood was the loss of *Graf Spee*'s Arado seaplane to terminal engine problems on 11 December. This might have given warning of the presence of a more powerful force than Langsdorff was bargaining for. As he neared the Plate, the German captain stripped his pocket battleship for action, removing the false turret and funnel that he had rigged to disguise its distinctive squared-off lines. The corsair was becoming the warship.

At 0522 on 13 December, an unlucky date for one side or the other, *Graf Spee* sighted smoke to the south. Its source was identified as one medium and two small sized warships, probably the expected escort. The navigating officer on the bridge reminded Langsdorff of standing instructions not to engage enemy warships, but Langsdorff had convinced himself that this enemy was within *Graf Spee*'s capabilities. At 0600 she turned south-westwards to close the target. The die was cast, for as she speeded up her worn diesels put up a billowing black cloud that was spotted by Harwood's ships. These were not what Langsdorff expected, but three cruisers. Harwood flew his broad pendant in the 6,840-ton light cruiser *Ajax*, armed with eight 6in guns. With him was Ajax's sister, *Achilles*, with a New Zealand crew, and the 8,390-ton heavy cruiser *Exeter*, armed with six 8in guns. All had been built when economy had been the order of the day, and they were individually far from strong vessels; but as a squadron of three they stood some chance against the pocket battleship. Moreover with a speed advantage in excess of 8 knots (*Graf Spee* could only make 24 knots with her foul bottom and worn-out engines) they could choose to engage or not as the situation demanded. Even if they were repulsed in action, Langsdorff could be shadowed until overwhelming force could be concentrated.

Harwood, a brave and aggressive officer with a flair for innovative tactics common in the late 1930s Royal Navy, hoped to deal with the pocket battleship himself. He had trained his squadron to divide the pocket battleship's fire. Two divisions would attack from separate directions. As Harwood's second heavy cruiser and largest and most powerful asset, *Cumberland*, was refitting in the Falklands, *Exeter* would have to form one of these divisions alone; the other would be formed by *Ajax* and *Achilles*. These would fire as one concentrated group on *Ajax*'s computerised fire control system while *Exeter* acted as a flank marker, radioing corrections to the flagship. The enemy would be deluged with fire and as much damage as possible inflicted in the hope of finding some flaw in the pocket battleship's armour, perhaps crippling it sufficiently for successful torpedo attack.

Captain F. S. Bell of *Exeter* needed no prompting to put Harwood's plan into action. He bore away to the westward on sighting *Graf Spee*'s smoke, as the Commodore continued to steam north-eastwards. Langsdorff concentrated his main armament on *Exeter*, which he considered to be the major threat; the secondary and tertiary armament of 5.9in and 4.1in guns were used to reply to the light cruisers. Range was just under 19,000 yards, but German fire was always accurate at the beginning of an engagement and *Exeter* was soon hit. After one 11in round had passed through the ship another hit 'B' turret, exploded and devastated the cruiser's bridge, killing all but the Captain and two others. As he retired to con the ship from aft, two more heavy shells slammed into the forward parts of *Exeter*, adding to the damage to the stricken ship. In return *Exeter* was able to straddle the *Graf Spee* with her third salvo. Although *Exeter* could not now act as flank marker, the concen-

Below: HMS *Ajax* opening fire on *Graf Spee* at 0740, as seen from HMS *Achilles*.

trated broadsides of the two light cruisers were also having telling effect on the *Panzerschiffe*'s upperworks, causing chaos to the secondary armament crews, only partially protected by the shields of their guns. This, combined with the threat of torpedo attack, caused Langsdorff to shift the attention of his main armament to *Ajax* and *Achilles*. In the event, it was *Exeter* which launched torpedoes, firing both sets of her tubes. This led Langsdorff to make a turn at 0636 and head off to the north-west. Langsdorff, a torpedo specialist and thus very sensitive to the torpedo threat, had decisively lost the initiative.

Having turned, Langsdorff shifted his main turret fire back towards *Exeter* and hit her again. 'A' 8-inch turret was knocked out and a shell amidships destroyed vital fire-control and compass communications. Then another heavy shell smashed into the hull forward, causing the ship to list. It seemed that *Exeter* only had minutes to live, but then Langsdorff shifted fire yet again to the other cruisers, which had turned to port in pursuit. Shortly after the turn, at 0646 the two light cruisers lost their radio link, and their gunnery was still further disrupted by *Ajax*'s Seafox floatplane spotting on *Achilles*' independent fire rather than the shells of its own ship, with which it was in communication. This gave Langsdorff a respite, the flagship's salvos falling over the target. At 0710, Harwood tried to shorten the range by turning to port, towards the enemy. This halved the armament available to both sides, and six minutes later Langsdorff altered course to the south and then turned back northwards, bringing all his armament to bear. Harwood's ship was straddled by 11in shells, and he opened his own arcs of fire by turning to starboard at

0720. Six-inch shells crashed into the *Graf Spee* amidships, causing the remains of the Arado seaplane to catch fire. Langsdorff got some revenge five minutes later when an 11in hit *Ajax*, putting both her after 6in turrets out of action and cutting the First Division's available firepower by 25 per cent.

Ajax next turned sharply to starboard and fired a spread of four 21in torpedoes. The pocket battleship turned sharply to port to avoid them and turned north-westwards once more to reply in kind. But the Seafox spotted *Graf Spee*'s torpedoes, and Harwood turned westwards to avoid them at 0730. He then moved south-westwards to open his firing arcs once more, cross the pocket battleship's stern and pursue, with the enemy on the starboard bow. As the range came down to 8,000 yards, both sides were still exchanging fire with every available weapon, *Graf Spee* even employing her 4.1in anti-aircraft guns. At 0738, Harwood was misinformed that his flagship was almost out of ammunition. This situation was not as bad as initially reported, but *Ajax* was down to only three 6in guns operational because of a defective hoist. Harwood therefore reluctantly ordered a ceasefire and at 0740 turned away to port under a smoke screen. *Exeter* had continued to use her after turret to pot away at the pocket battleship until 0730, when flooding put the mounting out of action. Having lost 61 men killed and 23 wounded, she had fought until she could do so no more. *Ajax* and *Achilles* lost eleven killed and five wounded between them.

Graf Spee was still able to damage her opponents, and *Ajax* suffered a final hit that collapsed her topmast with its vital radio aerials. But the German ship was in no position to pursue Harwood or even finish

Left: HMS *Ajax* moves in for a torpedo attack on *Graf Spee*, visible on the left horizon.

Right: View from HMS *Achilles* of the *Graf Spee*. The range is approximately 15,000 yards, *Achilles* has just fired and the *Graf Spee* has just fired a broadside in return.

off *Exeter*. *Graf Spee* had been badly knocked about, having suffered hits from three 8in and seventeen 6in shells. The Germans were shocked to find that one of *Exeter*'s 8in rounds had penetrated the armour belt – supposedly proof against such a calibre – and had narrowly failed to enter the machinery spaces. Another had penetrated two decks and destroyed the water purification plant. The peppering by 6in armour-piercing rounds had destroyed her galley, bakery and oil purification plant. The last was especially important, as *Graf Spee*'s engines were particularly vulnerable to impure fuel. Another key hit had holed the bows, making movement in heavy seas impossible. *Graf Spee* had lost 36 men dead and more than 50 wounded, including Langsdorff, who had insisted on conning his ship from the unprotected foretop gallery. The shaken Captain saw little alternative but to continue westwards to seek immediate help at Montevideo. His ship was incapable of a long voyage until her damage was repaired. Perhaps most importantly, she had expended her high-explosive ammunition, the most useful against lightly protected targets like cruisers. Even her remaining armour-piercing rounds were only enough for 40 minutes' firing. An extended engagement would have made *Graf Spee* totally defenceless against any threat called up by the enemy cruisers. Langsdorff's plan for glory for the Kriegsmarine had gone horribly, terribly wrong, and 36 of his crew, for whom he felt deeply, had paid the price for his misjudgement.

So the pocket battleship continued westwards, shadowed by *Ajax* and *Achilles*. *Graf Spee* kept the cruisers at arm's length by still well-directed 11in salvos. Brave, battered *Exeter* was ordered south to

the Falkland Islands, and *Cumberland* had already been ordered to make best speed northwards to replace her. *Ajax* and *Achilles* shadowed *Graf Spee* all the way to Montevideo, where the German ship dropped anchor just before midnight. The British ships had scored a remarkable success, but Harwood thought his chances of preventing a quick escape by the pocket battleship as only 30 per cent.

Langsdorff saw things very differently. He needed time, at least fifteen days, to lick his wounds. The British also wanted delay in order to bring to bear overwhelming force. As the Germans buried their dead – a ceremony attended by the released British prisoners in a remarkable testimony to Langsdorff's reputation as a gentlemanly opponent – a subtle campaign of disinformation and diplomatic duplicity was indulged in by both sides. Each was playing for time without revealing his own weaknesses. The Germans were made to believe that the battlecruiser *Renown* and the aircraft carrier *Ark Royal* were in the area. Then the pro-Allied Uruguayan government, wrongly thinking they were doing what the British wanted, told Langsdorff he had to leave by the evening of 17 December. The British sailed a merchantman from Montevideo, which tied Langsdorff to between 1815 and 2000 that evening. Intended merely to delay the German departure, it convinced Langsdorff that the British were laying a trap.

Langsdorff had three options: internment in Uruguay; a breakout, perhaps to pro-German Argentina; or scuttling. The first would be humiliating and mean a probable examination of the ship by the enemy, including its new radar system. A breakout would not necessarily be any better. The ship might be quickly disabled in shallow waters that would allow her to be ransacked by the enemy. Moreover her crew, who Langsdorff had personally led into unnecessary danger, would suffer heavy casualties in an unequal fight. The ship would have to be scuttled anyway as she ran out of ammunition. Better to take off her crew and send them safely to Argentina. Then take the ship out of harbour and destroy her and her secrets without further loss of life. By the time the unfortunate Captain returned to his *Panzerschiffe* at 0300 on the 17th, the decision had been taken.

All through the day the *Graf Spee* prepared for scuttling. Valuables were removed along with most of her crew. At 1800 the ship weighed anchor and moved out of Montevideo harbour. Harwood, now reinforced by *Cumberland*, prepared to fight a second

round. The *Graf Spee* dropped anchor, however, and evacuated the rest of her crew. At 2200, *Ajax*'s Seafox signalled the news back to the flagship: '*Graf Spee* has just blown up.' Harwood had won.

Langsdorff made sure his men were safely interned in friendly Argentina. He then bade his officers and men farewell, laid out the ship's ensign and shot himself upon it, after having written a suicide note that took full responsibility for the decisions, first to risk, and then to scuttle, his ship. Only he, Langsdorff felt, should 'bear the consequences' involved. He had disobeyed orders and hazarded the ship and ought, he felt, to pay the ultimate penalty.

The Battle of the River Plate was a great and welcome success for Britain. Harwood was given an immediate knighthood and promotion to rear admiral. The three cruiser captains were each awarded the CB. Five officers received DSOs and seventeen DSCs; 45 ratings received DSMs. At the celebration dinner in London, Winston Churchill, the First Lord of the Admiralty, said that in the long and dismal winter of the 'Phoney War', Harwood's victory had 'warmed the cockles' of the nation's heart. History had indeed repeated itself, but not in the way Langsdorff had intended.

Above: The British light cruisers HMS *Ajax* and HMS *Achilles* turn to open the range during the Battle of the River Plate. Painting by John Hamilton.

BIBLIOGRAPHY

Bennett, Geoffrey, *The Battle of the River Plate*, London 1972. A good relatively modern account with much technical detail.
Bidlingmaier, Kapitan zur Zee Gerhard, 'KM Graf Spee' in J. Wingate (Ed.) *Warships in Profile*, Vol.1, London, 1971. A crucial article that is the only source in English to give the German side of the story. Without this perspective both the battle and Langsdorff's suicide make much less sense.
Pope, Dudley, *The Battle of the River Plate*, London, 1956. The classic popular account.
Millington Drake, Sir Eugene, *The Drama of the Graf Spee and the Battle of the River Plate, A Documentary Anthology 1914–64*, London, 1964. An idiosyncratic but irreplaceably comprehensive source of information on the battle; a labour of love by the British ambassador in Montevideo in 1939.

LYSTER: TARANTO, 1940

by David Brown

'These naval airmen, bold fellows, always on for an adventurous attack...'
Sir Ian Hamilton, 1915

The midnight carrier aircraft attack on the Italian Fleet in its defended anchorage at Taranto on 11/12 November 1940 provided a striking example of minimum but concentrated force applied at a critical point and at a critical moment in a campaign. For the loss of just two aircraft and their crews, the Royal Navy's Mediterranean Fleet halved the immediate availability of the Italian battle fleet, achieving not only material parity but moral ascendancy over the only European navy that could mount an effective, though local, challenge.

The Mediterranean theatre was primarily a maritime theatre of war. Egypt and the Suez Canal occupied a central position in British grand strategy, for together they were regarded as the key to the 'gateway' to India. Opposing European armies in North Africa could only be reinforced and resupplied by sea. Britain, besides her general naval supremacy, had the advantage of a secure, if lengthy, route to the theatre around the African continent, but while Italy enjoyed very short trans-Mediterranean routes to her North African colonies, they were threatened by surface, submarine and air forces for their entire length; and even the few major destination ports – Tobruk, Benghazi and Tripoli – were by no means safe havens. If the Italians were to hold their initial shallow foothold in western Egypt, they would have to achieve at least temporary naval superiority to keep their army supplied; for victory on land, nothing less than supremacy at sea would do.

Although stronger than the Royal Navy's Mediterranean Fleet (vastly so in cruisers and destroyers), the Italian Navy made no attempt to seek out and destroy its primary adversary. Indeed, after a brush with the Mediterranean Fleet on 9 July 1940, when the battleship *Giulio Cesare* was damaged by a single shell fired by HMS *Warspite*, the Italian battleships made no serious attempt to interfere with British operations, let alone challenge for superiority. The Mediterranean Fleet was therefore permitted to go about its duties of reinforcing Malta and undertaking whatever offensive operations could be mounted against an enemy who appeared to be reluctant to come out and fight.

Attacks on enemy ports and anchorages are as old as naval warfare itself. In December 1904, at Port Arthur, the Imperial Japanese Navy demonstrated the potential of the torpedo-boat in this role (though surprise was achieved very largely by the expedient of not declaring war beforehand). By 1914, however, the threat posed by surfaced or submersible torpedo-boats was recognised by all the participants in the Great War and the main bases were so well defended by mines, guns and nets as to be virtually impregnable to conventional attack. As the German High Sea Fleet refused battle after Jutland, the British Admiralty developed means to attack it in its base, developing a completely new capability, which would today be described as an 'integrated weapons system' – an effective torpedo to be dropped in flight by a land-plane aircraft (the Sopwith T.1 Cuckoo) specifically designed for this role and flown from the world's first flat-topped aircraft carrier, HMS *Argus*. The ship was commissioned in September 1918 and began flying trials at the beginning of October, while

Left: Slow and obsolete but still the primary torpedo bomber of the Fleet Air Arm, the Fairey Swordfish achieved a vital success for the British at Taranto.

Right: A fitter at work on a Swordfish.

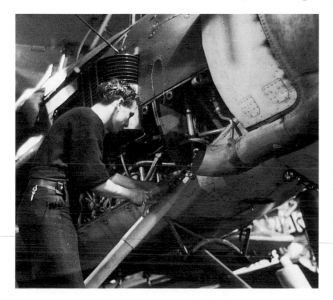

her torpedo-bomber squadron worked up in anticipation of an air torpedo strike on Wilhelmshaven in early 1919.

The Armistice intervened and, although the planned strike was never delivered, the Royal Navy remained the possessor of a sound offensive doctrine and means of delivery. Between the wars, steady if unspectacular progress was made in the development of aircraft and torpedoes. Tactical exercises had concentrated on the use of torpedo-bombers in open-sea, fleet engagements, but the 1938 Munich crisis had prompted Captain A. L. St. G. Lyster, commanding the Mediterranean Fleet carrier *Glorious*, to draw up a plan for an attack on the Italian fleet base at Taranto, on the 'heel' of Italy.

Admiral Sir Andrew Cunningham, the commander-in-chief of the Mediterranean Fleet, took full advantage of his carrier aircraft to take the war to the enemy in the opening months of the war in his theatre. Only HMS *Eagle* was at first available, but during July 1940 the experienced Swordfish aircrew of Nos 813 and 824 Naval Air Squadrons torpedoed and sank four Italian destroyers and a merchant ship in harbour, damaged a fifth destroyer and another merchant ship, besides sinking a submarine and its depot ship preparing to attack the Fleet base at Alexandria. The brand-new and larger carrier *Illustrious* joined the Fleet at the beginning of September, and, although her Swordfish squadrons (Nos 815 and 819) began rapidly to get into their stride, sinking two more destroyers and a pair of merchant ships in Tobruk harbour, it would not be until mid-October that all the aircrew would be fully proficient in night operations. With the *Illustrious* had arrived a Rear Admiral (Aircraft) to command the Mediterranean Fleet carriers; this was none other than the redoubtable Lumley Lyster, who promptly began the revision of his 1938 plans for a strike on Taranto.

Cunningham accepted the plan with enthusiasm and ordered that the attack should take place on 21 October, the 135th anniversary of the Battle of Trafalgar. Had this schedule been followed, the course of the war in the Mediterranean might conceivably have taken a very different turn, for Mussolini had decided

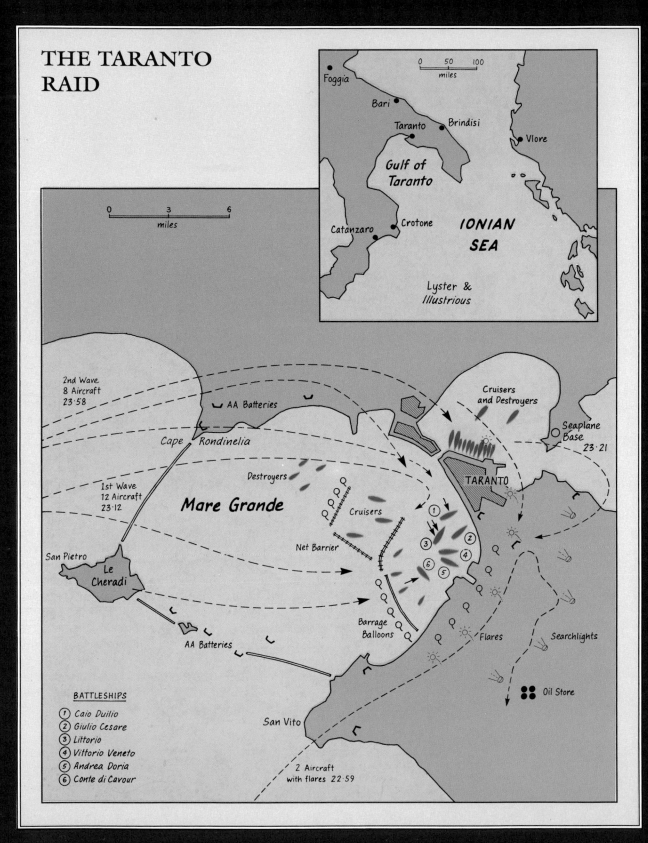

THE TARANTO RAID

Inset map:

Foggia
Bari
Taranto
Brindisi
Vlore
Gulf of Taranto
Catanzaro
Crotone
IONIAN SEA

0 50 100 miles

Lyster & Illustrious

Main map:

2nd Wave
8 Aircraft
23·58

AA Batteries

Cape Rondinelia

1st Wave
12 Aircraft
23·12

Mare Grande

Destroyers

Cruisers and Destroyers

Seaplane Base
23·21

TARANTO

Cruisers

Net Barrier

San Pietro

Le Cheradi

Barrage Balloons

Flares

Searchlights

AA Batteries

San Vito

Oil Store

2 Aircraft
with flares 22·59

0 3 6 miles

BATTLESHIPS

1 Caio Duilio
2 Giulio Cesare
3 Littorio
4 Vittorio Veneto
5 Andrea Doria
6 Conte di Cavour

Right: A Swordfish which has just been brought to a standstill by an arrestor wire aboard HMS *Illustrious* some time later in the war.

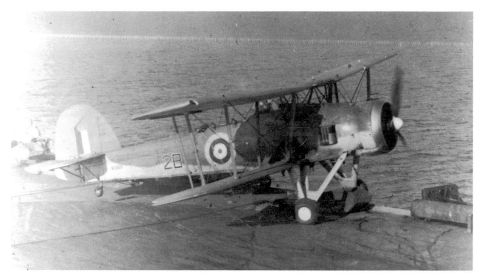

that Greece was to be invaded a week later, on 28 October. Not only was this unknown to the British, but Hitler, who was to meet Generalissimo Franco on the 23rd, was equally ignorant of the Italian dictator's plan; high on the Führer's list of priorities was Spanish assistance, or at least acquiescence, in the seizure of Gibraltar. In the event, the Taranto operation had to be postponed following a fire in the *Illustrious*: the invasion of Greece went ahead as programmed, and, at the summit meeting at Hendaye, Franco did not discourage Hitler's hopes.

The *Illustrious* was quickly repaired, but the deciding factor in the timing of the attack was the state of the moon, which was required for take-off and landing, and the need to provide the earliest possible assistance to Greece. 11 November was judged to be a suitable moonlit night and would also coincide with a propitious anniversary, that of the Armistice of 1918, which had prevented the first planned carrier-borne torpedo strike. Unfortunately, the *Eagle* had meanwhile suffered near-miss bomb damage, which affected her aviation fuel system, but the political imperatives were such that the operation could not be postponed again, and the number of Swordfish available was reduced from 36 to 24. More serious was the absence of the more experienced night-attack aircrew from the older ship, only five No 813 and 824 Squadron crews being transferred to the *Illustrious* with their aircraft.

Operation 'Judgement', as the Taranto attack was code-named, was but one phase of a most complex plan. 'MB.8' involved not only the Mediterranean Fleet but also the Gibraltar-based Force 'H', whose parish was the western Mediterranean and which was to cover cruisers and destroyers that would ferry troops and anti-aircraft guns to Malta from the west and then proceed to join the Fleet in the eastern basin; the carrier of Force 'H', *Ark Royal*, would create a diversion by bombing Cagliari, Sardinia, on 9 November. Warships of the Mediterranean Fleet would carry military personnel and stores to both Crete, where the Royal Navy was to develop a forward base at Suda Bay, and to Greece, while loaded convoys would be run to Malta, Crete and Greece from Egypt, with empty convoys returning from Malta and the Aegean. In all, five capital ships, one carrier, nine cruisers, 25 destroyers and four other warships, besides fourteen merchant ships, operated to the east of Malta during 'MB.8'.

'Judgement' was not the only offensive element of the plan. It was known that the Italians were running nightly supply convoys across the southern Adriatic, between Italy and Albania, and three cruisers and two destroyers were ordered to carry out a sweep through the Strait of Otranto while the attack on Taranto was in progress. If successful, the raiding sortie would relieve the pressure on the Greek army.

The *Illustrious* left Alexandria with the main body of the Mediterranean Fleet on 6 November 1940 and spent the next five days covering the convoys to and from Malta and the reinforcements from the west. The carrier's fighters dealt competently with the Regia Aeronautica shadowers and bombers that appeared up to 10 November, but three Swordfish were lost to petrol contamination which was traced to fuel supplied by one particular tanker. During the

Left: *Illustrious* seen here at high speed, her deck clear of aircraft. She was 170 miles from Taranto when she launched her aircraft for the attack.

forenoon of 11 November, recent aerial reconnaissance photographs of Taranto taken by the Royal Air Force, showing the latest positions of anti-torpedo nets and barrage balloons, were collected from Malta, and at 1800, as darkness fell, the *Illustrious* and four destroyers parted company with the Fleet and headed for the launch position, 170 miles south of the target.

Twenty-one Swordfish were launched, twelve in the first wave but only nine in the second, owing to the previous accidental losses. The first wave arrived in the area of the great harbour at 2255 to discover that the AA defences were already alert. (It would transpire that the Italian anti-aircraft sound detectors had picked up an RAF Sunderland flying-boat patrolling too close in to the coast.) Two aircraft were detached to illuminate the target area, and as soon as their flares ignited to the south-east of the outer anchorage (the Mar Grande), at about 2300, the batteries on shore opened fire in a general barrage. The six torpedo-carriers attacked from seaward between 2315 and 2320 and scored three hits, one on the *Conte di Cavour* and the other two on the new *Littorio*; the leader of the strike, Lieutenant Commander K. Williamson, RN, commanding officer of No 815 Squadron, was responsible for the hit on the *Cavour* and his aircraft was the only casualty from the first wave, although Williamson and his Observer, Lieutenant N. J. Scarlett, RN, survived to be taken prisoner.

Of the other six aircraft, the two flare-droppers dropped four 250lb (114kg) bombs apiece on the Fleet's oil storage depot while the remaining four, each armed with six 250-pounders, were briefed to dive-bomb ships in the inner harbour, the Mar Piccolo, and moored at the dockyard; one crew was unable to identify this target and bombed the adjacent seaplane base from low level.

By 2335 the last of the bombers had made its escape and there was to be a twenty-minute lull before the arrival of the second wave; the defenders do not appear to have noticed, for the intense barrage fire continued unabated. Only eight Swordfish reached the target area, one having had to return to the carrier after its long-range fuel tank became detached, but five of these carried torpedoes. At 2355 two aircraft dropped flares accurately and went on to bomb the fuel depot. On the stroke of midnight, the torpedo-bombers approached the outer anchorage from the north-west. These scored two more hits on the *Littorio* (only one of which exploded), hit the *Caio Duilio* and missed the *Vittorio Veneto* and the heavy cruiser *Gorizia*, this last aircraft being shot down with the loss of its crew, Lieutenants G. W. Bayley and H. J. Slaughter, RN, of *Eagle*'s No 813 Squadron. The single bomber dropped its bombs accurately on the ships moored in the Mar Piccolo.

The second strike was over in ten minutes, but the AA defences continued to fire for another 45 minutes – nearly 8,600 rounds of medium (76mm to 102mm) AA ammunition were expended during the night. All eighteen Swordfish that survived the attacks returned to the *Illustrious* between 0120 and 0250, two of them with minor damage. The crews knew that they had inflicted substantial damage on battleships in the outer anchorage, and fires had been seen in the dockyard area, but at that precise moment neither they nor the Italians, still struggling to keep the torpedoed ships afloat, had a precise idea of the extent of the damage.

At 0445, the crew of the *Duilio* fighting flooding caused by a 77m² hole abreast the forward main magazine, had to admit defeat and beached their ship. Fifteen minutes later, the *Cavour* was deliberately run aground, but with an even larger, 96m², hole forward, she flooded completely up to the level of the weather deck, with her after turret completely submerged, and she was abandoned at 0545. The new *Littorio* was better protected than these modernised old battleships, but she finally succumbed to two holes forward and a smaller one aft, near her steering gear, with a total area of 270m², and was beached at 0625. Between them, the three battleships had lost 52 men.

Elsewhere, the damage caused by the bombing was negligible. Two aircraft were destroyed and buildings set on fire at the seaplane station; the cruiser *Trento* and the destroyer *Libeccio* were superficially damaged by direct hits that failed to explode, while the destroyer *Pessagno* suffered some strained plates and flooding from near-misses. Ashore, the oil fuel depot escaped, although the pipeline connecting it to the Mar Grande was damaged, and the dockyard water supply was cut by a hit on the San Giorgio aqueduct. Regret-tably, one aircraft's stick of bombs fell on a residential area of the town, destroying several houses and causing civilian casualties.

The carrier and her screen rejoined the main body of the Fleet at 0700, welcomed back by a brief signal from the flagship – '*Illustrious* BZ' ('Manoeuvre well executed'). The cruiser force returned from the Adriatic four hours later, having destroyed a four-ship convoy in the early hours of 12 November. Preparations had meanwhile begun for a re-strike on the night of 12 November (prompting one aviator to remark that 'even the Light Brigade had only been asked to do it once'), six torpedo-bombers, seven dive-bombers and two flare-droppers being readied for an attack by a single wave. But in the late afternoon, with low cloud and rain forecast in the Taranto area, the follow-up attack was cancelled and the Fleet began its return to Alexandria.

Had the second strike been mounted, it would have found only the three derelicts form the previous night's attack. During the afternoon of 12 November, the three surviving battleships – the *Vittorio Veneto*, which had been attacked but missed, and the *Andrea Doria* and *Giulio Cesare*, which had not been attacked – and the heavy cruiser and modern destroyer divisions sailed for the greater security of Naples. There they would be safer from attack but would be in no position to react quickly to British activity in the central and eastern basins. The Mediterranean Fleet now had a capital ship superiority that would continue until late May 1941 – the *Littorio* returned to service

Right: The remains of Williamson's aircraft after the attack.

Left: 'The Attack on Taranto' by John Hamilton. Flares were used by the attacking Swordfish to illuminate the Italian fleet, but there is doubt if any searchlights were used by the defences.

Left: The *Caio Duilio* sank at her moorings after receiving one torpedo hit. She is seen here with her keel resting on the floor of the harbour.

Right: An aerial reconnaissance photograph of Taranto harbour taken shortly after the attack.

after repairs in late March 1941, but by that time Royal Navy torpedo aircraft had caught up with her sister ship, *Vittorio Veneto*, damaging her off Cape Matapan in the same month (see next chapter). The *Duilio* was raised and repaired, rejoining the fleet in mid-May 1941, but although the *Cavour* was refloated and taken to Trieste for repair, this work was never completed.

The Swordfish crews' success drew unwelcome German attention which shortened their own ship's successful career and had even wider repercussions. On 20 November, Hitler, thwarted by Spanish refusal to assist in the seizure of Gibraltar or agree to the German occupation of the Canary Islands, and frustrated by his Italian ally's lack of success at sea, offered Mussolini a Luftwaffe specialist anti-shipping force, Fliegerkorps X. With no alternative means of countering the Mediterranean Fleet, Mussolini accepted the offer, and the German aircraft began arriving on Sicilian airfields in December 1940. The British army in Egypt had meanwhile begun a successful offensive, its seaward flank secure and supplies by sea through captured ports assured, which was to drive the Italian forces back to the gates of Tripoli and result in the dispatch of a German expeditionary

force to North Africa. In its first full-scale attack, in January 1941, Fliegerkorps X succeeded in depriving the Mediterranean Fleet of its one modern carrier, putting HMS *Illustrious* out of action for more than a year. After the loss of a cruiser shortly afterwards, Admiral Cunningham virtually abandoned the central basin, leaving the German bombers with no shipping targets within range. They therefore turned their attention to Malta in an attempt to neutralise its base facilities. After their ship was damaged, the *Illustrious*'s Swordfish crews operated ashore, from a remote valley in northern Greece, against shipping in Valona Harbour, from Crete during the battle of Matapan and some from Malta, where No 830 Squadron operated effectively against shipping supplying the Axis armies in North Africa. As at Taranto, their later successes were achieved with marked economy of effort – a claim that can be justified only with difficulty on behalf of their supposed imitators, the Japanese naval aviators who flew 360 aircraft from six carriers to strike at Pearl Harbor thirteen months after the 'Battle of Taranto'.

CUNNINGHAM: MATAPAN, 1941

by James Goldrick

'The whole principle of naval fighting is to be free
to go anywhere with every damned thing the Navy possesses.
Sir John Fisher, 1919

The origins of the Battle of Cape Matapan derive from German pressure on the Italians to interrupt the seaborne reinforcement of British forces in Greece. The Italian battle line had been grievously reduced by the British air attack on Taranto the previous November, but the Axis powers were confident that the British had suffered in their turn after the arrival of German air units in theatre early in 1941. The Germans assessed that the Mediterranean Fleet could only deploy one battleship, without the support of an operational fast carrier. In these circumstances, the fast battleship Vittorio Veneto and the Italian Navy's powerful heavy cruisers would be more than enough. Britain had only one heavy cruiser in the theatre (immobilised by light attack craft in Suda Bay on 26 March) and the covering forces for the convoys to Greece consisted of a handful of 6in-gun cruisers and destroyers. The Italian aim was to surprise a detachment of British ships and achieve defeat in detail through sweeps to the north and south of Crete,

forcing the interruption of convoy movements between Egypt and Greece.

From the beginning, however, the Italian effort was hamstrung by inadequate intelligence and air support. The British had signals intelligence warning of the sortie and the commander-in-chief, Admiral Sir Andrew Cunningham, was able to suspend convoy sailings and dispose his forces to search for the Italians. In fact, he had at his disposal not one operational battleship, but three, and was willing to use them. A further vital element was air cover. The carrier *Formidable* had recently arrived on station to replace the damaged *Illustrious*. Her air group was small and its Fulmars, Albacores and Swordfish barely adequate for their tasks, but Cunningham could also call upon shore-based naval aircraft and RAF units from both Crete and Greece. By comparison, the Italians were to enjoy no direct support from either their own air force or that of the Germans.

The British possessed other advantages. The fit of surface warning radar was not yet general, but it was carried by sufficient ships and had been in service long enough for its tactical potential to be at least partially understood. The Mediterranean Fleet also maintained a legacy of expertise from the extensive pre-war training of the Royal Navy in night fighting. Although the destroyers and newly commissioned big ships possessed relatively little experience, the crews of units such as the battleship *Warspite* knew their job – and Cunningham was arguably the most expert 'night fighter' in the Royal Navy, having had two subordinate flag commands at the peak of the pre-war efforts. The Italians, by comparison, did not expect to fight at night and had neither developed a doctrine nor trained in the art.

The British used their forewarning to deploy a force of cruisers and destroyers under Vice Admiral H. D. Pridham-Whippell south of Crete and to lay on extensive air searches. By 27 March there were definite indications that the Italians were out, but the latter had decided against what they assessed to be the greater risk of a sortie north of Crete in favour of concentrating south of the island. After a series of deceptive measures to convince watchers ashore in Alexandria that the heavy ships were not ready for sea, Cunningham sailed his battle fleet after dusk the same evening, intending a rendezvous with Pridham-Whippell the next day.

The morning of 28 March found the Italian Admiral Iachino's forces divided into three groups: two

Below: Admiral Sir
Andrew Cunningham.

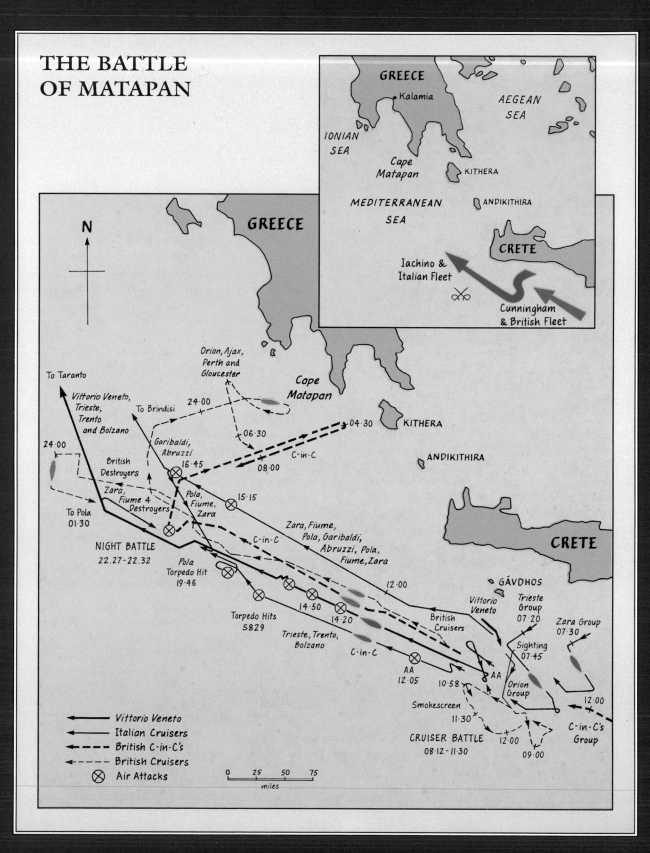

THE BATTLE
OF MATAPAN

N

GREECE

GREECE

Kalamia

IONIAN
SEA

AEGEAN
SEA

Cape
Matapan

KITHERA

MEDITERRANEAN
SEA

ANDIKITHIRA

Iachino &
Italian Fleet

CRETE

Cunningham
& British Fleet

To Taranto

Vittorio Veneto,
Trieste,
Trento
and Bolzano

24·00

To Brindisi

Orion, Ajax,
Perth and
Gloucester

Cape
Matapan

24·00

Garibaldi,
Abruzzi

16·45

06·30

04·30

C-in-C

08·00

KITHERA

British
Destroyers

Zara,
Fiume 4
Destroyers

Pola,
Fiume,
Zara

15·15

ANDIKITHIRA

To Pola
01·30

Zara, Fiume,
Pola, Garibaldi,
Abruzzi, Pola,
Fiume, Zara

C-in-C

CRETE

NIGHT BATTLE
22.27 – 22.32

Pola
Torpedo Hit
19·46

12·00

Vittorio
Veneto

GÁVDHOS

Trieste
Group
07·20

Zara Group
07·30

Torpedo Hits
S829

14·50

14·20

British
Cruisers

Sighting
07·45

Trieste, Trento,
Bolzano

C-in-C

AA
12·05

AA

Orion
Group

12·00

10·58

C-in-C's
Group

Smokescreen

11·30

12·00

09·00

CRUISER BATTLE
08·12 – 11·30

→ Vittorio Veneto
→ Italian Cruisers
→ British C-in-C's
→ British Cruisers
⊗ Air Attacks

0   25   50   75
miles

Left: Stern view of *Zara*. Caught unawares by the radar assisted *Valiant* and *Warspite*, she was finished off by the destroyer *Jervis*.

Right: The Italian heavy cruiser *Fiume*.

The reality became evident after 0745, when the three cruisers and three destroyers under Vice Admiral Sansonetti sighted the British cruiser force. Knowing the heavier metal of the Italians, Pridham-Whippell immediately altered course southeast in an attempt to draw the enemy on to the battle fleet. The stern chase and intermittent gunnery action that followed lasted just over an hour until Admiral Iachino ordered his ships to turn away. Suspicious of the reason for the British withdrawal, Iachino wanted to set his own trap. If Pridham-Whippell followed the Italians, he would be drawn on to the guns of *Vittorio Veneto*, with Iachino's detached units in a position to cut off his retreat.

When Pridham-Whippell turned to shadow the Italians, *Vittorio Veneto* began to work her way east. Still unknown to Iachino, however, Cunningham had closed part of the distance and was now just over 70 miles astern of his subordinate. A six-aircraft torpedo-bomber strike was readied aboard *Formidable*, but the C-in-C initially held his hand, afraid that it would indicate to the Italians the presence of a carrier and thus that the battle fleet was at sea, and anxious that he be close enough to catch any ship disabled by the raid. Cunningham's hand was forced by the fact that the Albacores were the only force capable of slowing the Italian cruisers. Pridham-Whippell had no speed advantage and the shore-based

cruiser forces to the north-east and just over the horizon from Pridham-Whippell's ships, and the *Vittorio Veneto* to the north-west. Cunningham was more than a hundred miles to the south-east, his presence at sea unknown to the Italians. For his part, the British C-in-C was attempting to locate the enemy forces with reconnaissance sorties from Crete and from the *Formidable*. It was these aircraft that made sighting reports of cruisers and destroyers at 0720 and 0739, but the reported positions and the force composition so closely matched those of Pridham-Whippell's group that they were not at first assessed as Italian.

Below: The 35,000 ton Italian battleship *Vittorio Veneto* seen here at the Italian fleet surrender in October 1943, with the cruiser *Duca d'Aosta* in the background.

units could muster only a few aircraft for their attacks. At 0939 the strike was launched.

The Albacores were still out-bound when the cruiser *Orion* sighted *Vittorio Veneto* to the north. The Italian battleship immediately opened fire and was soon straddling the British cruisers, damaging *Orion*. Pridham-Whippell turned south and made smoke. While this measure proved effective in the short term, his situation was dangerous – the *Vittorio Veneto* was quite capable of keeping up with the British ships, and the Italian heavy cruisers were faster. Pridham-Whippell was saved by the arrival of the Albacores at 1127. They attacked *Vittorio Veneto* and, although no torpedoes struck, Iachino knew that he could not continue without air cover. The Italian forces turned for home at high speed. Masked by smoke, Pridham-Whippell was initially slow to appreciate that the chase was over and, in any case, uncertain as to the strength of the Italian forces in the area. He turned east to join Cunningham.

Under the false impression that the *Vittorio Veneto* had been hit and slowed down, Cunningham chased

westwards. Apart from a small and unsuccessful torpedo-bomber attack on *Formidable*, the British remained undisturbed from the air, and both the carrier and battleships were able to launch fresh aircraft. The difficulties of maintaining a picture on three separate enemy groups and the scouting aircraft's own navigational uncertainties meant that it took some time for Cunningham to appreciate that Iachino was drawing away from him.

The situation was recovered for the British by a second strike from *Formidable*, whose aircraft proved more effective than the repeated efforts of the shore-based bombers. A six-aircraft attack just after 1515 resulted in one torpedo hitting *Vittorio Veneto* aft on the port side, bringing the ship to a stop and causing severe flooding. The battleship was eventually able to work up to 16 knots, but the British now had the chance to catch up, if not in daylight, then at least during the night hours.

Accurate reports from *Warspite*'s scouting aircraft began to make the situation a little more clear to Cun-

Right: An action shot of the torpedo attack on the Italian warships at Matapan.

ningham. A third strike was launched from *Formidable*, and preparations were made to dispatch destroyers from the main body to conduct a night torpedo attack as a prelude to intervention by the battle fleet and cruisers. Pridham-Whippell was already well ahead of the main body and, by darkness, assessed that he would soon gain contact with the rear of the Italian fleet.

Formidable's last strike proved a limited success. The torpedo aircraft did not harm *Vittorio Veneto* but left the heavy cruiser *Pola* stopped in the water, a fact that the darkness and confusion prevented Iachino knowing for more than an hour. The Italian admiral now turned north-west and increased speed to nineteen knots. This proved critical in preventing interaction with the British light forces. Cunningham had learned that the strike had not achieved enough, and he detached eight destroyers led by Captain P. J. Mack in the *Jervis* to attack the Italian fleet. The British mistake was to assess that the Italian main body was 24 miles closer and steaming nearly six knots less than they really were, and the destroyers in consequence biased their approach too much towards the west, Mack having the idea of passing to the north of the Italians and attacking from ahead. Another difficulty for the British was that the destroyers' presence constrained Pridham-Whippell, already forced to concentrate his cruisers against the possibility of unexpected encounters with Italian units he believed to be in the vicinity. Thus, when a stationary contact was eventually detected, the cruisers kept clear in the expectation that this was the *Vittorio Veneto* and the target intended for the destroyers. Furthermore, communications problems – and mistaken identities – prevented both cruisers and destroyers from attacking contacts that later proved to be Italian heavy cruisers which had turned back to assist the *Pola*.

After some debate, Iachino had dispatched the cruisers *Zara* and *Fiume* and four destroyers under Vice Admiral Cattaneo with instructions to assess the situation and render what assistance they could. Iachino still discounted the close proximity of British heavy forces; although he had information of British ships within range for night attack, he believed them to be cruisers or destroyers, with which he had some confidence in dealing. Cattaneo's forces passed clear of the

Below: The Italian cruisers take avoiding action during the aerial torpedo attack.

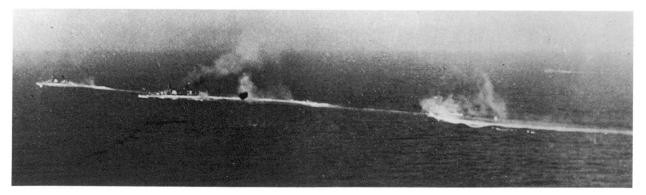

British destroyers and Pridham-Whippell's cruisers, but their course for the *Pola* put them in the path of the enemy battle fleet.

Cunningham now knew of the presence of a disabled heavy unit from Pridham-Whippell's reports. If the destroyers and cruisers were pursuing other quarry farther west, he reasoned that it was up to the battleships and their depleted escort to finish this target off. Despite warnings from his staff, Cunningham discounted the risk of torpedo attack and directed the battle fleet – with *Formidable* still in the line – to close the *Pola*, soon held on the battleship *Valiant*'s radar. Cunningham's ships were approaching the crippled Italian cruiser on a line of bearing, with gun arcs open, when at 2220 they sighted Cattaneo's ships crossing ahead at a range of only a few thousand yards. Cunningham immediately turned his force into line ahead, clearing *Formidable* away to the north. The battleships shortly afterwards opened fire at point-blank range – which Cunningham himself defined as a 'range even a gunnery officer cannot miss'. Their salvoes had immediate and catastrophic effect. *Zara*, *Fiume* and the destroyer *Alfieri* were soon burning furiously while the remainder of the screen made a forlorn attempt to

close the British. By 2315, *Fiume* would have sunk.

Cunningham's aggression and determination were matched by his prudence. Barely four minutes after opening fire, by which time it was apparent that the battleships had done their work, the C-in-C ordered an emergency turn together to the north. This allowed the heavy ships to clear away from possible torpedoes and meant that Cunningham could release his remaining quartet of escorts to deal with the Italian destroyers. The Australian *Stuart* and the *Greyhound*, *Griffin* and *Havock* had a confused and exciting two hours. Although two of the Italian destroyers escaped, the *Alfieri* and *Carducci* were sunk. Given the British and Australian destroyer crews' inexperience in night fighting, which forced them to operate independently rather than as a coordinated unit, and the Italians' superior speed, such results were probably as good as could be expected.

In the meantime, Pridham-Whippell and Mack were continuing their pursuit of *Vittorio Veneto*, amidst some confusion as to each other's location and intentions. Repeated false alarms and the sighting of flares to the north-west resulted in signal traffic that gave the C-in-C the impression his scouts were already in contact with the Italian main body. In fact, they were still some 30 miles astern and unsure of the enemy's line of advance. All hope of catching *Vittorio Veneto* effectively disappeared when Pridham-Whippell received a general signal from Cunningham directing that all forces not engaged in sinking the enemy should retire north-east. The intention of this directive was to clear the battleships from the destroyer action taking place around the crippled Italian cruisers, but it had the understandable effect of causing Pridham-Whippell to break off his search.

Mack's efforts against the *Vittorio Veneto* ended when *Havock*, mistaking the *Pola* for a battleship, reported that she had found a unit of the *Littorio* class. This caused Mack to alter course east-south-east, away from Iachino. By the time *Havock* had corrected her mistake, there was little else that *Jervis* and her consorts could do but continue towards the *Pola*. In the event, it was the *Zara* which they met first. *Jervis* disposed of her in short order. The next victim was *Pola* herself, around which several of the battle fleet's destroyers had already gathered. Mack briefly considered the possibility of taking the Italian cruiser as a prize, but the tow to Alexandria would have been too long and dangerous. After removing survivors, *Jervis* ordered *Nubian* to dispose of *Pola*, which was accomplished with two torpedoes.

As dawn broke the next morning, *Formidable*'s scouts were in the air again, but their searches drew the expected blank, and Cunningham had little hesitation in ordering a withdrawal to Alexandria. The confusion of the night action had been such that he feared at least one destroyer had fallen victim to friendly fire, but to his 'inexpressible relief' not a ship had been lost. That good fortune continued during the British fleet's progress home. An attack by German bombers had been beaten off and several ASDIC contacts proven false by the time the force entered Alexandria harbour on the evening of 30 March.

The Mediterranean Fleet regarded the victory and its performance with mixed feelings. Cunningham, in his disappointment over the escape of the *Vittorio Veneto*, evinced very much the same attitude as Nelson's comment that a success however large, if incomplete, could not be called well done. The results were good, but no more. The reality was that the British had operated on what was no more than a residue of night fighting expertise, which was effective more because of its relative superiority to that of the Italians than its absolute quality. In both men and material, the Royal Navy was hard-pressed – and the situation would worsen in the months ahead.

Yet Cape Matapan measurably reduced the threat posed by the Italian fleet and confined the Axis to waging an air and submarine war against the British Mediterranean Fleet. Without better training and some integration of air assets with surface forces, the Italian Navy would not risk another fleet encounter. Had they done so at the time when the British were most worn down by the strain of the evacuations from Greece and Crete, the war in the Mediterranean might have taken a very different course.

BIBLIOGRAPHY

Bragadin, M. A., *The Italian Navy in World War II*, trans G. Hoffman, Annapolis, 1957. The first comprehensive official history of the Italian Navy in the war, making clear many of the operational and logistic difficulties under which the Italians were operating.

Cunningham, A. B., *A Sailor's Odyssey: The Autobiography of Admiral of the Fleet Viscount Cunningham of Hyndhope*, London, 1951. Provides remarkable insight into a sea commander's thinking.

Pack, S. W. C., *Night Action off Cape Matapan*, Annapolis, 1972. A good summary of the action if not yet privy to the full range of the archives.

Roskill, S. W., *The War at Sea, 1939–1945*, vol I, London, 1954. The original British official history, shrewdly and judiciously written.

Seth, R., *Two Fleets Surprised: The Story of the Battle of Cape Matapan*, London, 1960. A popular narrative drawing on both the British and Italian official accounts.

Warner, O., *Cunningham of Hyndhope, Admiral of the Fleet*, London, 1967. Includes a useful summary of the battle.

FRASER: NORTH CAPE, 1943

by Geoffrey Till

'Not alone is the strength of the Fleet measured by the number of its fighting units, but by its efficiency, by its ability to proceed promptly where it is needed and to engage and overcome an enemy.'
Admiral Richard Wainwright, USN, 1911

As 1943 drew to a close, both the German and the British navies had real incentives for a significant naval engagement in the frozen waters of the Arctic. The German surface fleet had never been able to operate as a coherent force in the way that pre-war planners had wanted and by now was reduced to the battleship *Tirpitz*, the battlecruiser *Scharnhorst* and a number of cruisers that were sometimes deployed to join them in the north. Their generally passive performance to date had led to Hitler's making one of his 'unalterable decisions' to scrap them. Doenitz, the commander-in-chief of the German Navy, had managed to win them a stay of execution but realised only too well that they would need to prove themselves. On 4 December he declared: 'Should the opportunity arise for the battle group to strike, I will under all circumstances go at the enemy.' Only this would ensure their safety against Hitler.

But there was another, more serious, reason for the Germans to put to sea again, and that was the rapidly deteriorating situation in the war against the Soviet Union. After the gigantic defeat at Kursk in the summer of 1943, the German army was in deadly peril; the Navy would simply have to do something to help. It was not hard to see what this might be, for since November 1943 the British had resumed running supply convoys to northern Russia. Since a twenty-ship Arctic convoy could easily be carrying between 300 and 400 aircraft, more than 4,000 tanks or other military vehicles, guns, ammunition and so on, its safe arrival in Murmansk or Archangel could make a material difference to the bitter struggle on the Eastern Front. By this stage of the war, neither the Luftwaffe nor the German submarine service could seriously threaten the Allied convoys. It was therefore up to the surface ships. At the Führer Conference of 19–20 December 1943, Doenitz therefore announced that Battle Group 1 would attack the next Arctic Convoy passing by on its way to Russia. As it happened, the convoy in question, JW 55B, left Loch Ewe that very afternoon, on its way for Murmansk. Significantly, Doenitz christened the operation 'Eastern Front'.

In some ways, this was just what Admiral Sir Bruce Fraser, commander-in-chief of the British Home Fleet, had been waiting for. Occasional forays such as that of the battleship *Bismarck* in 1941 had conclusively demonstrated both the technical quality and the fighting spirit of the larger German naval units. From time to time, moreover, the Germans had managed to accumulate quite a substantial force in Norway's northern waters, and there was even the faint possibility that they might one day be joined by the unfinished aircraft carrier *Graf Zeppelin*. Such a battle group certainly needed to be taken seriously. It might try and stage a destructive foray against Allied shipping in the Atlantic, perhaps putting new life into a strategic U-boat campaign that the Allies had only just mastered. The Arctic convoys were an even more tempting target. The British had therefore to keep enough battleships, aircraft carriers and cruisers in the Home Fleet to provide the necessary cover if ever the Germans came out.

This was easier said than done. Only the Germans would know if and when they would make their challenge; the British on the other hand, needed to be

Below: The *King George V* class battleship HMS *Duke of York* making smoke.

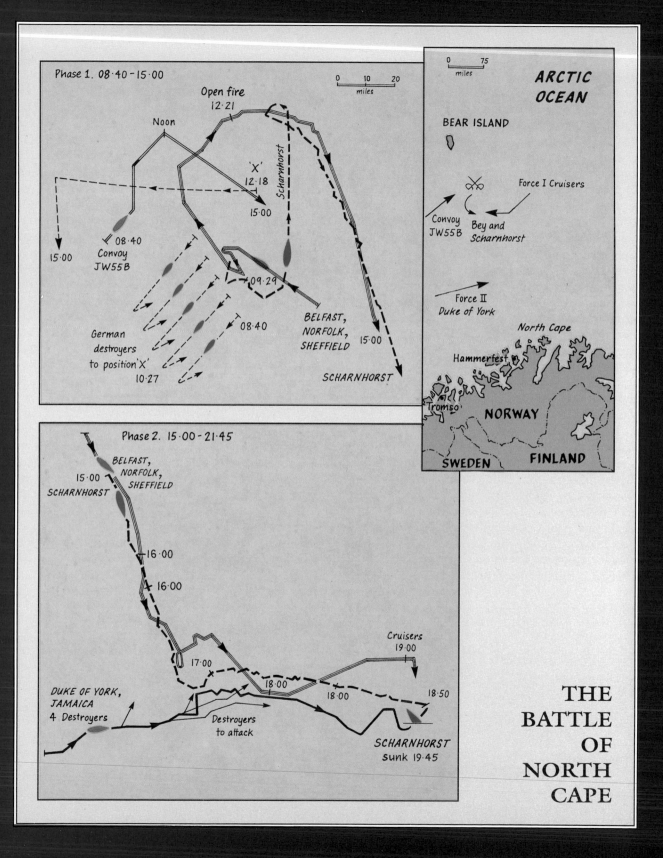

Phase 1. 08·40 – 15·00

Open fire
12·21

Noon

0   10   20
miles

'X'
12·18

15·00

Scharnhorst

08·40
Convoy
JW55B

15·00

09·29

German
destroyers
to position 'X'

08·40

10·27

BELFAST,
NORFOLK,
SHEFFIELD

15·00

SCHARNHORST

Phase 2. 15·00 – 21·45

BELFAST,
NORFOLK,
SHEFFIELD

15·00
SCHARNHORST

16·00

16·00

17·00

Cruisers
19·00

18·00

18·00

18·50

DUKE OF YORK,
JAMAICA
4 Destroyers

Destroyers
to attack

SCHARNHORST
Sunk 19·45

0   75
miles

ARCTIC
OCEAN

BEAR ISLAND

Force I Cruisers

Convoy
JW55B

Bey and
Scharnhorst

Force II
Duke of York

North Cape

Hammerfest

Tromso

NORWAY

SWEDEN   FINLAND

THE
BATTLE
OF
NORTH
CAPE

ready all the time, and this was an exhausting business. Moreover, the Home Fleet had other things to do as well. It had to support naval operations taking place outside the Arctic theatre, provide work-up facilities and support the northern blockade. Sometimes the Home Fleet simply ran out of ships and had either to be reinforced from outside or to cut down on its commitments. Thus in March 1943, to his embarrassment and Stalin's fury, Churchill reluctantly concluded that he would have to call a temporary halt to the Arctic convoys.

This explains why the British made such determined efforts to attack the German ships that Hitler mistakenly thought so useless. But it was not easy. The ships were tough and very well hidden away in Norway's difficult fjords. The *Tirpitz* even had trees planted on her decks! On the rare occasions when they went to sea the larger German units were handled with extreme circumspection. None the less, by a combination of midget submarine and air attacks, which put the *Tirpitz* temporarily out of commission, and by the requirement for most of the German cruisers to return to the Baltic for refits, the situation slowly improved through 1943. In November of that year, Fraser felt he could afford to start up the Arctic convoys again.

The sleek and dangerous battlecruiser *Scharnhorst* still remained to be dealt with. But now the situation was different. Fraser was sure that the strategic situation would soon force the Germans to make a move. The first three east-bound and two west-bound convoys passed by without incident, but the last of the east-bound convoys, number JW 55A was known to have been spotted by the Germans. Fraser was so sure that the Germans would attack one of the next pair, JW 55B, which left Loch Ewe on 20 December (as we have seen) and RA 55A, returning empty from the Kola Peninsula on 23 December, that he took his flag-

ship, the battleship *Duke of York*, to sea on the same day, and twice rehearsed his force in the tactics of night interception he was to use 24 hours later. His expectations of a foray by the Germans was reinforced by the degree of air shadowing to which JW 55B was subjected. Fraser was quite clear, however, that his first priority was to get the convoy through safely.

Had he but known it, there was still a great deal of uncertainty on the German side as to whether an attack should take place at all and, if so, what form it should take. The complicated German command system was one of the reasons for this. Doenitz, keen on the concept of an attack, was away in Paris on his way to spend Christmas with his U-boat crews; from here he and his chief of staff urged his forces on. Admiral Schniewind at Group Headquarters North, in Kiel, was much less confident about the wisdom of the foray and wanted it postponed. Arctic Command at Narvik was even more doubtful. The weather was appalling. This would reduce the operational effectiveness of the German destroyer squadrons (whose big 5.9in guns made them bad sea boats) and further weakened an already hard-pushed Luftwaffe operating out of the Lofoten islands. The Air Commander Lofoten frankly admitted the reconnaissance deficiencies of his force. And rightly so: throughout the approaching battle, the Luftwaffe's reports were to be sparse, inaccurate, vague about the composition or position of the forces reported on, and inordinately slow in reaching the *Scharnhorst*. Both of these things worried Arctic Command because it increased the chance that the German force could be surprised by the British. And there were rumours that the British had developed a highly effective radar fire control that would give them a decisive edge in a night action; at that time of the year, moreover, the Arctic day was nearly all 'night'.

Left: The 34-knot German battlecruiser, sunk in the last capital ship duel in Royal Navy history.

Right: Admiral Bey, commander of the *Scharnhorst* on her last operational sortie. He perished with his ship.

Right: HMS *Belfast* played a vital part in the action with *Scharnhorst*, discovering and tracking the German battlecruiser with her radar.

Lastly, there was Admiral Bey himself. A born destroyer commander, he had only temporarily assumed command of the *Scharnhorst* group in November when Admiral Kummetz had gone off on leave. Immensely popular with his crew, and perhaps swayed by their enthusiasm, he was aware of all the problems but none the less confident he could do what Doenitz wanted.

The result of all this was a dangerous imprecision in the stream of orders that Admiral Bey received. The degree of his authority either in running risks in his bid to attack convoy JW 55B, or in calling the operation off, was quite uncertain. Nor was it very clear whether the convoy was to be attacked by his destroyers with *Scharnhorst* in support or the other way about. Finally, it was far from clear where the various British forces were, how strong they were and, most crucially, whether heavy units were in the area. But on one point his orders *were* clear: 'You must disengage if a superior enemy force is encountered.'

When, on the afternoon of 25 December, the order came for the *Scharnhorst* to sail, spontaneous cheers rang across the fjord, and her crew, some 2,000 men, set to work with a will, taking down the Christmas decorations and preparing the ship for action. *Scharnhorst* left her anchorage accompanied by five destroyers late in the afternoon of Christmas Day. In the words of one observer, 'the long slender shadow of the handsomely proportioned ship gliding past and slowly gathering speed, without light, without sound. Beautiful and lethal, she came speeding from her mountain lair to hunt in the open.'

Although no specific orders were given to them, two minesweepers left as well, their captains assuming that they were supposed to prepare the way for the German squadron to leave in safety. But *Scharnhorst* left so quickly that they could not keep up and, to their dismay and concern, fell astern unheeded. It was an ominous early indication of poor coordination between *Scharnhorst* and her consorts.

Worse was to follow. Out in the open sea conditions were terrible. Dense snow squalls seriously impaired visibility, and the waves were 30 feet high. 'They rolled up in long roaring swells, dark foam-flecked, white crested. The gale tore shreds of spray from the crests and shot them flat across the water. The eddying snow was thicker and heavier than the men had ever known it... and it was as cold as the icy breath of the Pole itself.' The destroyers found it very difficult to keep company as the force ploughed northwards through Christmas night. At 0730 on the following morning, 26 December, Admiral Bey pushed his destroyers forward to see if they could find the convoy, but within an hour, through poor signalling and station-keeping, the destroyers had lost touch with *Scharnhorst* and even with each other for a while. Agitated signalling between them led Bey to suppose, wrongly, that they were in action; his confusion was complete, but he ploughed on northwards, never to regain company with his all-important destroyers.

All this was in strong contrast to the meticulous, professional approach of the British forces closing on *Scharnhorst*. Admiral Fraser had a much more complicated task on his hands than his adversary. First he had two convoys to protect, and he envisaged that they would pass each other in the dangerous narrows to the south of Bear Island. He suspected that German submarines and aircraft were in the vicinity, waiting for them, and expected *Scharnhorst* to be on the scene as well, doubtless supported by destroyers. Both convoys had their own escorting forces, but there was in addition a supporting cruiser group, comprising

Above: HMS *Duke of York* opens fire on the *Scharnhorst*. Painting by John Hamilton.

Above right: HMS *Belfast* at the Battle of North Cape. With the rest of the cruiser squadron she shadowed the *Scharnhorst* until the arrival of the *Duke of York*. Painting by John Hamilton.

Belfast, *Norfolk* and *Sheffield* under the command of Vice Admiral R. L. Burnett, approaching from the east and offering cover to RA 55A. Finally, Fraser's own force, consisted of the battleship *Duke of York*, the cruiser *Jamaica* and four destroyers, was approaching from the west.

When it became clear to Fraser that RA 55A had after all escaped the notice of the Germans and was clear of Bear Island, he detached four of its screening destroyers and these joined JW 55B early on Christmas morning. Fraser ordered this convoy to alter course to the north, taking it farther away from any German force approaching from the south. At 0400 on Boxing Day morning, Burnett was 150 miles away, approaching *Scharnhorst* and her base. As it happened, Bey, who then was still in company with his destroyers, was on a course that would indeed bring him on to his prey, convoy JW 55B steaming slowly eastwards towards Russia.

The weather on Christmas night was appalling, causing discomfort and damage even on the battleship *Duke of York* as she battled through a full gale and heavy seas. By Boxing Day morning, however, conditions were improving, with the wind and sea abating.

There was still a heavy swell and no more than moderate visibility.

At 0834 Burnett picked up *Scharnhorst* by radar at 25,000 yards, about 30 miles south of the convoy. Forty minutes later, *Sheffield* reported the enemy to be in sight, about 13,000 yards away, and at 0924 fired star-shell. This failed to illuminate the target, so *Norfolk* fired blind, relying on her radar range-finding, five minutes later. *Scharnhorst* was caught completely by surprise; she hauled away to the north, took one, and possibly two, hits from *Norfolk*, but did not reply. During this opening skirmish, Bey lost his forward radar, putting him at still more of a disadvantage.

Below: HMS *Norfolk*, part of Vice Admiral Burnett's supporting cruiser group

Bey told his crew that he would try once more to get at the convoy, a few miles away, and used his superior speed to work his way round to the north. Burnett realised his three cruisers could not keep up with the speedy German battlecruiser, and shrewdly accepted a loss of contact, steering a shorter, more direct, course that would keep him between the convoy and *Scharnhorst*, should Bey try to approach it again. Not unnaturally, Fraser was concerned at the risk Burnett was taking. 'Unless touch can be regained,' he signalled at 1058, 'there is no chance of my finding the enemy.'

But things worked out just as Burnett had anticipated. Shortly after noon, *Belfast* regained radar contact as Bey closed on the convoy again, and at 1221 *Sheffield* signalled 'Enemy in sight' for a second time. Shortly afterwards Burnett's cruisers opened fire at 11,000 yards. Bey was dismayed to find himself caught again – even more so when he realised it was

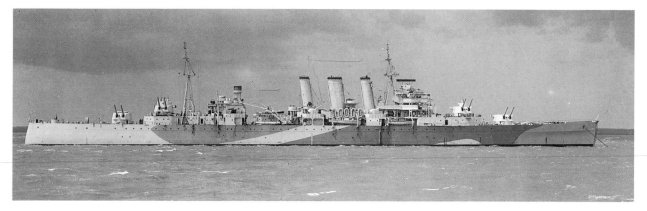

Above: One of the two 11-inch shell hits on HMS *Norfolk*.

the same three ships. In this second action there was general firing for about twenty minutes, this time *Scharnhorst* getting the better of it. One of her 11in shells ploughed into *Norfolk*, whose lack of flashless cordite made her the obvious target. A turret was knocked out and most of her radars were destroyed; one officer and six ratings were killed. *Sheffield* took some punishment too. *Scharnhorst* herself was probably not hit in this second skirmish, but Bey decided it would be pointless to try to get at the convoy a third time and turned away, breaking off the action. Firing ceased at 1241, and Bey steered for home, heading, had he but known it, straight for Fraser in the *Duke of York*. To compound the error, Bey signalled his destroyers also to stop looking for the convoy and to turn for home, not realising that they were then within eight miles of their prey.

Burnett was delighted that the Germans were speeding off in just the direction he wished them to take and chased along behind. He kept contact by radar just outside visibility range, sending accurate and timely reports that kept Fraser completely in the picture. Carefully, Fraser orchestrated his forces, closing the net on the fleeing *Scharnhorst*. On the *Duke of York*, the men had pork chops for their Boxing Day lunch, but those in the control positions found it difficult to eat them with their bare hands.

To spring his trap, it was necessary for Fraser to send and receive many signals, but German direction-finders failed either to pick them up or pass the information on to Bey. A German reconnaissance aircraft was seen shadowing Fraser's force, but again Bey heard nothing from it. He tried in vain to shake Burnett's cruisers off but had no idea there were any significant units between him and Norway, and confidently signalled Arctic Command of his estimated time of arrival.

For the next four hours or so, *Scharnhorst* sped southwards, deeper into the trap. Suddenly at 1648, and completely without warning, the battlecruiser was bathed silver grey in the light of star-shells, with her turrets unsuspectingly trained fore and aft. A British officer on the destroyer *Scorpion* thought 'what a lovely sight she was at full speed. She was almost at once obliterated by a wall of water form the *Duke of York*'s first salvo.'

Fraser had caught his prey brilliantly, but he knew that *Scharnhorst* was the fastest ship present and still might get away in the confusion of battle and in poor visibility. The British knew it was therefore essential to slow the battlecruiser down. At the first salvo, *Scharnhorst* pulled away from Fraser around to the north, twisting and turning, but ran into fire from *Belfast* and *Norfolk*.

At 1724, Bey signalled, 'Am surrounded by heavy units', and was soon enveloped in a succession of salvoes from the *Duke of York*'s 14in guns. One hit knocked out her foremost turret, putting three of her 11in guns out of action. Another hit the quarter-deck, causing havoc. *Duke of York* fired 52 broadsides, achieving 31 straddles, sixteen within 200 yards of *Scharnhorst*. It was remarkable shooting. After her initial confusion, *Scharnhorst* too produced effective shooting. The 'large orange flashes' on the horizon seemed very menacing to the *Duke of York*'s crew, but in fact there were no hits; two of *Scharnhorst*'s 11in shells went through the *Duke of York*'s masts, but without exploding.

Once again *Scharnhorst* was able to use her speed to open up the range, and at 1824 the *Duke of York* checked her fire. There was 'a distinct atmosphere of gloom and disappointment' aboard when it seemed as though the wounded battlecruiser might yet escape.

In fact, *Scharnhorst* had sustained damage in a boiler room, which slowed her down to 8–10 knots for a time. This was fatal. Two pairs of destroyers, bucketing after her through heavy seas, were able to work themselves into a torpedo firing position on the

Right: Few survived the Arctic waters after *Scharnhorst* sank – only 36 were picked up by the British ships. Some are seen here on the catapult deck of HMS *Duke of York*.

Right: One of *Scharnhorst*'s wounded is transferred to a hospital ship from *Duke of York*.

Right: A photograph taken after the battle aboard the *Duke of York*, a group portrait of the victorious commanders at the Battle of North Cape. Fraser is fifth from the left, with Hughes Hallet, captain of *Jamaica*, to his left.

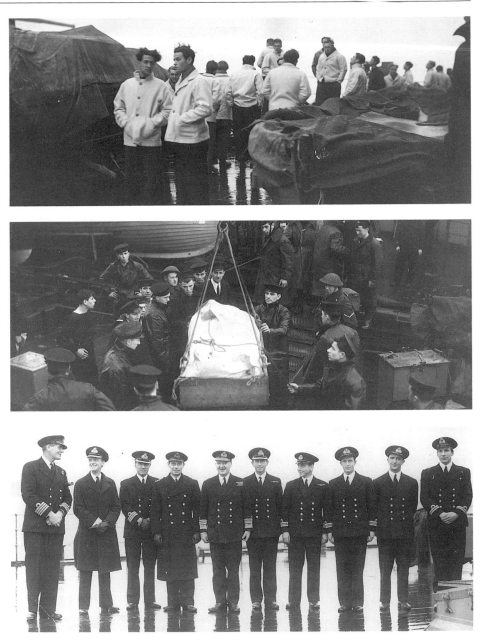

battlecruiser. To the north-west were *Savage* and *Saumarez*; Scharnhorst spotted them and used her secondary armament against them. Unseen, the other pair crept up from the south. *Scorpion* and the Norwegian *Stord* were in fact the only ships between *Scharnhorst*, the open sea and her base. To the destroyers, the brightly illuminated battlecruiser looked enormous, filling the control officer's binoculars. 'Get out the wires and fenders,' shouted one sailor on *Scorpion*, 'We're going alongside the bastard.' Instead of turning to obliterate the British destroyers, Bey tried to outrun them and to dodge their torpedoes, but he could not avoid the attack from both directions and took four devastating hits.

Scharnhorst's speed fell off completely, and by 1901 both *Duke of York* and *Jamaica* had caught up and resumed their shooting at 10,400 yards. Burnett's cruisers joined in as well. To one observer on *Duke of York*, 'the enemy appeared as the dark source at the centre of a veritable mass of diverging and converging tracer and gunfire'. The cruisers and destroyers joined in too, firing torpedoes into the murk. *Scharnhorst*

Left: The *Sharnhorst* sinks, probably due to a torpedo delivered by HMS *Jamaica*. Painting by John Hamilton.

finally sank at about 1745, leaving only 36 survivors out of her crew of 2,000.

She had fought gallantly to the very end and demonstrated once again the remarkable resilience of German capital ships. It had taken thirteen 14in hits from the *Duke of York*, twelve 8in hits from the cruisers and eleven torpedo hits to sink her. She had been defeated by the sheer professionalism of the British, whose superior command and control had been the decisive element at every level and stage of the battle. The harassing action of the destroyers and cruisers had been crucial in providing the conditions for the final execution by the *Duke of York*'s first-rate gunnery. Altogether, the battle of the North Cape was a triumphant vindication of the enormous effort devoted to the perfection of every aspect of battle fleet tactics so assiduously practised by the Royal Navy during the inter-war period, and since. The sinking of the *Scharnhorst* was the effective end not only of the German surface naval threat to British seapower but of an era of naval battles where the gun was the main weapon. Never again would a British battleship fight its own kind.

BIBLIOGRAPHY

Watts, A. J., *The Loss of the Scharnhorst*. A no-nonsense, concise guide to the battle complete with plans, ships' particulars, etc.

Roskill, S. W., *The War at Sea, 1939–1945*, vol III, London. An authoritative, reliable and informed account in this, the official history.

Hinsley, F. W., *British Intelligence in the Second World War*, vol III. This book shows the importance of Ultra intelligence in establishing the conditions for the battle; but also makes clear its limitations.

Padfield, P., *Doenitz: The Last Führer*. He explains the idiosyncratic role played in his battle by Doenitz and the higher levels of command back in Germany.

Busch, F.-O., *The Drama of the Scharnhorst*. Indispensable account of the German side of the battle, written with imagination and style.

Schofield, Vice Admiral B. B., *The Arctic Convoys*. Popular history and analysis of Britain's maritime support for Russia, providing the necessary perspective for understanding the significance of the *Scharnhorst* operation.

WOODWARD: FALKLANDS, 1982

by Eric Grove

'Anyone can see the risk from air attack which we run...
This risk will have to be faced. Warships are meant to go under fire.'
Winston Churchill, 1940

The first day of May 1982 was the 50th birthday of Rear Admiral John 'Sandy' Woodward. He was celebrating it in the aircraft carrier *Hermes* in command of Task Group 317.8 to the east of the Falkland Islands. TG 317.8 was a major component of Task Force 317 commanded by Admiral Fieldhouse, Commander in Chief Fleet, in Northwood, north London. Formation of the task force had begun in response to clear evidence at the end of March that Argentina was about to invade the Falkland Islands. In a dramatic meeting at the Houses of Parliament on the evening of 30 March, Sir Henry Leach, the First Sea Lord, convinced the Prime Minister that a maritime counter-attack to recapture the islands was practical. Margaret Thatcher, knowing her political survival rested on the success of this venture, had to agree – despite the doubts of the Minister of Defence, John Nott who, the previous year, had carried out a major defence review in which the Navy had borne the brunt of the cuts. This was Leach's opportunity to strike back, not just at the Argentines, but perhaps even more at his political chief.

On 2 April, even before the islands had been captured by the Argentines, Operation 'Corporate' had been ordered. The closest available major naval force was a squadron of destroyers and frigates exercising off Gibraltar. These were commanded by Woodward in his role as Flag Officer First Flotilla. He was ordered to proceed south to Ascension Island with his most suitable general-purpose assets, the large 'County' class guided-missile destroyers *Glamorgan* and *Antrim*, the Type 42 air-defence destroyers *Sheffield*, *Glasgow* and *Coventry*, and the frigates *Brilliant* (Type 22), *Arrow* (Type 21) and *Plymouth* (Type 12). The core of Woodward's group was to be the Anti-Submarine Warfare support carriers *Hermes* and *Invincible*, which were sailed from Portsmouth on 5 April with maximum publicity. The main fighting power of these ships were, respectively, twelve and eight Sea Harrier fighter/attack aircraft, short take-off/vertical landing aircraft operated to maximum effect by the use of 'ski-jumps'.

On 7 April, Woodward was ordered to send *Antrim* and *Plymouth* together with the auxiliary *Tidespring* to proceed with all speed ahead. They were intended to form Task Group 317.9 to recapture South Georgia, which had also fallen to the Argentines. A week later, as the carriers approached a rendezvous with Woodward, he detached his Type 42s together with *Brilliant* and *Arrow* and the auxiliary *Appleleaf* to get as many assets as close to the Falklands as possible in case the last-minute political negotiations taking place forced a freeze on deployment. The following day, 15 April, Woodward shifted his flag to *Hermes*, which had the most comprehensive flag and communication facilities available. The carriers brought with them the first units of a complementary amphibious task group under Commodore Mike Clapp in the assault ship (LPD) *Fearless*, carrying the Marine Task Group commander, Brigadier

Below: HMS *Invincible* leaving Portmouth on 5 April 1982.

Right: HMS *Plymouth* bombarding Argentine positions around Brown Mountain on South Georgia to cover the British advance at Grytviken, 25 April 1982.

Julian Thompson. There were also more frigates for TG 317.8 to replace those already sent on ahead, including the Type 21 *Alacrity* and the Type 12 *Yarmouth*. In a series of conferences between the Task Group commanders and the Task Force C-in-C, who flew down from Northwood, it was decided that Woodward would go ahead with his battle group to be in position on 1 May to enter and enforce a Total Exclusion Zone (TEZ) declared around the islands. The battle group would then simulate a landing to draw out the Argentine Navy and Air force and engage them in battle for over two weeks before the amphibious group, which had to wait at Ascension Island for vital reinforcement and reorganisation, eventually arrived.

On 18 April, Woodward's battle group set sail southwards, accompanied by the fleet auxiliaries *Olmeda* and *Resource*. On 24 April the carrier group joined up with the forward surface action group, minus *Brilliant*, which had been sent to reinforce TG 317.9 when the South Georgia operation began to go awry. The situation had been saved, however, and on the 26th *Antrim*'s captain reported that South Georgia was again under the Union Flag. Three days later *Brilliant* and *Plymouth* rejoined the flag. On 30 April orders came from Northwood that once inside the TEZ any combat ship or aircraft identified as Argentine was to be fired upon. Fieldhouse also told Woodward via satellite telephone that he was to proceed inside the TEZ the following day. The weeks of diplomacy had proved abortive; the second naval Battle of the Falkland Islands was about to begin.

Before dawn on the 1st, an RAF Vulcan bomber flying from Ascension Island dropped bombs on the runway at Port Stanley. This was followed by a carrier strike by twelve Sea Harriers on aircraft and buildings at the same airfield and on the airstrip at Goose Green, where three Pucara light attack aircraft were destroyed by cluster bombs. No Sea Harriers were lost. Woodward also dispatched *Glamorgan*, *Arrow* and *Alacrity* to take the airfield under 4.5in gunfire. An anti-submarine unit made up of *Brilliant* and *Yarmouth* was also sent to search the likeliest area of enemy submarine activity and to threaten a possible landing to the north-east, north of Berkeley Head. A flight of Turbo Mentor light strike aircraft managed to take off from Port Stanley to attack this pair but was chased off by two Sea Harriers. Argentine Mirage III fighters also appeared from the mainland to probe the Task Group's defences. One fired missiles at a Sea Harrier, but to little effect. The Argentine fighter pilots were unwilling to close the more nimble British carrier fighters. They also knew that the British had a decisive technical advantage, the AIM-9L version of the Sidewinder heat-seeking missile, capable of being fired with great reliability from any angle. The Argentines had no equivalent. AIM-9L was the key to British success that evening when the Argentines put in a full scale strike with Canberra, Dagger and Skyhawk bombers covered by Mirages and more Daggers. Strike Daggers took on the bombardment group. Close to shore, the ships had difficulty replying, but the only hits were scored by cannon fire on *Arrow*, causing the first British casualty of the battle. Directed by fighter controllers in *Brilliant*, *Coventry* and *Glamorgan*, the Sea Harriers claimed a Mirage, a Dagger and a Canberra. A second Mirage was also so badly damaged that it tried to put down at Stanley – only to be shot down by jumpy Argentine AA crews.

This was a decisive defeat for the Argentines, who would never again take on the Sea Harriers in fighter *versus* fighter combat. All subsequent air attacks on Woodward's forces would be carried out by small groups of aircraft trying to slip through the defences.

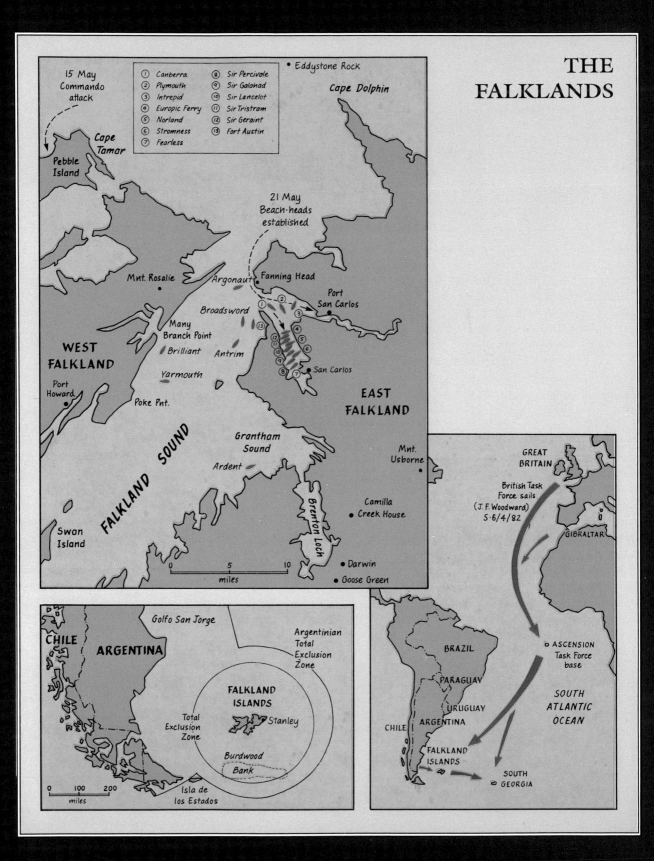

THE FALKLANDS

15 May Commando attack

Legend:
① Canberra
② Plymouth
③ Intrepid
④ Europic Ferry
⑤ Norland
⑥ Stromness
⑦ Fearless
⑧ Sir Percivale
⑨ Sir Galahad
⑩ Sir Lancelot
⑪ Sir Tristram
⑫ Sir Geraint
⑬ Fort Austin

• Eddystone Rock
Cape Dolphin

Cape Tamar
Pebble Island

21 May Beach-heads established

Mnt. Rosalie
Argonaut Fanning Head
Broadsword
Port San Carlos
Many Branch Point
Brilliant
Antrim
WEST FALKLAND
Yarmouth
Port Howard
Poke Pnt.
San Carlos
EAST FALKLAND

FALKLAND SOUND

Grantham Sound
Mnt. Usborne
Ardent

Swan Island

Brenton Loch

Camilla Creek House

0   5   10
miles

Darwin
• Goose Green

CHILE
ARGENTINA
Golfo San Jorge

Argentinian Total Exclusion Zone

FALKLAND ISLANDS
• Stanley

Total Exclusion Zone

Burdwood Bank

0   100   200
miles

Isla de los Estados

GREAT BRITAIN

British Task Force sails
(J. F. Woodward)
5·6/4/82

GIBRALTAR

BRAZIL

PARAGUAY

URUGUAY

CHILE   ARGENTINA

FALKLAND ISLANDS

ASCENSION Task Force base

SOUTH ATLANTIC OCEAN

SOUTH GEORGIA

These could be more easily countered than massed escorted strikes. The ASW ships together with carrier-based Sea King helicopters carried out a series of depth-charge attacks on a submarine contact. This seems to have been the *San Luis*, which reported replying with a torpedo, the guidance wire of which broke. After more harrying by depth-charge and torpedo-carrying helicopters from the frigates and the carriers, the 1,000-ton boat beat a retreat.

Woodward's attention now turned to the Argentine surface fleet. It was known that the carrier *Veinticinco de Mayo* was at sea, escorted by Argentina's two British-built Type 42 destroyers. A frigate group equipped with Exocet anti-ship missiles was also on the prowl, as was the old 6in-gunned cruiser *General Belgrano*, forming a surface action group (SAG) with two Exocet-equipped former American 'Gearing' class destroyers. These should have been covered by Britain's second naval Task Force in the area, TF 324, a battle squadron of nuclear powered attack submarines (SSNs). Such was the threat of the Argentine carrier that its sinking had been authorised outside the TEZ, but the closest submarine, *Splendid*, was unable to locate her. The only SSN in contact with the enemy was Commander Chris Wreford Brown's *Conqueror* trailing the *Belgrano* SAG. Woodward could have sunk *Belgrano* with his own ships, but much to his chagrin he had no control over TF 324, which was limited to targets within the TEZ.

The *Belgrano* group was a real threat. Six months previously, Woodward himself, on exercise in HMS *Glamorgan* in the Indian Ocean, had been able to close in for a perfect simulated missile attack on the US carrier *Coral Sea*. What he could do the Argentines might also be able to achieve, and it would be the more difficult to deal with the SAG if a carrier air strike were expected simultaneously. Woodward needed to simplify his tactical problem, and as a submariner recognised the problems *Conqueror* might face if the *Belgrano* group tried a rush over the shallow water of the Burdwood Bank. The only option open to him seemed to be to try as quickly as possible to provoke an attack on the cruiser and destroyers. So he signalled *Conqueror* by satellite to attack. Although the signal was intercepted at Northwood by Flag Officer Submarines and a signal sent to *Conqueror* not to attack the *Belgrano* (a communication that mystified Wreford Brown, who had not received Woodward's message and would not have acted upon it even if he had done so), Woodward's remarkable *démarche* had

Above: Admiral Sir Terence, later Lord, Lewin

the intended effect. Fieldhouse and the Chief of Defence Staff, Admiral Sir Terence Lewin, drove to Chequers (the Prime Minister's country house) where they briefed the War Cabinet on the situation. Mrs Thatcher was unwilling to overrule the commander on the spot, and a signal changing TF 324's Rules of Engagement to allow attacks outside the TEZ was sent to the SSNs.

On receipt of this – and prudently checking its veracity in the context of recently received orders not to attack the enemy – Wreford Brown closed the *Belgrano* group and fired three old Mk 8 torpedoes. Two hit the *Belgrano* herself, which quickly sank. Another probably hit the destroyer *Hipolito Bouchard* but failed to explode. The remaining ship, *Piedra Buena* dropped depth-charges, which helped keep *Conqueror* from mounting a subsequent attack on the destroyers. By the time it seemed sensible to go after them with Mk 24 guided torpedoes, *Conqueror* had been ordered not to interfere with rescue work.

Left: HMS *Invincible* with six Sea Harriers and a Sea King helicopter on her flight deck.

As Woodward waited for the results of his calculated insubordination, he ordered TG 317.8 into air defence formation with his Type 42s acting as forward pickets 30 miles 'up-threat', *Glamorgan* and the Type 12s and 21s in an inner anti-air and anti-submarine screen, and a Type 22 to cover each carrier as 'goalkeeper' with its Sea Wolf point-defence missiles.

No attack came. The Argentine carrier group had indeed been authorised on 1 May to carry out an attack on the British, supported by the Exocet frigates to the south, but the attack had been called off when it became clear that the British were not landing in the islands after all. It had also become clear that there was insufficient wind over-deck in the unseasonably calm conditions to launch the *Veinticinco de Mayo*'s Skyhawks, and the Argentine strike had to be aborted. If it had gone in, the combination of well trained Naval pilots, retarded bombs effective at low altitude and inexperienced defenders might have seen another Midway. As it was, the best opportunity for the Argentines to prevent a landing in the *Malvinas* passed, never to return. On the news that the *Belgrano* had been sunk, all Argentine surface ships were ordered back to port. This outcome had been expected by the admirals in London when they had pressed for a change in the Rules of Engagement. With no effective counter to SSNs, the Argentine Navy had little alternative but to stay in its territorial waters for the rest of the war. This was the second major British success of the battle .

During the following night Lynx helicopters from *Coventry* and *Glasgow* attacked surface contacts with the newly developed Sea Skua missiles. The outcome (at the time of writing this account) is still not entirely clear, but one Argentine patrol vessel, the *Alfarez Sobral*, was badly damaged. During 3 May, Woodward took his group to the south-east into foggy weather, then turned back towards the islands to make another bombing attack. The Argentine Navy's Second Attack Squadron equipped with newly delivered Super Etendard aircraft and five Exocet anti-ship missiles had attempted an attack on 2 May, but the aircraft had failed to meet their refuelling tanker. Now they had another chance.

Guided by a Neptune reconnaissance aircraft, and benefiting both from exercises against Argentina's Type 42s and the British Task Group's lack of airborne early warning, the Super Etendards were able to close Woodward at low level, 'pop up' to find contacts and launch their missiles. They penetrated a hole in the Task Group's defences caused when two Sea Harriers on combat air patrol were directed to carry out a surface probe mission. One Exocet was decoyed away by *Glasgow*'s 'chaff', but the other struck *Sheffield* on the starboard side. The destroyer had been taken by surprise in part because the air situation over the Task Group was insufficiently well coordinated. *Invincible*, the air defence control ship, was grappling with repeated false alarms and chose not to act upon the alert *Glasgow*'s warning. Just as important,

Right: HMS *Sheffield* on fire after being struck by an Exocet anti-ship missile on 4 May 1982.

Sheffield's electronic warning receiver was blanked out by satellite communications. The Exocet set fire to the destroyer and broke the main water main, making fire-fighting difficult. A late twentieth century warship contains much flammable material, notably the rubber coatings of its miles of wire, and the blaze was soon out of control. The destroyer was abandoned and burnt out, eventually sinking on 10 May. To add to Woodward's woes a Sea Harrier was shot down by AA fire while bombing Goose Green airfield.

The setbacks of 4 May caused Woodward to decide to husband his resources and move farther to the east. Sadly, however, this did not prevent the loss of two more Sea Harriers, which collided in cloud on 6 May.

Two days later Woodward decided to begin to turn up the heat once more. On the night of 8/9 May, high-level bombing missions began using Sea Harriers. Ships were sent in back to the islands to put pressure back on the garrison. On the 9th, the first 'Combo' of a type 42 destroyer and Type 22 frigate was formed of *Coventry* and *Broadsword* to shoot down any air traffic over Stanley airfield. The complementary weapons-fits of the two ships electronically data-linked together provided both area- and self-defence capability. The Combo scored an unexpected success when it diverted two Sea Harriers on a high-level bombing mission to disable the Argentine intelligence gathering trawler *Narwhal*, which was later boarded by helicopter and left to sink. Captains Hart Dyke of *Coventry* and Canning of *Broadsword* then took up station. The first Sea Dart missile shots only succeeded in turning back a Hercules transport, but a Puma helicopter was eventually shot down, the first kill for the system.

Of all the possible landing beaches for the invasion of the Falkland Islands, San Carlos at the north end of Falkland Sound seemed to offer the most promise. In order to test the sound for mines, *Alacrity* was sent in during the night of 10/11 May. The frigate passed unscathed and sank for good measure the transport *Islos de los Estados* with 4.5in gunfire. After joining her sister ship, *Arrow*, north of the islands, the group was attacked by the submarine *San Luis*, but again the submarine's torpedo wire broke and the frigates continued on their way.

On the 12th the Task Group succeeded a little too well in drawing out the Argentine Air force to give battle. The *Glasgow/Brilliant* Combo was attacked by eight Skyhawks. The British pair had problems both in acquiring the targets and engaging with Sea Dart because of a salt-encrusted launcher. Then the destroyer's gun jammed! *Brilliant*'s Sea Wolf came to the rescue, dealing with three of the first wave of attacking aircraft, two directly and one by forcing it into the sea. The fourth Skyhawk was able to drop its bombs, which narrowly missed. The next wave then came in. *Glasgow* cleared her gun but not the missile launcher and then suffered a failure in her ADAWS control system. Paul Hodinott, her captain, could only reply with machine-guns when the destroyer had

to cease-fire with her 4.5 as it was interfering with the Sea Wolf radar. The attackers succeeded in confusing Sea Wolf, and *Brilliant* was near-missed. *Glasgow* was hit, but the bomb was dropped at too low an altitude to explode, the first of many such weapons to be so misused. It passed straight through the destroyer and out the other side. *Glasgow*'s damage-control crews were able to contain the serious damage and after further repairs she was later able to rejoin Woodward's screen until replacement with an undamaged Sea Dart ship was possible.

With the amphibious group fast approaching, Special Forces operations could help mitigate the air threat. On the night of 14/15 May, supported by *Glamorgan*, SAS personnel landed from *Hermes* and destroyed the light aircraft parked on the airfield at Pebble Island – disturbingly close to the likely beachhead. On the 17th, *Invincible* briefly left her station to land SAS personnel in Argentina by helicopter to report on the departure of raids from the mainland. On the 18th, the 21-strong amphibious force, which included the liner *Canberra*, arrived, escorted by *Antrim*, the Type 12 frigate *Plymouth*, the Type 21 *Antelope* and the 'Leander' class frigate *Argonaut*, which were added to Woodward's fleet. The transport *Atlantic Conveyor* also brought eight more Sea Harriers and six of a squadron of ten RAF Harrier ground-attack aircraft. These were distributed to *Invincible* and *Hermes* (the last four RAF Harriers later flew down using in-flight refuelling). Woodward persuaded Clapp and Thompson that a night run-in for the landing was preferable. It was decided to mount the

operation on the night of 20/21 May, when bad weather would help cover the approach.

After a massive helicopter cross-decking to spread *Canberra*'s troops between the amphibious ships on the 19th, the Task Force commander gave Woodward permission to proceed with the landing at his preferred moment, which was the day after. The Carrier Task Group commander detached seven ships directly to support Clapp: *Antrim*, *Argonaut*, *Ardent*, *Plymouth*, *Yarmouth*, *Brilliant* and *Broadsword*. These ships fought a heroic battle of attrition with the Argentine Air Force and Naval Air Force in the days after the landings. On the 21st, *Argonaut* was hit by rocket fire from a small Macchi 339 attack aircraft. The first major air strike was mounted at about 1235 GMT using Daggers. One was shot down by a Sea Cat missile from *Plymouth*, but *Antrim*, the air defence coordinator stationed off Cat Island, was hit by a 1,000lb bomb. Dropped from too low an altitude, it failed to explode; if it had done so, the guided missile destroyer would have blown up as the bomb passed through the missile magazine. *Broadsword* was strafed with cannon shells. The next wave of Daggers succeeded in completing the neutralisation of *Antrim* with gunfire, but one was shot down by a Sea Wolf from *Broadsword*, and *Brilliant* took over the fighter controller's role, placing herself at the entrance to San Carlos Water to cover it with her missiles.

Ardent was bombarding Goose Green, destroying a Pucara as it tried to take off. The Pucaras tried to take out *Ardent*, but some were driven off by the ship's

Left: HMS *Hermes* **recovering Sea Harriers.**

Above: San Carlos Water. Painting by D. Gardiner.

own weapons and another was shot down by a Sea Harrier. Then *Ardent* was taken on by four Skyhawks, which missed; two of these were shot down by Sea Harriers as they escaped. Then more Skyhawks attacked *Argonaut*, hitting her with two out of eight bombs. Again the over-enthusiastic pilots dropped too low and the frigate escaped, albeit seriously damaged. Four Daggers formed the next wave. One was shot down by a Sea Harrier, but the other three penetrated the Sound, avoiding Sea Cat missiles. *Brilliant* had problems engaging a crossing target, but *Broadsword* near-missed a Dagger, causing it to miss *Brilliant*. However, its cannon fire penetrated the ship, temporarily disabling the computer and wounding, but not disabling, the vital fighter controller, Lieutenant Commander Lee Hulme. *Ardent* was next to suffer. She was the target of repeated attacks, first from Daggers that exploited a malfunctioning Sea Cat system to put one bomb into her stern. Air Force Skyhawks then scored more hits as did the formidable Skyhawks of the Argentine Navy with their retarded bombs. Finally Air Force Skyhawks put yet more bombs into the stricken ship to make a total of nine hits, just two of which failed to explode. Sea Harriers shot down three of the Naval attackers, but the frigate had to be abandoned. In all, the British carrier fighters that day shot down four Daggers, five Skyhawks and a Pucara.

The British were dissatisfied with the apparent ineffectiveness of their air defences, but this was more apparent than real. The Argentines had failed to inflict damage on the vital amphibians and had been forced to bomb from too low an altitude for many of their bombs to work. The story was the same when the air attacks were resumed on the 23rd. The Task Group had been reinforced by the Type 42 *Exeter* and two more Type 21s, *Ambuscade* and *Antelope*. The latter was ordered in to support the 'amphibs' but, after finishing off a supply vessel at Port King with Lynx-fired Sea Skuas, was hit by a Skyhawk with a bomb that did not initially explode – until later, when being made safe, sinking the newly arrived frigate. Two Argentine aircraft were lost, one to several weapons simultaneously, the other to a Sea Harrier. On the 24th, Sea Harriers claimed three Daggers while the various ships contributed to a Skyhawk shot down. Two landing ships were hit but the bombs failed to explode.

The story was not quite so happy on the 25th. The *Coventry/Broadsword* Combo had been placed to the north of the sound to act as a missile trap, and it was singled out for attack by the Argentines after scoring two Sea Dart successes against Skyhawks. Four Skyhawks made the attack, the first two taking on *Broadsword*, whose Sea Wolf malfunctioned. The bombs missed, one bouncing up through the flight deck without exploding. Then it was *Coventry's* turn. The ship thought she had a Sea Dart solution on the attackers and hauled off the Sea Harriers coming to her aid. But the enemy aircraft were able to attack successfully, and *Broadsword* could give no aid as the destroyer obscured her firing arcs. *Coventry* was hit by three 1,000lb bombs and quickly sank. Then disaster struck the main Task Group in the shape of another Super Etendard strike with two Exocets. The warship's 'chaff' proved effective enough, but the *Atlantic Conveyor* was sunk, taking with her the ground troops' helicopter support.

This was the Argentine's best day in the sea battle for the Falklands, but it did not avail them much. Most of the British troops ashore, now two brigades strong and commanded by Major General Sir Jeremy Moore, were able to march across the island; the landing ship *Sir Galahad* was lost and *Sir Tristram* seriously damaged in a badly handled sea-lift of those who could not. As the advance continued, the Carrier Task Group continued to give active support to operations ashore as well as vital air cover. The last major reinforcement for Woodward arrived on 26 May, the unique Type 82 destroyer *Bristol*, Type 42 *Cardiff*, the rebuilt Seawolf-equipped 'Leander' *Andromeda*, the more normal 'Leanders' *Minerva* and *Penelope* and the Type 21s *Active* and *Avenger*. The Argentines made their last major air attack four days later with a Super Etendard carrying their last air-launched Exocet and four Air Force Skyhawks in support. They met the frigate *Avenger* leaving the Task Group on a Special Forces mission and attacked her. The missile was, however, decoyed by 'chaff' and the bombs missed. *Exeter* shot down one of the Skyhawks with Sea Dart, and another with gunfire, while the survivors returned to Argentina convinced they had bombed and hit *Invincible*. In fact, despite having to manoeuvre to remain within her 'chaff' cloud (having fired initially on the wrong beam!) *Avenger* was unscathed, as was the rest of the Task Group.

Woodward's ships helped support the final assault on Port Stanley with gunfire, the only untoward event being a hit on *Glamorgan* by an Exocet taken off a warship and flown into the islands. A navigational error took the destroyer across its danger zone. When the British flag was hoisted once more at Port Stanley, the naval battle of the Falklands came to a victorious end. It was not before time, for the ships were showing signs of wear and tear and could not have gone on much longer.

It was always a closer run thing than the British public imagined, which made the achievement of Fieldhouse and the other commanders all the greater. Woodward's own achievement as commander of TG 317.8 had been, together with the submarine task force operating in association with him, the defeat of the surface, air and sub-surface components of the Argentine Navy and the Argentine Air Force. He had inserted and supported a powerful amphibious force, whose own battle had reasserted British sovereignty. Aircraft from *Hermes* and *Invincible* had accounted for 33 enemy aircraft in the air and on the ground for the loss of no aircraft in air-to-air combat – but six Sea Harriers and four RAF Harriers had been lost to ground fire and operational accidents. Eighty-four Royal Navy personnel were killed, a remarkably low loss rate considering the losses of ships. The helicopter and survival suit transformed the chances of living through a sinking. It was a famous victory. Moreover, not only the Argentines were defeated. The Royal Navy's achievements led to some clawing back of the losses of the John Nott defence review and some useful improvements in capability, notably early warning helicopters. Just as the Falkland Islanders were returned to British rule, the Royal Navy itself survived to fight another day, in Whitehall as well as on the oceans of the world.

BIBLIOGRAPHY

British Aviation Study Group, *The Falklands War*, Twickenham, 1986. By far the fullest reference work on the forces engaged in the sea/air war; a remarkable work of reference.
Blakeway, Denys, *The Falklands War*, London 1992. An excellent modern short account that benefits from the latest research.
Brown, J. D., *The Royal Navy and the Falklands War*, London, 1987. The nearest thing to an official history of the Royal Navy's role in the war; essential reading.
Ethell, J., and Alfred Price, *Air War South Atlantic*, London, 1983. The first detailed operational study of the air-sea war; still useful.
Freedman, L. and V. Gamba-Stonehouse, *Signals of War*, London 1990. The most comprehensive politico-military account of the war, seen from both sides.
Ward, Cdr. 'Sharkey', *Sea Harrier Over The Falklands*, London, 1992. A delightfully provocative account from the Fleet Air Arm perspective.
Woodward, Admiral Sandy (with Patrick Robinson), *One Hundred Days: The memoirs of the Falklands Battle Group Commander*, London, 1992. An irreplaceable source, as it gives access to Woodward's diaries that he used as a decision making aid. However, readers must bear in mind that they are reading the personal views of the Battle Group commander, not the definitive, fully informed memoirs of the Task Force commander.

EPILOGUE
by Sir Julian Oswald

The reader who has enjoyed this splendid book as much as I have may well wonder whether an Epilogue is either appropriate or necessary. Possibly it is neither, but it does furnish an opportunity for an independent pen to pay tribute to this fascinating volume. And it is a delightful happenstance that the hand that holds this pen is the same as that which transferred victuals (a much more naval word than food) from the oak tables of the Senior Gunroom at Britannia Royal Naval College, Dartmouth, to the mouth of a young cadet, who can hardly have imagined that he was to spend the next 46 years of his life serving under the White Ensign, in eleven ranks, always conscious of the Royal Navy's proud inheritance of honour, valour and humanity, so well represented by the pictures lining the walls of that majestic Gunroom. Nor was he to know, in the hopeful days of 1947, when the world had so recently concluded the second 'war to end all wars', that further conflicts were to be added to the history of the Royal Navy during his time in the service.

It would indeed be surprising if any youngster's mind was not filled with the excitement of these battles depicted around the walls of his Mess – but it would have been a very percipient youth who foresaw that for the next four decades the Service he had just joined would be engaged in a unique war – a war short of open hostilities – the Cold War, in which, together with allies, it was pitted against the second most powerful Navy in the world in an unceasing round of marking and counter-marking, watching and assessing, surveillance, intelligence gathering, exercising and training. Our youngster would have needed at least second-sight to realise that during the long years of the Cold War the Navy would also find itself engaged, many times, in hostilities and in the exercise of maritime power around the world, largely away from home waters. The 1982 Falklands Campaign fully merits its place of honour in this book, but it should not obscure the fact that the Royal Navy has been called upon to exercise maritime power, some-times including open hostilities and often short of actual fighting, over 300 times since 1945.

So what does this book capture? Is it the soul of the Royal Navy, its ethos or its mores? Jesuits of old might well be diverted from considering the number of angels that could dance on the head of a pin to debate this issue, but in truth modern Jesuits are far too busy on much more vital issues and the question is not important; the answer is probably a bit of all three. Reviewing, with all the wisdom of hindsight and the happy inhibition that comes with age, my four years education at Dartmouth I am interested and almost amazed at how well we were led (not forced) to imbibe, digest and appreciate the traditions of the Royal Navy by techniques that today would definitely be described as 'soft sell'. Of course we learnt some naval history, and we read Geoffrey Callender's *Sea Kings of Britain* – I have mine at my elbow now. But the study of our maritime heritage certainly did not occupy a disproportionate amount of our time, and when I was allowed to specialise in History in my final terms it was neither Nelson nor Jellicoe I studied, but Garibaldi. In this I was totally supported by my tutor, who wanted to further my interest in strategic matters, and felt I had a poor understanding of the development and importance of the nation state!

So we learnt of our naval tradition and heritage by osmosis, indirectly and as a natural, not an enforced, process. But always it was there, and three times a day, at breakfast, dinner (not lunch for Cadets!) and supper our eyes roamed around the walls and read Alfred and the Danes, Sluys, The Armada, North Foreland, Barfleur, Finisterre, Quiberon Bay, Copenhagen, Trafalgar and more. They must have entered our minds as surely as our rations entered our mouths.

Of course, the day of the thirteen-year-old Naval Cadet has long gone – and rightly so. As the age of joining for naval officers has risen, so has the number and complexity of the entry schemes. More and more, Dartmouth has become the training establishment for all Naval Officers: full career, short career, supply officers, seamen, engineers, pilots, submariners, officers promoted from the lower deck, female officers, doctors, dentists, chaplains and reservists; all spend some time here nowadays. The emphasis of the various courses is now less academic, more concerned with professional aspects of life at sea and strongly centred on leadership. Whereas Dartmouth was a school with a strong naval flavour, it is now a Naval College – with the task, for the most part, of turning already well-educated civilians into Naval Officers. This immediately brings us back to the emphasis on, and value of, tradition and the ability to draw on past successes, acts of bravery, battles fought and campaigns won to encourage future sailors that the Navy of today and tomorrow can, and if called upon so to do will, face up to whatever demands the country may put upon it as bravely and loyally as ever its predecessors did – and, as this book shows, that says a very great deal.

This is not a political book, and the Epilogue certainly should not end on a sour note. But it is important to remember that after the more than 1,000 years of British naval warfare, largely successful, which this volume illustrates so well, things *could* change, and change dramatically for the worse, if the Royal Navy and its sister services are starved of funds, equipment and people. The cost of maintaining peace is high, and that cost is fully justified if the far worse and infinitely more expensive alternative, war, is to be avoided. The 'peace dividend' is not surplus cash that can be raided to bolster other socially desirable programmes: the true peace dividend is peace itself.

Since the battles that adorn the walls of the Senior Gunroom at Dartmouth were chosen, two World Wars have been fought, many more great naval actions have been added to the roll, and countless sailors have died. Our best chance of ensuring that the inhabitants of our islands can continue to enjoy, in peace and quietness, the blessings of our land lies in maintaining the capabilities of our armed forces at a viable level, which cannot be much less than those they enjoy today.

We might all with benefit recall the preamble to the *Articles of War*, proudly depicted on the front of Britannia Royal Naval College, Dartmouth:

'It is upon the Navy, under the good Providence of God, that the safety, honour and welfare of this realm do chiefly attend.'

APPENDIX A:
THE OTHER BATTLES

Space precluded full descriptions being given of all the battles commemorated in the Gunroom, so short notes follow on those engagements that are recorded there and which have not been described in the preceding pages.

De Burgh: Sandwich, 1217

On St. Bartholemew's Day, 24 August, a fleet of 36 ships from the Cinque Ports, commanded by Hubert de Burgh, Governor of Dover Castle and a key supporter of the infant King Henry III, overcame a larger fleet, about 80 vessels strong, commanded by a colourful naval mercenary called Eustace the Monk. Eustace was attempting to reinforce the French army landed in England the previous year in support of Prince Louis of France, installed to replace King John by a post-Magna-Carta baronial revolt. The English ships got to windward of their opponents and used lime to blind their enemy before a classic boarding and entering contest began. The heavily laden French vessels could not move against the wind to aid the ships attacked by the English, and all but fifteen of the French ships were taken or sunk. Eustace was captured and beheaded. Prince Louis made a negotiated withdrawal to France. This engagement is also referred to as the Battle of Dover, or the Battle of South Foreland.

Duke of Bedford: Harfleur, 1416

Following Henry V's return to England after Agincourt, a French army laid siege to Harfleur. It was supported by a fleet of French and Genoese ships. The relieving English fleet was led by Admiral Sir Walter Hungerford Morely, with the King's brother, the Duke of Bedford, in charge of the embarked troops and thus in overall command. On 15 August the two fleets engaged each other. The larger size of the English fleet was balanced by the large size of the nine Genoese carracks, and the fighting was fierce. As the day began to go against them, some of the Allied fleet deserted and this began a rout. Four of the nine large Genoese carracks were captured. A final attack by French galleys during the landing of the army was also driven off, and Harfleur was relieved.

Sir Francis Drake: Cadiz, 1587

In an attempt to pre-empt the Spanish Armada (see pages 31–40), Sir Francis Drake led an expedition of twenty ships to disrupt its preparations. The expedition was on normal joint stock lines, and was expected to make a profit for its investors, which included the Queen. The fleet made for Cadiz, where, on 19 April, it defeated the defending galleys with superior firepower and then took, looted and destroyed at least 24 Spanish ships. On the following day, Drake attacked and burnt the Armada flagship. After, in Drake's words, 'singeing the beard of the King of Spain', the fleet destroyed much of the fishing fleet off Sagres before proceeding finally to 'make the voyage' with the capture of the treasure carrack *San Felipe* en route from the East Indies to Lisbon. The Queen made £44,000 and Drake £17,000; and the Armada was delayed until 1588.

Essex: Cadiz, 1596

In an attempt to pre-empt another Spanish Armada while making a profit, Howard of Effingham, with the Earl of Essex commanding troops and in overall charge, took a large Anglo-Dutch fleet to Cadiz, where they found a large fleet with goods bound for the Indies. An attempt to charge the Spanish a large ransom was refused, whereupon the Anglo-Dutch fleet attacked the ships and landed troops, who sacked the town. Because of fierce Spanish resistance, only two ships were taken intact and little booty gained; most of the Spanish ships and their contents were burnt. The expedition inflicted financial and material losses and disrupted Spanish activities, but it was a disappointment in terms of profit.

Duke of York: Lowestoft, 1665

Fought 40 miles off Lowestoft on 3 June, this was a typically fierce but rather indecisive clash between the large fleets of the period, with 109 ships on the English side and 103 on the Dutch, under Admiral Opdam. Once the two fleets engaged, the two lines lost formation and a mêlée ensued. The two flagships, *Royal Charles* and *Endracht*, fought each other, and James was lucky to escape when a chain-shot killed many of those around him. Opdam was killed when *Endracht* suddenly blew up, and command devolved upon Vice Admiral Jan Evertsen. Assisted by Tromp, he extricated his ships and withdrew towards the Netherlands. The Dutch had lost 32 ships, but only nine were brought in as prizes by the English. The English lost only one ship, taken early in the engagement, and were clearly the victors, although the Dutch fleet was far from being completely beaten.

Benbow: West Indies, 1702

On 19 August, shortly after the outbreak of the War of the Spanish Succession, Vice Admiral John Benbow, commanding in the West Indies with seven ships of the line, found Captain Ducassé with a French mixed squadron of eleven ships off Santa Marta (now Cartagena, Colombia). After an initial brief engagement, a pursuit ensued, with Benbow and his flagship *Breda* supported only by *Ruby* and *Falmouth*: the rest of the squadron stood aloof during the following five days while Benbow tried to bring the enemy to battle. The explanation for his subordinates' disobedience was a mixture of Benbow's relatively low social background coupled with his fiery temper and outspoken criticism of his captains, who thus felt no loyalty to their commander-in-chief. On the 24th, Benbow was finally able to inflict heavy damage on one of the French ships, but attempts to take her, led in person by the Admiral, failed, and Benbow was badly wounded by a chain-shot. The French were able to tow their ship to safety, and the other senior captains refused to obey the Admiral's order to continue the chase. When the fleet returned to Jamaica, Benbow died of his wounds. Two captains who had not engaged were court-martialled and shot, and another was cashiered. The sad affair only became famous because of Benbow's great courage.

Rooke: Vigo, 1702

The Spanish silver fleet of seventeen ships, escorted by a powerful French squadron of similar size under Chateaurenault, put into Vigo, where it was assailed by about 37 vessels of Sir George Rooke's 70-strong Anglo-Dutch fleet sent against Spain at the outbreak of the war. The fleet included twenty troopships carrying 4,000 Dutch soldiers. The treasure ships were also protected by a boom and shore batteries. After a fierce fight, the boom was breached by the British *Torbay* and the Dutch *De Zeven Provincien*. As Sir Cloudesley Shovell's flagship *Association* gave covering fire to Dutch troops who were landed to capture the forts, the squadron entered the harbour to engage the enemy in a fierce battle. Chateaurenault gave the order to burn the ships rather than give them up, but some eleven treasure ships seem to have been captured with their cargoes of silver. All of the French and Spanish ships were captured or destroyed. Allied casualties were light.

Rooke: Gibraltar, 1704

On 24 July, Rooke assaulted Gibraltar with an Anglo-Dutch force of marines, who suffered 277 casualties, including 60 dead, despite heavy covering fire from eighteen English warships led by Rooke's flagship, *Royal Catherine*. The Rock surrendered the following day. 'Gibraltar' remains the Royal Marines' only battle honour.

Hawke: Finisterre, 1747

For eight weeks in the autumn of 1747, Rear Admiral Hawke, with fourteen of the line, patrolled off Finisterre, waiting for an expected French convoy. On 14 October he found it, escorted by only eight enemy ships of the line. In a heroic covering battle, the French had all but two of their covering force taken by the British, but the convoy escaped. The ships involved received the battle honour 'Ushant' to distinguish the action from Anson's earlier in the year (see page 71).

Boscawen: Lagos, 1759

Admiral Edward Boscawen had been blockading De La Clue's fleet at Toulon but had to go to Gibraltar for refit. This allowed the French to escape, and Boscawen gave chase as soon as he heard of the sortie. On 18 August off Portugal he sighted some units of the enemy fleet, the rest having taken refuge in Cadiz. A French 74 was taken, but Boscawen had to transfer his flag because of the damage to HMS *Namur*. During the transfer he was forced to repair a damaged and leaky boat with his wig. Overnight, four French ships of the line took refuge in Lagos bay, pursued by the British. De La Clue's flagship went aground and was abandoned and burnt; the

Admiral died of his wounds. A French 74 suffered a similar fate after being deliberately wrecked, and another 74 and a 64 were taken. Half of De La Clue's original force of ten of the line had been destroyed or captured.

Rodney: St. Vincent, 1780

Better known as 'The Moonlight Battle', this earlier Battle of Cape St. Vincent took place during the War of American Independence when, following Spain's entry into the war against Britain in 1779, Admiral Sir George Rodney, flying his flag in HMS *Sandwich*, was dispatched with a fleet of seventeen other ships of the line and five frigates to escort a convoy sent to relieve Gibraltar and Minorca, Britain's major bases in the Western Mediterranean and under siege by the Spanish. On 8 January 1780, 300 miles off Finisterre, the British force met a Spanish convoy of seventeen vessels escorted by five men of war: all the Spanish ships were taken. Just over a week later, on 16 January, off Cape St. Vincent, Rodney's force sighted a squadron of eleven Spanish ships of the line and two frigates commanded by Admiral Don Juan de Langara. Rodney signalled for a general chase and tried to cut the enemy off from making back to Spain. The battle began in the late afternoon and continued in bright moonlight, but in increasingly stormy weather, until

1400 the following morning. Six Spanish ships of the line were taken, two later having to be abandoned, and the *Santo Domingo* exploded. Rodney's success relieved Gibraltar and secured Britain's position in the western Mediterranean.

Duncan: Camperdown, 1797

During the summer of 1797, Admiral Adam Duncan was sent to blockade the fleet of the Batavian Republic (as the Netherlands had been renamed after conquest by revolutionary France). The mutiny at the Nore forced Duncan to simulate the presence of a larger fleet, but by October his force was back to full strength. However, he was forced to make for Yarmouth roads to refit and take on stores. This enticed the Dutch out. Duncan rejoined the small squadron shadowing the enemy on 11 October, and battle was joined, sixteen British ships of the line and eight frigates confronting eighteen Dutch ships of the line and seven frigates. Fighting was very fierce for more than three hours, but the British had the best of the engagement and ten Dutch ships struck, including *Vrijheid*, flagship of Vice Admiral de Winter, the Bata-

Below: The Battle of Camperdown. Engraving by Dodd.

Left: The morning during the Battle of Camperdown. Engraving by Dodd.

Below left: Duncan. Portrait by Sir Joshua Reynolds.

ranean Fleet under Lord Exmouth, supported by a Dutch squadron, offered the *deys* (governors) of Tunis, Tripoli and Algiers treaties prohibiting the taking of Christian slaves. Algiers refused, and a punitive bombardment was carried out on 27 August to force compliance. Rocket boats were used in addition to more conventional ships and gunboats led by the flagship *Queen Charlotte*. Rocket troops and sappers and miners were landed. Their combined activities destroyed the Dey's fortifications and he gave up his studded scimitar in token of surrender. He also released 1,200 of his Christian slaves.

Codrington: Navarino, 1827

During the Greek War of Independence, an international fleet was formed by Britain, France and Russia to enforce the Treaty of London, which demanded that the Turks agree to an armistice and that the supporting Egyptian army withdraw. The fleet assembled off Navarino under the command of Admiral Sir Edward Codrington. He had been told to use force only as a last resort but was drawn into confrontation on 20 October by reports of atrocities ashore. With twelve ships of the line, eight frigates and six smaller ships, he sailed into Navarino harbour and into the midst of the Turkish-Egyptian fleet of seven of the line, fifteen frigates and 43 smaller vessels. Shooting broke out, and a general action ensued, which lasted for four hours. The Turks lost a ship of the line, twelve frigates and 22 other ships, as well as suffering 4,000 casualties. Allied casualties were 696, but no ships were lost. Codrington was recalled, but his victory was a factor in the final ejection of the Turks from Greece.

vian commander-in-chief, which was taken by Duncan's flagship, *Venerable*. The prizes were so heavily damaged that two sank on the way home, and none could be used again. Duncan's ability both to handle his mutinous crews and defeat an unusually capable opponent was noteworthy.

Exmouth: Algiers, 1816

With the end of the Napoleonic War, attention turned to suppressing the Barbary pirates. The Mediter-

APPENDIX B:
SPLENDID ISOLATION IN STONE AND BRICK
by Evan Davies (with Eric Grove)

'We have stood alone in that which is called isolation – our splendid isolation, as one of our colonial friends was good enough to call it.' – George Goschen on 26 February 1896.[1]

I will never forget my first sight of Britannia Royal Naval College. It was a really beautiful August day. The sun was shining from what seemed a deeper blue sky than usual, with perfect white clouds. The grass was green, and as I drove through the morning roads of Devon, I was more keyed up than I could express. I needed a job badly. I had found one, apparently. Now I was heading to see my place of work for the first time, and to meet, other than in the curious anonymity of the interview room, my future bosses.

I had never seen the College before, not even in a photograph. I had no idea what to expect, except that it was going to be formidable. Clearly the Royal Navy was not going to turn young men (for this was before the Women's Royal Naval Service Officers' Training Course came to Dartmouth) into officers in the tradition of St. Vincent, Nelson and Cunningham in some inconspicuous shed. Dartmouth was one of those words which had a special meaning to a Briton with an interest in service matters.

The road from Totnes to Halwell and Dartmouth seemed a very long one to me. I was anxious not to start my new career with a 'black' for being late. Fortunately I did not at that time know that my two bosses were a sometime colonel in the Royal Signals and a sometime captain in the Royal Marines, neither of whom was very good at suffering fools. At last I came to the top of the hill on the slope of which Townstal is built, above the newer town of Dartmouth nestling along the west bank of the Dart. Still no College. Down the hill. Still no college. Somehow I missed the small bit of the College you can see from the top of College Way. Perhaps I was concentrating on the problem of College Way's steepness in the borrowed and battered old farm Land Rover I was driving and of whose brakes I was not entirely confident. Then a

road sign for BRNC: left through a gateway, which in those less security-conscious days was without a sentry, and I received the full force of the College, from what all agree is its best angle.

The grass of the hill was very green and very well cut. The Bracknell brick was very orange, the granite and Portland stone were very clean. Aston Webb's original façade, uncluttered by the monstrous First World War addition of D Block because of the low angle of view, stood clear and confident against this hugely blue sky. No one, not even a very civilian would-be lecturer, could miss this message. Here was pride, propaganda and pomp writ in huge letters across the join between earth and sky. I was lost.

Actually I was *very* lost. The College was on leave, and there was no one about to tell me how to get into this magnificent pile. Some hours, it seemed, of stumbling brought me to an open door, tucked discretely at the back, and into a maze of empty, and gleaming parquet-floored corridors. Eventually, I found a tall, distinguished man in a beautifully tailored suit who courteously showed me to the door of the Director of Studies' office. I arrived five minutes ahead of time, and so I had accidentally achieved a 'pass' in the test of naval time, which is five minutes ahead of all else. I knocked, entered, and was very shortly taken next door to meet the Captain in his office, a tall distinguished man in a beautifully tailored suit.

The experience of entering Dartmouth can be shattering. A few weeks later I was walking up the hill from the main college towards Hawke Division at the end of my first day on the College staff with a young man who was completing his first day in the Navy. We walked in companionable, confused silence, both tired as the dusk of a September day fell around us. Just as I was about to turn off into the masters' hostel, where my cabin was, he turned to me and formulated, perfectly, the effect of the day upon him and me: 'You know, sir, I am thinking of becoming a pacifist.' He was stunned. I was stunned. But we were both learning. I knew it was a cabin, not a bedroom.

And he was the first person ever to call me 'Sir'.

The College stands on its hill, like the statement of some eternal verity, overlooking the estuary of the Dart and the ancient port of Dartmouth. From here part of Richard I's fleet sailed to the crusades in the Holy Land. From *Dertemouthe* sailed Chaucer's archetypal seaman. And from Dartmouth sailed part of the fleet for that Crusade in Europe in 1944.

Consciously Sir Aston Webb sought to put a millennium and more of naval activity into the very structure of the College and to condition young people to an awareness of the tradition to which they should be proud heirs. The Navy's article of faith is strongly proclaimed from the front of the College:

'IT IS UPON THE NAVY, UNDER THE GOOD PROVIDENCE OF GOD, THAT THE SAFETY, HONOUR AND WELFARE OF THIS REALM DO CHIEFLY ATTEND.'

Variations of this proud statement appear in the successive naval discipline acts since the first in 1661. Whether it is compatible with naval discipline and the drill regulations for young officers, as they stand on the parade ground to be inspected at Divisions to look up high enough to read this statement, I could not say, but as I have been frequently assured that they have counted all the windows and window panes while parading, I feel sure that the message reaches them.

Actually this statement of fundamental truths is but one of the tensions the College represents. Indeed the very self-confidence that the college seems to embody was less secure than the stone and brick on such a site seem to imply. The College is built around this huge sweep of history, yet it is less than one hundred years old. The College opened in September 1905, to carry forward a new scheme for the training and education of young officers, the Selborne Scheme. Sir John Fisher, the architect of this scheme, saw it as revolutionary, and it was opposed by all those who saw themselves as the embodiment of tradition. Since then the battle between the differing concepts of naval officership have been fought endlessly; the place of education, of training, and of socialisation have been argued about and changes made with bewildering frequency.

However, to understand the College it is necessary to go back a good way. Navies have always depended upon seamanship, but for much of the Middle Ages that skill was subordinate, socially and hierarchically, to the military skills of soldiering. Ships became warships largely by the importation into them of some weapons and platforms for their operation, and of a squad of soldiers, under their own officers to fight them. The military captain was likely to be the social as well as military superior of the ship's master. With the arrival of the heavy gun as the ship's main weapon, the skills of the soldier declined in relative importance and the navigational skills of the seaman became more important. As the Royal (or Cromwellian) Navy emerged as a permanent institution with a permanent officer corps, so the recognition came that the merger of the two types of officer implied a need for definite skills among naval officers. The Royal Navy, unlike the British Army, has almost from its first days as a permanent institution insisted upon a test of competence for officers before commissioning them. The Royal Proclamation of 18 December 1677 set out the ground rules:

'And our further will and pleasure is, that the qualifications without which no person shall from henceforward be accounted capable of the employment of lieutenant in any of our ships be...
1. To have spent so much time actually at sea... in our service... as... shall... amount to 3 entire years at least...
2. Nor be under 20 years of age...
3. To produce good certificates under the hand of the several commanders under whom he hath served, testifying the several voyages he hath been employed in, with his sobriety, diligence, obedience to order, application to the study and practice of the Art of Navigation... and his strict performance of the duty of midshipman for one year...
4. To produce a like certificate, under the hand of at least one of our Principal Officers and Commanders... as also of two other commanders... jointly signifying their being (upon examination of the said person...) fully satisfied in his ability to judge and perform the duty of an able seaman and midshipman, and of his having attained to a sufficient degree of knowledge in the Theory of Navigation capacitating him thereto.[2]

Charles II and Pepys did not accompany this regulation by any training institutions. They created an apprenticeship scheme, and that is the way that almost all naval officers joined and were trained until 1857. As has been pointed out, 'There were obvious defects in such a system. For, although an alert and observant lad might learn the rudiments of seamanship, his opportunities for improving his general education,

Above: *Britannia* and *Hindustan* at Dartmouth. (Reproduced by courtesy of Philip Jarrett)

and for mastering the essential arts of his profession... were uncertain.'[3] These defects may have been part of the motivation for the decision in 1729 to establish the Royal Navy's first officer shore-training establishment, the Royal Academy, at Portsmouth. However, there was also probably a wish to increase the Admiralty's control over who might join the Navy as a potential officer. The Academy opened in the summer of 1733 in a building which still exists in Portsmouth Dockyard. Its students were recruited on an unashamedly *élitist* basis from the sons of nobility and gentry, and took a course of at least two and no more than three years in writing, arithmetic, drawing, gunnery, fortification, other 'useful parts of the mathematics', French, dancing and the exercise of the firelock. The second year at the Academy also included a considerable practical element: one afternoon they were to be shown the manner of rigging a ship or do boatwork, or do useful jobs about the dockyard with the Master Attendant; another afternoon they were to be instructed by the Master Shipwright.

The old college did produce some distinguished officers, like Jane Austen's two sailor brothers, Francis and Charles, Thomas Byam Martin and Philip Broke. However, the Royal Academy was not an unalloyed success: the students were an ineffectively disciplined lot, and it was not generally the favoured route into the Navy. It was shut down in 1806, reformed and reopened in 1808, as the Royal Naval College, and survived until 1837.

From 1837 until 1857 the Royal Navy went back to sending all potential officers straight to sea. In 1857 things changed. In 1854 HMS *Illustrious*, an old two-decked line-of-battle ship[4] was moored in Haslar Creek as a floating training ship for boy seamen, 'Jemmy Graham's novices' as they were called. Her captain was Robert Harris, who had not himself been to the old college, who came to believe that a similar institution for the training of young officers would be an improvement. His initial first efforts failed, but he persuaded the Admiralty to allow him to put his son, the future Admiral Sir Robert Hastings Harris, to do the course in *Illustrious* before going to sea. Harris junior was entered in the books of HMS *Illustrious* on 10 January 1856. On 23 February 1857, only six weeks after he completed his course, the Admiralty issued a circular making the *Illustrious* course general from August 1857. In November 1856 Captain Harris had been arguing that the desirable ship for the new establishment would be a three-decker, but it was not until 1 January 1859 that the Royal Navy's fourth HMS *Britannia* was substituted for *Illustrious*.[5] Soon it became clear that Haslar Creek was not really a very suitable place for the *Britannia*. Towards the end of 1861 the decision was taken to move her to Portland, and she sailed there on 7 February 1862, escorted by HMS *Trafalgar*.

'If plenty of open air and a generous supply of ozone were particularly in request, Portland is a very good place to go to; but other considerations will naturally crop up in selecting an anchorage for a training ship. But for the breakwater, there would be practically no harbour at all. The breakwater, though it certainly forms a shelter against any sweep of the swell in the channel, cannot in any degree break the force of an easterly gale; and even the Chesil Bank does not modify to any great extent the fury of winter gales from the south-west, though it ensures more or less smooth water; while northerly gales sweep across Weymouth Bay with unrestrained violence. As a port of assembly for a large fleet it is... admirably suited; but they have to take their chance of being occasionally cut off from communication with the shore for a day or two. There was no possibility of acquiring ground for playing fields...' [6]

Portland's unsuitability as a place for the ship soon became accepted, and in September 1863 her second Captain was ordered to look for a more suitable place to put her. He selected Dartmouth, and on 29 September 1863 the tugs *Geyser* and *Prospero* towed her from Portland to Dartmouth. She took up her moorings off Sandquay about 0900 on 30 September 1863.

Above: HMS *Britannia* and HMS *Trafalgar* at Portland *c.*1862.

By 1864, *Britannia* was too small for the number of cadets which rose sharply in that year, and then fell away, and in that year she was joined by HMS *Hindostan*[7]. The old *Britannia* was by 1869 too small because better accommodation was required and more studies[8] were needed, so in July she was replaced by HMS *Prince of Wales*[9] which was renamed *Britannia*.

Despite this improvement, the problems created by crowding 200–300 boys into two static wooden ships still caused concern, and in 1874 a Committee was appointed chaired by Rear Admiral E. B. Rice to look into the health and general training of cadets. In its report of 1875 it recommended that a college building should be constructed on shore, and in July of the following year another committee, on the acquisition of a site for a Naval Cadets' College, met under the chairmanship of Admiral G. G. Wellesley. It considered 32 sites, not only at Dartmouth and Kingswear but on the Isle of Wight and Southampton Water, at Gosport, Hayling Island, Portsmouth, Weymouth,

Devonport, Milford Haven and even Westward Ho! Advertisements were placed in the newspapers and both local pride and hopes for financial gain were enlisted to obtain and evaluate proposals. The dispute became public and rather acrimonious, the front-runners emerging as Wootton in the Isle of Wight and Mount Boon [*sic*] at Dartmouth. In the end the Wellesley Committee came down heavily in favour of the latter, the location of the existing *Britannia* playing fields. It was a site 'admirable... in all respects, possessing every requisite, the only drawback being the large mount of rainfall and a certain amount of inconvenience in the movements of a training vessel without the use of steam'.

Nothing happened. The exact reasons are unclear, but expense was probably the main culprit. In the 'Dark Ages of the Victorian Navy' economy was the watchword and the decision of the Prince of Wales to send his sons to the existing *Britannia* seemed a vote of confidence in the old ship. Criticism continued and yet another Committee, in 1885, raised local hackles by recommending the removal of training to the Solent. This proposal was forgotten when further public grumbles about *Britannia*'s 'gaol-like' atmosphere and discipline problems resurrected the College idea in the mid-1890s. Naval expenditure had regained popularity, and the Admiralty was committing itself to ambitious programmes funded by an almost profligate series of financial loans. Preliminary discussion of the *Britannia* establishment, sick quarters and so on took place at Board of Admiralty level on 15 November 1895 together with proposals to revise the existing training scheme. When presenting the Naval Estimates in March 1896, Mr George Goschen, the First Lord of the Admiralty, announced that the decision to build a college at Dartmouth had been taken and that the scheme of training offered, first in the ship and then in the new shore establishment, would be altered to four shorter terms of four months each. Cadets would enter at between 14½ and 15½, a year older than previously. The instruction to begin negotiations to buy the land for the new College had in fact been given in February, and Treasury clearance for the expenditure was requested. The chosen site at Mount Boone was already used for the *Britannia*'s playing fields and the kennels for the beagle pack, but it would now have to be purchased outright. The Raleigh Estate, to which it belonged, was in Chancery. The negotiations soon became complex and difficult. By October they had effectively broken down and the Admiralty began to consider compulsory purchase for £25,000. It hoped that the legislation under which the college was to be funded, the Naval Works Loan Act of 1895, gave it the required powers, but legal advice was to the contrary and the Defence Act of 1842 had to be resorted to instead. By December the land for purchase had been marked out, but acquisition was still held up because of disputes over Dartmouth's status as a fortress or garrison town. Judgement was not finally given in favour of the Admiralty until 13 November 1897, and the owners' representatives, seeing the futility of further resistance, became more cooperative in order to secure the best possible price. The final settlement seems to have been made at the end of June 1898.

The site chosen had certain obvious advantages, especially in terms of 'straight-line' decisions, but it also had some very obvious disadvantages. The hill was fairly steep, and it would be impossible to produce a level area for the building. Much work would have to be done to produce any sort of flat area, save rather higher up the hill than the college was actually built. This could only be done by sacrificing the existing playing fields. Getting building materials to the bottom of the hill by water or train to Kingswear was no problem, but an inclined plane had to be built to the top of the site to carry them up to the hospital, now Hawke Division, and the main buildings.

Aston Webb[10] was chosen as architect, and work began on the terraces that year: not until later were tenders requested for the constructions of the buildings themselves. On 18 April 1900, the Admiralty accepted the submission from Higgs and Hill who estimated they could build the College in three and a half years at a cost of £220,600. Work proceeded through 1901, a year that saw a particularly serious influenza epidemic in the ships, with the death of two cadets. This may have led to the work on the new sick quarters being speeded up, for they soon began to take shape ahead of the rest of the College. By March 1902 the main building had also begun to rise, and on the 7th of that month King Edward VII laid the foundation stone. The new hospital took its first patient at the beginning of the autumn term.

The original new College, as designed in 1899, was much smaller than the present structure. It consisted of the captain's house, the chapel, now the Church of England Chapel, the long main corridor of the building, the Messroom, now known as the Senior Gunroom, and then apparently called Nelson, the wardroom block, and the modern A, B and O blocks. However, the back portion of the present O Block, where the library, fleet display room and science laboratories are now located, were not part of the original building; nor were the Sky Studies, the second storey at the back of the original O block behind the quarter-deck.

The new College was a very literal representation of the old ships. The new College was arranged in multiples of four, designed to accommodate four entries of cadets. They would, as in the old ship, lead separate lives. There would be separate dormitory spaces for them, in what are now known as A and B blocks. There would be separate recreation spaces for each term. These are the old gunrooms along the front of the original college, now used for other purposes, but still clearly marked by the four bay windows that accent the front on the ground storey. There were even four tables in the Messroom, and there usually are, even to this day.

Ironically, well before the College was finished, the four-entry system was abandoned, as from 1902 the fourth term was spent in training cruisers at sea, not the old wooden ships in the Dart. This seems to have been a further response to the pressure of numbers, as the Navy continued to grow. The new College was somewhat more flexible. There was space to push more cadets into the large dormitories, which there had not been in the mess-decks of the old ships. By 1914, the College was coping with terms of more than 100, as opposed to the 75 for which it was designed.

It is easy to see Aston Webb's structure as splendid assertion of that massive naval superiority which had given Britain and her empire security through *Pax Britannica* for so much of the nineteenth century. In a very important sense this vision is true, and, it seems to me, that is certainly the intention behind the original building. Its propagandistic and didactic purpose is obvious. However, there is a clear tension between appearances and the reality for the Navy's, and the Empire's, situation in 1896 or 1902 or 1905. In early March 1896, the Board of Admiralty took the decision to build Britain's second Naval Academy. In 1897, at the Diamond Jubilee Fleet Review, the Prince of Wales had reviewed, on his mother's behalf, the greatest fleet in the world, asserting the dominance of the seas, and announcing, yet again, to all and sundry how Britain wished her place in the world to be understood. It is easy to see the new Naval College which was built as a result of the Admiralty's decision as a version of the Diamond Jubilee Fleet Review built from stone and brick. The College was not so much a 'stone frigate' as a 'stone fleet' or a 'stone strategic posture'. In part that view is fair. It is hard to imagine that so confident a building could have been built in the 1950s, let alone the 1990s. The Royal Naval College is and always has been propaganda. But BRNC is propaganda on a number of levels.

A fortnight before the decision to build the College was taken in March 1896, the First Lord of the Admiralty, George Goschen, had, in a speech at Lewes in Sussex, used the phrase 'splendid isolation' for the first time. Splendid isolation has a wonderfully arrogant ring, but again appearances are deceptive. Goschen was using splendid isolation as part of an argument for increasing naval estimates, for he was worried about the extent to which Britain stood isolated in a hostile world. Naval estimates were rising fast. They had risen by nearly 22 per cent from 1893–4 to 1894–5 and then by 13.5 per cent in 1895–6. Goschen wanted another rise, by nearly 11 per cent, for 1896–7. Britain was feeling less secure.

The new Naval college was also the institutionalisation of the failure of the strategy implicit in the Northbrook and Spencer programmes. The Navy and the nation had been woken by the scares of the 1880s from the slumber of the Dark Ages of the Victorian Navy – the 1870s – to realise that its impressive advantage, held since the early eighteenth century, of owning more than 50 per cent of the world's major warships had gone, and that rivals were growing stronger. The spirit of the 1890s was very *Navalist*. Mahan had ridden a wave of opinion which saw the Navy as Britain's formula for greatness, and wished to develop the same weapons. The United States Navy had risen from its post-1865 torpor and was developing fast. Admiral Togo[11] and the Japanese Navy were to show exactly what the new navies could do, at Tsushima. Britain's old enmities with France and Russia were yet unsettled. Indeed, as work on the terraces of the new college began in 1898, the Fashoda Incident was to bring the United Kingdom and France close to war. The new German Navy was just, in 1896, beginning its expansion: Tirpitz became State Secretary for the Navy in 1897. Britain had responded to the new threat, as to previous nineteenth-century scares, by building newer, bigger and better warships. However, unlike former scares and similar responses, the strategy had not worked. The huge

Above: A view from the hills overlooking the college. Note the *Britannia* moored to the right.

expansion of the 1888–9 and 1893 programmes had not persuaded rivals to give up the race. The Royal Navy would have to remain at an expanded and expanding level for the foreseeable future. The temporary expedient of cramming more and more students into the training ships would no longer do: in the spring of 1881 the number of students in the old ships had been about 129; by March 1896 there were at least 287. This was intolerable for the cadets, and something had to be done to ensure that the new Navy would be officered. The new College was clearly designed to accommodate those sorts of numbers.

However, even before the new College was complete, another fundamental reform was introduced. On Christmas Day 1902, the 'Selborne Memorandum'[12] was published. Under the new system all officers of the Executive and Engineer branches of the Royal Navy, and of the Royal Marines, were to enter the Service between the ages of twelve and thirteen and be trained on exactly the same system until passing for the rank of Sub Lieutenant at the age of nineteen or twenty. The public stress of the new scheme was on the importance of study for the creation of a competent officer for the new technological era.

The real power behind the new scheme was not the First Lord but Admiral Sir John Fisher, the Second Sea Lord. He wanted to put the proposals into effect as soon as possible. Britannia Royal Naval College was

still far from ready and was unsuitable for the new scheme without modification. The new scheme would more than double the number of cadets from roughly 225–250 a year under the old scheme, meaning the College had originally to accommodate about 300 to 330 cadets at one time. The new scheme would require more officers to be educated as the College was now to accommodate Engineers and Marines as well as the Executive branch officers of the ships, and it would now need to house twelve entries, making nearly 1,000 cadets. This was done by building the present C block running back behind the chapel on the east side of the existing works at Dartmouth, with space for two extra terms in a single large Gunroom.

More difficult was the fact that the new College would not be ready in time, so before the end of 1902 plans had been made for a new college in the grounds of Queen Victoria's house at Osborne on the Isle of Wight. Construction began in March 1903. Within six months the new institution was opened by the King and its first term joined in September. They and their successors were to spend six terms (two years), at

Osborne, before passing on for a similar period to Dartmouth.

As the revised College took shape during 1904, it was decided not to open it until September of the following year, when the first new-scheme term would be ready to move from Osborne. The old scheme had had to be kept going in order to keep a steady flow of officers into the service, and when the College opened, there would still be two terms in the ships. There would need to have been at least two further terms of the old entry in order to maintain a continuous flow of cadets into the fleet.[13]

Captain Cross of *Britannia* assumed the old-scheme cadets, and his staff, would transfer up the hill to the new College that had, after all, been built for them. He was soon disabused. The creators of the 'new scheme' wanted the College to maintain as few of the old *Britannia*'s traditions as possible. The *Britannia*'s teaching, which emphasised cramming for examinations, was anathema to educational progressives such as Professor J. A. Ewing, who had been appointed Director of Naval Education from Cambridge in 1903, and Cyril Ashford, first headmaster of Osborne and headmaster designate of Dartmouth. They wished the new College to emphasise the responsibility of the pupil to educate himself. They were joined by Rosslyn Wemyss, Captain of Osborne, in stressing the need for a 'fresh start'. As Wemyss and Ewing put it in the summer of 1904, 'the development of the College should proceed with the least possible influence on the part of the old system of training.' Ewing was even stronger in a slightly later paper: 'I am very anxious to see that Dartmouth College develops on entirely new lines without *Britannia* interference or even influence.'

Opening with three *Britannia* terms to only one moved up from Osborne would mean that the scene would be dominated by the older boys, prejudiced against the new order. Captain Cross was totally outgunned in this bureaucratic engagement and, supported by Selborne, the Admiralty concocted a radical plan to deal with the problem. When the new College opened, the third old-scheme term would depart to the cruiser *Isis* in the normal way. The other two terms would also be loaded into cruisers to be taken to a foreign port to complete the work they would have done in *Britannia* or the new College. HMS *Eclipse* would take the second term and *Highflyer* the first. Various sites were evaluated, all in warmer climates than Britain's, so that money could be saved on heating. Gibraltar, Malta, Alexandria, Las Palmas and the West Indies were all considered, and the choice eventually fell on Bermuda. So the *Britannia* contribution to the new College was kept to a minimum, and Wemyss, who left Osborne in the spring of 1905, was given the supervision of both Colleges to make sure the Admiralty's intentions were carried out.

Cross left *Britannia* at the end of the spring and was replaced by Captain Goodenough, who would be directly responsible for the change-over. Commander Brand and nine other officers would also be from the *Britannia*, but almost half the initial naval staff would be new. Although the penultimate 'old scheme' term would arrive at the same time as the ex-Osborne cadets, it was the former who would be outnumbered by the latter, rather than vice-versa. Although the old-scheme cadets would be nearly a year older, the new-scheme cadets would have two years of experience of the naval system and would be in a good position to dictate customs to the new College. All the cadets would be taught by a new teaching staff in an institution firmly dedicated to the new scheme. The *Britannia* name might remain for a short time and, indeed, rather contrary to Ewing's wishes, the administration of the new College would owe a great deal to that of the old ships. Nevertheless, a remarkable amount had been done to ensure that September 1905 would indeed mark that 'clean break' with the past that Ewing and Ashford desired so much.

Britannia Royal Naval College opened at last on 14 September 1905. The new building, 'a cross between a workhouse and a stable', as one critic had denounced it, stood out rather harshly in red and white on Mount Boone. Opinion on Aston Webb's achievement remains divided. Pevsner is mildly carping:

'In the picture of twentieth century Dartmouth the dominant motif is no longer the castle or the harbour but [the] enormous college buildings stretching out along the hill... They are of brick and stone on a revised and camped-up eighteenth-century tradition, not successful as an ensemble, because the Edwardian-Palladian motifs are not of sufficient bombast to fit the scale adopted. The tower is not high and broad enough for a distant view, and the side cupolas are niggling. The towers at the far ends are far too small too – the same mistake as made by Webb in the Victoria and Albert Museum... In the middle, stretching out behind and at right-angles to the main block, **is** the great hall. This has an open timber roof with traverse stone arches.'[14]

From which, I suppose, one concludes that Pevsner or his researchers had not entered the building and had certainly not looked at it carefully. Indeed it would appear that there is nothing in that account which could not have been gained by looking at the published plans in *The Builder* or some similar journal, which were not exactly executed, and glancing up from the town. Another commentator, who certainly *had* entered the building, for he was a cadet there for nearly four years, described it thus: 'To the right the Captain's house, a handsome building in red brick with white facings, imparting, as indeed did the whole College to those who viewed it for the first time, an air, as of marzipan, of costly edibility.

'The architects, faced no doubt by the conflicting opinions and absolute ignorance in matters artistic of their lordships, had emerged from their long ordeal with credit, producing a building which possessed dignity and, at the same time, the geometrical virtues of those pictures on a child's brick set. This, one felt, was precisely what a grateful government, whose taste was still Victorian, not yet Edwardian, might have offered Nelson had he lived a century later. Here was all the magnificence of Blenheim Place and something of the order and austerity of Wellington Barracks.'[15]

The College symbolised the new approach to naval education that Fisher and his lieutenants were imposing on a doubting service. In fact it effectively disguised the conservatism and poverty of invention that lay at the heart of the Selborne Scheme. Fisher had inherited a whole series of personnel problems when he came to be Second Naval Lord in June 1902. Many of them were to do with ratings' concerns, and are not relevant here. However, the crucial officer issues, apart from a serious and growing shortage of numbers of officers, especially of middle and junior officers, were the worrying social fissures in the officer corps. The most critical of these was between the dominant and socially and professionally privileged Executive branch officers and the non-military branches, especially the Engineers. The Navy was the target at this time, and indeed had been the target for a good many years, of pressure and protest from the professional engineering lobby within and without the service. That Fisher recognised a problem existed can clearly be seen in the memorandum he wrote while Commander-in-Chief Mediterranean Fleet in

February 1902, just after he had learned that he was to become an exceptionally senior Second Naval Lord.[16] This problem the Selborne Scheme deliberately did not address. Rather, Fisher was seeking to abolish the problem, by ensuring that the officers of the Royal Navy would all be drawn from the same social group. In other words, Fisher was not seeking to solve the 'Engineer Problem'. He was seeking to abolish the old style engineer, and replace him with something more 'socially acceptable'.

Fisher was really arguing a much older but still live case.[17] His view quite clearly was that naval officership was a matter of experience, character and conditioning rather than an intellectual pursuit. He was opposed to shore-based training. He wanted officers *in ships*, learning by doing. He regarded engineering as something akin to machine minding, exactly the opposite of the view the engineering lobby tended to take. Therefore he was not interested in the intellectual content of the new colleges. Originally, Fisher seems to have been content that the extemporised college in the Isle of Wight should be in an old iron-clad, HMS *Sultan*, in the Medina Estuary.

Fisher took the view that the education of officers could best be done by the practical elements of naval engineering and then by spending long periods attending to the crises in the engine room of high-revving reciprocating machinery. Fisher thought the very unreliability of naval engines could be turned to educational, training and conditioning advantage. He subsequently claimed much credit for the educational reforms of the new scheme, but they seem to have been foisted upon him, largely by senior academic engineers who wanted schoolboys to have more general education at the new colleges, and less engineering.

In September 1905, the College contained only two terms, the 63 survivors of the original 73 new-scheme cadets who had joined Osborne in September 1903, called the St. Vincents, and the 42 Hawkes, who, as old-schemers, were new entries. The term system kept the two groups almost entirely apart: there was no doubt who were regarded as the most important.

In the summer of 1907 the College finally began to operate as intended, with six new-scheme terms, St. Vincent, Drake, Blake, Hawke, Grenville and Rodney, the last two sharing 'C' Block. Each term was divided into 'watches', each of which was, in turn, subdivided into classes. 'Port A' was the most advanced class, while

'Starboard B' the least. The College now contained 359 cadets; the maximum capacity was rated at more than 400. Even so, there was too much pressure on the teaching accommodation of the original design. This situation was improved a little by the opening in 1907 of a new one-storey block with five additional studies and a reference library (the present E Block), and the building of a third storey at the back of O block, the present sky studies, which provided additional class rooms and office space. Naturally the staff also grew, and at the beginning of 1908, when the *Britannia* was dropped even from the College title, Captain T. D. W. Napier of HMS *Espiegle*, Royal Naval College, Dartmouth, was commanding a naval staff that had increased from 20 to 29. Ashford now controlled 26 masters and four naval instructors.

The education offered by Ashford and his masters seems to have been notable both for its quality and novelty. The mathematics and science, supplemented by considerable practical engineering instruction, combined to create a grounding in applied science unique in contemporary secondary education. It even produced one winner of the Nobel Prize for Physics, Professor Lord Blackett, who entered Dartmouth as a Hawke in 1912. The humanities were not forgotten. Indeed, the attempt to develop the intellects of the boys through the medium of Modern Languages, History and English rather than the Classics was as novel as the technological emphasis of the Royal Naval College Course. It is, perhaps, not too much to say that, in the context of its time, the early Dartmouth was one of the most progressive schools in the land.

As the Royal Navy expanded, the terms tended to increase in size, with 70 cadets in each becoming the norm. Among them was the Prince of Wales, later King Edward VIII and the Duke of Windsor. He joined as an Exmouth in 1909, this name having replaced Rodney. Prince Albert, later King George VI, arrived as a Grenville in 1911. The demand for officers was still increasing and the Selborne Scheme was not producing enough engineers. In 1913, a committee chaired by a former Captain of RNC Dartmouth, Rear Admiral Hugh Evan-Thomas, recommended the creation of the Special Entry for boys who had completed their education at public school. They would be trained separately from the cadets of the Selborne Scheme. It was also planned to increase the entries at the Royal Naval Colleges to an average of 110 per term. This was almost double the original numbers, so extra accommodation would be required at both Colleges. A new block was therefore projected at Dartmouth to house three new large gunrooms, an extra dining hall and dormitories for the junior terms. Its construction allowed much needed extra laboratories, classrooms and a masters' common room also to be added. Construction began in the summer of 1914 to the designs of Aston Webb's offices in 19 Queen Anne's Gate. It appears that Aston Webb played no part in the actual design. Certainly the inspiration of the original buildings was lacking in the new block which, much to the original architect's regret, ruined the roof line of the old College when seen from afar.

The First World War rudely interrupted life at Dartmouth. The Admiralty wanted the cadets to provide midshipmen for the older ships of the Reserve Fleet, and the boys took part in the test mobilisation of July 1914. They had been back in College for less than a week when Captain Stanley received the order to stand by to mobilise in earnest. Within seven hours the cadets and ship's company reservists were on their way to their war stations by train.

It was rumoured that the College building would be used as a naval hospital, but a term of 79 cadets joined from Osborne in September. The staff had been transformed. Stanley and almost all the other officers had gone to active service and been replaced by officers from the retired list. Rear Admiral T. D. W. Napier was commanding officer, and the deputy headmaster, Arkwright, and ten other masters had been lent to Osborne, where three acted for a time as term officers as well as masters. McMullen, the Head of Science, and three others had gone to sea as RNVR officers together with a mobilised retired-list RN officer, and two others were serving with the Royal Engineers. M. Charbonnier of Modern Languages was serving in the French Army, and two other modern linguists were at the Admiralty assisting Ewing with his secret intelligence work in 'Room 40'. Only Ashford, half a dozen masters and a naval instructor remained.

The College began to fill up again at the beginning of 1915 when two terms moved up from Osborne simultaneously, with most of the borrowed masters, and there were four terms back in residence by the start of the summer term. In 1915–16 the time spent at Dartmouth by cadets fluctuated between three and five terms, but the Exmouths who entered in 1917 only spent a mere two terms at the College. Together with the two senior terms, they were sent to sea in the summer of 1917. The Admiralty was considering Osborne's future, and one of the options being explored was its abolition and the halving of the cadets' course. Moving three terms out of Dartmouth meant that the process could be begun, and the same number of terms duly arrived from Osborne in September, with four masters. The scheme was soon shelved, however, and the junior of these prematurely promoted terms spent an unprecedented eight terms at Dartmouth, as did the following two entries.

The fluctuations in course length must have put a great strain on the academic staff and prevented them achieving even satisfactory results. The supervision of the superannuated naval officers also seems to have left something to be desired. Nevertheless, the College did not become overcrowded, even though the first of the larger terms arrived in 1916, long before the completion of the new buildings. The studies connecting the old buildings with the new were completed in May 1917, but the new block did not house its first cadets until the beginning of the next year. The opening of the new common room allowed the Headmaster to use the old one as a larger office.

The end of the war and the consequent contraction of the Royal Navy soon created considerable problems. Instead of recruiting reservists from civilian life (as would happen in the Second World War), the Admiralty had increased the numbers of regular officers, and there were now far too many. The new terms arriving at Osborne were halved in numbers from the summer of 1919, but more drastic pruning was required. The blow fell on 30 March 1920. Captain Leatham announced to the cadets assembled on the quarter-deck that, although the present senior term would pass out as it stood, the other four large terms, and the three similar-sized terms at Osborne, would have to be cut by 40 per cent. The departures seem to have been voluntary and not as great as originally intended. Nevertheless, the new small entries meant that Dartmouth's enlarged accommodation could now include Osborne's cadets as well as the older boys. The junior college's reputation for disease had for some time rivalled that of the old *Britannia*, and the contemporary financial climate ruled out new, properly built accommodation. Therefore the Admiralty decided to close RNC Osborne, and in May 1920 two terms moved up to Dartmouth instead of one. In January 1921 two more arrived, and in May the four remaining Osborne terms moved up with the first new entries to join Dartmouth since the end of

the old scheme. Captain Marten of Osborne had already replaced Leatham, who had been promoted rear admiral. The last cadets left Osborne on 5 April and the junior college officially closed on 20 May.

Dartmouth settled down once more, but now with eleven terms totalling more than 500 cadets. Engineering was reduced in importance and treated less practically as, with the Special Entry providing suitable candidates for the other branches, Dartmouth cadets were now intended to be Executive officers only. The new names chosen for the extra terms were Anson, Benbow, Hood, Rodney and Duncan. The large D Block gunrooms were divided by partitions and the terms began their progression around the College from the west end of that building. Junior terms messed in D Block mess-room, seniors in the main building. The teaching staff was swelled by ex-Osborne masters to 55 and the naval staff, also including ex-Osborne members, now totalled 39.

The 1920s were in some ways a golden age in Dartmouth's history. Changes were few and, after the traumas of the Geddes Axe, things seemed secure. Routine rather than innovation became the order of the day. As HM Inspector of Schools reported in 1926 in an otherwise complimentary report, 'the staff was tending to become a smooth-running, efficient machine rather than a body of pioneers developing new ideas and a new system'. There does, however, seem to have been a little tension around this time between the Headmaster and the Captain over the control of engineering instruction.. It was a pity that this slight cloud marred Ashford's final years at Dartmouth, for at the end of the summer term of 1927 Dartmouth's first headmaster retired. A knighthood was a fitting reward for his magnificent services to naval education.

The new academic head was E. W. E. Kempson, who had originally worked as an engineer and had taught at the College before the war as both a Naval Instructor and a civilian master. In 1911 he had gone to Rugby to head the science department and, after the war, in which he had served in the Royal Engineers and won a Military Cross, he had become an Inspector of Schools. In their 1926 report the Inspectors had commented on the care given to the weaker pupils rather at the expense of the brighter cadets. Accordingly Kempson soon announced that 'Alpha' classes would be chosen in the three senior terms, members of which would concentrate on three main subjects at the expense of a fourth. These cadets were also given a slightly relaxed routine and expected to work more on their own.

As the economic horizon began to darken in 1929, the College began to come under attack in Parliament and the Press. As the number of cadets dropped faster than the numbers of staff employed in the College, concern and criticism mounted over the apparently lavish ratio of staff to pupils. In 1932 there were indeed 412 officers, masters, ship's company and civilian workers to only 408 cadets. It was suggested that Dartmouth might take pupils not intended for a Service career, but this proved unnecessary. Favourable reports from the schools' inspectorate, the support of the Admiralty and cuts in staff all helped stave off closure. All terms except the first were grouped into pairs, and by 1934, when the number of cadets was reduced to 368, there were only twenty officers and thirty-six masters (including two Naval Instructors). Total college staff had been cut to 308.

One important problem at this time was that parents, worried about the long-term prospects of the naval profession, were preferring the flexibility of the Special Entry rather than committing their sons to Dartmouth at the age of thirteen. By 1936 the numbers at the College had risen to 415 but only at some cost. As Kempson reported that year to the Admiralty, of the 45 places available for a recent term only 26 had passed for entrance but seventeen failures had been allowed in to boost numbers, and even then the term had not been filled. This was in turn causing doubts to be expressed about RNC cadets when compared with the quality of the Special Entry. It was recognised by some that there were indeed features of College life that were becoming unattractive. These

defects seem to have become clear to Admiral Sir Martin Dunbar-Nasmyth, Captain of the College from 1926 to 1929. When he was Second Sea Lord in 1936 he was the force behind the decision taken that year to introduce a House system. The new Captain, F. H. G. Dalrymple-Hamilton, arrived in January to supervise the change-over, and he found Kempson to be an enthusiastic supporter of the idea. The two seem to have got on very well together. After a meeting with term officers, the original proposal of seven houses was reduced to five, and in March the Captain, with Lieutenant Commander Sladen, the Duncan term officer, left on a whistle-stop tour of public schools to see houses in action. After further discussion the new system was duly introduced at the beginning of the summer term. The houses were called St. Vincent, Exmouth, Hawke, Blake and Grenville (new spelling, the first three to be accommodated in D block, the last two in the front buildings (A and B blocks respectively). C block with its large gunroom was to be a junior Drake house for the first two terms. The process, which has seen the emphasis at Dartmouth swing from academic study to professional training, began in 1939. The deteriorating international situation had led to the Special Entries' training cruiser *Frobisher* being refitted for active service. In May, therefore, the eighteen-year-olds who should have gone to sea in her were sent instead to Dartmouth's ship's company barracks block.

Far from the exodus of 1914, the outbreak of war in 1939 saw the College dramatically increase in size. Another group of Special Entry cadets arrived and were housed in C block, owing to the barracks being still occupied by the Frobishers and the RNC passing-out term, who would also normally have been at sea. Extra huts had to be constructed to provide sufficient accommodation. The Drakes were temporarily reduced to one term only and to sleeping in the old D block mess-room that had latterly been used as a cinema. In April 1940, Captain Cunliffe was appointed Naval Officer in Charge of the port of Dartmouth and the College became still more crowded as dormitories had to be converted into offices and a full operations room constructed. WRNS officers and ratings also began to appear for the first time.

Kempson retired in 1942, to be succeeded by J. W. Stock from Portsmouth Grammar School. His first term had not started when the College was bombed, on 18 September. The damage was quite severe, and it was necessary to send the junior cadets to Muller's

Orphanage in Bristol, commissioned as HMS *Bristol*. Only the four senior terms of RNC cadets returned to Dartmouth, but the Admiralty decided to use the buildings as a Combined Operations training centre. After a year as such, first as HMS *Dartmouth II* and then as HMS *Effingham*, the establishment was passed to the US Navy as an advanced base. It was from Dartmouth that the ill-fated Exercise 'Tiger' shipping sailed in April 1944, to meet disaster when E-boats struck the convoy in Lyme Bay, and it was from Dartmouth and neighbouring ports that the forces that landed on 'Utah' beach in Normandy sailed.

By February 1943, HMS *Britannia* had re-assembled at Eaton Hall, the Duke of Westminster's impressive house near Chester, where it would remain until the summer of 1946. The return to Dartmouth was delayed by the need to repair the bomb damage, and the opportunity was also taken to improve the College buildings. The library was doubled in size, the science laboratories were expanded and a new F block was begun to provide extra classrooms.

A system of scholarships to Dartmouth had been introduced in 1941 by A. V. Alexander, the First Lord, but they did not go far enough to widen the college entry. The Admiralty announced, therefore, that from September 1948 cadets were to enter Dartmouth at sixteen. This was the age that many boys of the required qualifications left state secondary schools, and it removed the advantage that private-sector boys had in applying to enter Dartmouth at the natural break-point in their education. In any case, it was felt that thirteen was too early an age to choose a career and to be able to detect whether a candidate had the right qualities to become an officer. Fees for boarding and tuition would be abolished. The Special Entry would continue at Dartmouth alongside the Sixteen Entry. Thirteen-year-olds would still join RNC until May 1949.

The end of the younger entry caused the number of Darts to decline as the extra sixteen-year-olds did not make up for the loss of the junior terms. The low birth-rate of the 1930s was limiting the number of suitable candidates, but the new age of entry presented particular problems as the headmasters of public and grammar schools became increasingly reluctant to lose boys in the middle of their school careers. By the summer term of 1953, at the end of which the last thirteen entries passed out, the College was down to 202 Darts and 45 Benbows. There were only four

houses, Blake, Exmouth, Grenville and St. Vincent, and both C and F blocks were closed, the newest building after only very brief use. These buildings had been used by the Benbows who had moved up the hill in 1950 to be more closely integrated with the rest of the College. The following year their old barracks had been taken over by HMS *Hawke*, the training establishment for Upper Yardmen, young officer candidates from the lower deck.

The Admiralty had recognised that the existing cadet entry situation was most unsatisfactory and, in July 1952, a 'Committee on Cadet Entry' had been appointed under the chairmanship of the Hon. Ewen Montague, Judge Advocate of the Fleet. This duly reported, in April 1953. Its report was a confused affair, and one member submitted a radically different minority report. The majority report argued that the thirteen entry was unloved and did not really work, but should be retained. However (and this seemed to be the *real* favourite of the majority report) they also wanted a return to a modified version of the old thirteen entry. They attempted to get over the objection that had been inherent in the system since 1902, and to which Kempson had pointed when it was visibly failing in the 1930s, that parents were less and less inclined to sign their sons up for the navy at thirteen. The old deal had been that a boy who passed through Dartmouth was obliged to accept a commission should he be offered one. However, the Admiralty was not obliged to offer commissions to successful candidates, an option it had exercised at the time of the Geddes' Axe. This manifestly unfair commitment, and the awareness that a boy who failed at Dartmouth was unlikely to be effectively educated for anything else, had obviously deterred parents. The Montague committee report recommended that the thirteen entry should offer a general public school type education, and that those who went through it should no longer be obliged to accept commissions.

The majority report also recommended that there should be an eighteen entry. A decision to enter at eighteen meant that the boy had a much more adult chance to make up his own mind, and could have received a general education as well. While Dartmouth was almost unique in offering a high quality technical education as it was before the First World War, the Selborne Scheme had much to recommend it. In the post-1944 Education Act world, the arguments were much less strong. The majority report went on, in essence, to recommend that the BRNC campus should become three establishments. The first would be the thirteen- and sixteen-entry school under the direction of a civilian headmaster. The second would be an officer basic training establishment to which those from the school who chose to go on into the Navy and the eighteen-entry candidates should go, which would be headed by a Royal Navy commander. The third would be the Admiralty Interview Board, under a rear admiral, who would also superintend the other two establishments.

It is refreshing to turn from this nostalgic mirage to the report by Mr F. Barraclough, the Chief Education Officer for the North Riding of Yorkshire. He disagreed so fundamentally with these recommendations that he wrote his own minority report. This recommended retaining the sixteen entry but argued in favour of an eventual move to an all-eighteen entry when practicable. This was the natural break in a young man's education and would be more likely to provide the quantity and quality of candidates the Navy wanted, given the contemporary trend to staying on at school. Barraclough did not think the time was yet ripe to make such a change, but the Admiralty disagreed and decided to go ahead and make it immediately. When the 'Committee on Officer Structure and Training' (COST) was set up at the beginning of 1954 under the chairmanship of Vice Admiral Sir Aubrey Mansergh, its first and most urgent task was to design a new Eighteen Entry training scheme.

In its initial report presented in March, COST welcomed the end of the old Dartmouth scheme and argued that all officers could now be given a comprehensive professional training before going to sea. Dartmouth should become a Naval Academy with an attached training squadron where officers could undertake a 28-month course before going to sea as midshipmen. This would begin with a two-term academic levelling process to cover deficiencies in scientific knowledge or self-expression abilities. After the weaker cadets had been weeded out by examinations, the rest would proceed to the Dartmouth Training Squadron, where they would serve as the ships' companies to get sea experience and knowledge of lower-deck conditions of service. They would then return to Dartmouth for four terms of professional instruction, reinforced by further education in academic subjects, short courses in the DTS and a visit to a naval air station. It was subsequently decided to promote cadets to midshipmen on completion of their squadron time and they would go to sea as acting sub-lieutenants.

This amendment, which temporarily abolished the sea-going midshipman, was to help doom the scheme to a short life.

The new scheme was to begin in the summer of 1955, and at the end of the Easter term, as the College prepared to celebrate its 50th anniversary, there was a distinct feeling that an era was ending. The Benbows and Hawkes would disappear, the former into the new scheme. The existing sixteen entries would have to complete their education before moving on to the new scheme. Dartmouth would have to be transformed for its new role. Dormitories had to be converted into single cabins for the midshipmen and four-berthers for the cadets to allow for study as well as sleeping. The gunroom accommodation had to be improved to reflect the more relaxed atmosphere. The traditional classrooms were no longer adequate on their own, and tutorial rooms were required to replace many of them.

This pushed the victualling stores, which themselves had to be enlarged, out into a new block adjoining the west end of the College. Expanded naval and clothing stores also took over a wing of the hospital. A new gunnery block was begun and the neglected F block became a well-equipped navigation and communications instruction building. The foundations were also laid for an annex to D block to contain cabins, tutorial rooms and new administrative offices. The Hawke barracks was also modified for the expanded ship's company and became Beatty Division.

Although the conversion to a tertiary college was in principle more radical than the changes of 1902, the process was slow, gentle and more subtle. There was no question of replacing the academic staff. Mr Stork did, however, become Director of Studies at the beginning of 1956, and his masters became lecturers. They were also now full members of the Wardroom Mess. 1956 also saw the end of the Houses and the beginning of five new Divisions in which all the officers under training were integrated. The names were traditional: Blake, Drake, Exmouth, Grenville and St. Vincent. The Dartmouth Training Squadron also became operational. By summer 1957 there were more than five hundred officers under training at the new BRNC: 171 cadets and 419 midshipmen. These included young men from Australia, Ceylon, Malaya, New Zealand and Pakistan as well as Britain. The staff totalled 57 officers and 42 lecturers. They were not, however, to be given the chance to settle down to the new scheme. The COST training was due for early review as a result of another of the Committee's proposals, the setting-up of the General List of officers from the various specialisations. A committee was duly appointed on 1 April 1958, chaired by the late Sir Keith Murray, Chairman of the University Grants Committee. It reported on 26 September 1958. Despite the fact that the 1955 scheme had barely begun and its products had not yet reached the fleet as fully qualified officers, the Committee felt it had too many defects and ought to be changed forthwith. Entrance standards were both too low and too variable; the close interweaving of academic and professional studies at BRNC gave insufficient time for proper development in either. The academic staff at Dartmouth was praised for its work in bringing the least able cadets up to standard, but it was felt that the better cadets suffered, and there was no external qualification to show for the course afterwards. The DTS time was not properly exploited, and officer-like qualities were being neglected, not only in the intellectual but in the character and leadership sense. The Murray Committee would have liked to restore the old thirteen entry. Instead it put forward a radically changed eighteen entry system. First, the entrance qualifications would be increased to a minimum of two A levels. To give a proper professional and Character and Leadership grounding, a whole cadet year would be spent at Dartmouth, including a term in the DTS, where proper instruction would be given. After a second year at sea with the fleet as a midshipman, the young officer would return to Dartmouth as acting sub-lieutenant for a year's academic course at first year university degree standard.

The Committee specifically wished to keep Dartmouth, which they praised for its traditions, situation and buildings, Most of all, however, they felt it lent itself to keeping all specialisations together for as long as possible in accordance with the new GL concept. To satisfy London University, whose external degree would be completed by the Engineers at RNEC Manadon, there might have to be a considerable expansion of the laboratories, not to mention a radical reorganisation and strengthening of the academic staff. Nevertheless there was enough room for the 370 cadets and sub-lieutenants expected annually.

Although the suggested scheme was adopted in basics, not all the 'Murray' suggestions were put into effect exactly as planned. By the time the first cadet entry arrived in September 1960 there had been some significant changes. The most important was that the Engineers were not to come to Dartmouth for their third year, and this allowed the problems of external approval and validation to be avoided. Indeed G. W. E. Ghey's appointment as Director of Studies in 1959 had reinforced continuity of academic staff; he had first joined as a master in 1926.

The return of the Murray Scheme sub-lieutenants in September 1962 meant that the higher standard of academic teaching called for by the report could begin. The officers-under-training could now concentrate on it, their professional indoctrination being over, although the sub-lieutenants' leadership would be consolidated and extended by their role in helping run the College. The independence of the academic course from external examinations was turned to advantage as it allowed flexible mixtures of navally-orientated academic subjects to evolve. The new stress on tutorials and private study was in the finest tradition of Ewing and Ashford, albeit now at a higher level.

Although the Murray Scheme was the main College task of the 1960s, that decade saw a great increase in the number of different entries coming to the College and different courses offered to them. The Royal Marine Young Officers Courses of one term's introduction to the Navy were carried out in DTS rather than the College, following the new scheme's introduction, but the Upper Yardmen returned from their northern exile in HMS *Téméraire* in 1960. They took up residence in the hospital, which had ceased to operate as such in 1958 and had been used since by the Admiralty Interview Board. The course lasted two years before they went to sea as midshipmen. The Temeraires were integrated with the other five divisions two years later. 1960 had also seen the start of a new Supplementary List Aircrew entry, who began to come to Dartmouth for a two-term combined professional and academic course before flying training. The Supplementary List was extended to Seamen in 1961 with a course of similar length at the College plus a term in DTS before proceeding to the fleet as midshipmen. They were later joined by SL Engineer officers, who did the first two terms of the Dartmouth course before proceeding to Manadon. Instructor officers-under-training (IOUTs) began to attend Dartmouth for a one-term naval training course in 1962. That year also saw the beginning of a special course for New Commonwealth and foreign officers who were beginning to come to the

College in increasing numbers. At first a New Commonwealth Year was offered instead of the RN Academic course, which could also be done by Commonwealth and foreign officers if sufficiently qualified, and Internationals were also entered in the SL Seaman Scheme. By 1967, however, a special package had been devised for all these officers with a term's academic work in their third cadet term and an International Senior Term of more advanced study. In the mid-1960s the College contained almost 700 officers-under-training and the staff comprised 54 officers and 34 lecturers. It was again divided into five divisions, a new Hawke having been re-born in the hospital buildings in 1963 to concentrate the SL (Air) entry. The year after, however, it became a division like the others. Other new names that appeared were Cunningham, which replaced Exmouth as a divisional title in 1968, and Jellicoe which replaced Grenville at the same time. Numbers began to decline once more, and even in a busy winter term there were only 477 OUTs in the College by 1970. Drake Division was therefore abolished, yet again, at the end of that year's summer term.

One reason for this decline, and a factor that was by then threatening the College's very existence as an academic institution, was the move towards a graduate entry. The 1960s was a decade of expansion in higher education associated with the Robbins Report, and the Services felt that they would lose the very best officer candidates if they did not follow this trend. In 1963 the first five cadets were nominated to go to university instead of doing the Dartmouth third year. In September 1964, Seaman Officers Under Training arrived at Dartmouth to inaugurate what later became known as the Direct Graduate Entry (DGE) scheme. In 1965 the University Cadet Entry (UCE) was begun whereby young men leaving school with university places would take them up sponsored by the Navy. On graduation they would do professional training at Dartmouth together with a course in technological subjects for arts graduates. It seemed to some, however, that Service education needed a more fundamental shake-up in the era of both an expanded graduate entry and the moves to greater unification of the armed forces. In 1966 in a thorough-going study of Service education, Michael Howard, Professor of War Studies at King's College London, and Cyril English, Senior Chief Inspector, Department of Education and Science, came to the conclusion that new entry academic instruction should be centralised at a

Royal Defence College where the top 20 per cent of candidates would read for degrees. This appealed to Mr Healey, the Secretary of State for Defence, and the scheme was adopted and announced in the 1967 Defence White Paper. Plans were made to establish the institution on the site of the Royal Military College of Science at Shrivenham. The scheme was subjected to considerable criticisms, but it finally grounded on the rocks of financial stringency and the emergency defence cuts of 1967–8.

It seemed, though, that when H. G. Stewart, a member of the science staff since 1947, was appointed Dartmouth's Director of Studies in September 1967, he could well be the last. Although the College survived the abortive Howard-English exercise, it was almost immediately under a fresh attack. The Defence White Paper of 1968 had stated that possible ways of giving officers degree-standard academic training would continue to be investigated. The Navy now proposed to begin at Greenwich a course run by City University, which would be attended by all Seamen and Supply sub-lieutenants instead of the Dartmouth third year. At the end of this period the best students would go on to complete a full degree course at City while the others would pass on to further training courses as usual. Civilians would join the naval officers. This threatened to reduce the College to an initial training establishment without both its senior officers under training and its best academic staff, and was strongly opposed.

Although this battle was eventually won, the tide was running too strongly against the Murray scheme for it to survive. Trust was placed in the UCE scheme to provide an increasing number of officers, but to supplement it a new Naval College Entry was being mooted in 1971. Officers-under-training of all three branches would come to Dartmouth to do a common period of Naval General Training involving both professional and Character and Leadership subjects. One term would be taken in the College and another in a Dartmouth Training Ship. After that the students would split up. Engineers would go to Manadon or Cambridge and some qualified Seamen and Supply officers-under-training with no university places would be nominated, either to City for the RN-sponsored Systems and management course or to another university. The General List non-graduate would go on to two terms of academic instruction at BRNC and the SL Seamen and Supply officers to one term. As many UCEs as possible would be encouraged to defer going up to university so that they might do their Naval general training course at Dartmouth first. The other entries' training would not be changed very much, although they would have to fit in with the new syllabus and timing. In 1972 as a sign of the new system all the junior officers under training became midshipmen and the rank of Cadet was abolished after 128 years. The Naval College Entry course has seen a little evolution too: a more extensive four-week period of introductory training was introduced in the mid-1970s, while the General List academic course has been extended to three terms.

Until the 1970s, Dartmouth remained an all-male bastion, at least so far as students were concerned, but the advent of two- and four-week Short Introductory Courses for doctors, nurses, dentists, chaplains, reservists and constructors brought about a change. The course of QARNNS in spring 1973 had the distinction of being the first women officers-under-training at BRNC. They were soon followed by lady dentists, doctors and naval constructors. In 1976 the WRNS decided to confirm this co-educational policy, transferring their officer training course of one term's professional and academic work to Dartmouth from Greenwich to form a separate Talbot division.

In September 1978, C. H. Christie became BRNC's fourth Director of Studies. The varied look of the College's student body was very apparent, and nothing could better illustrate that the balance at BRNC between academic and professional instruction has swung firmly in favour of the latter. Fewer than half the 493 students were now on academic courses, though many courses were mixed academic and professional. The balance of the College staff reflected this change: there were then only 32 lecturers but more than 60 officers. With so many of the College's courses now lasting only one term, the atmosphere had altered fundamentally compared with the more leisurely pace of ten years previously. Now most new naval officers did their long-term academic work at university: in September 1978 there were 136 UCEs and 57 nominations.

The last ten years have continued the story of frequent changes. The early 1980s saw the abolition of the fifth term for the General List, an end to projects to redevelop and modernise the college, and a series of attempts to bring the education and training of officers on track while numbers of officers being trained continued to decline. The new Officer Training System was a reversion to a sort of poor man's Murray Scheme. The lengthening of the basic Naval General Training package from thirteen weeks to nineteen followed by a shortened training ship cruise, then a year away from the College in the fleet to reach fleet board standard and then a 26-week Naval Studies package certificated by the Polytechnic South-West, now Plymouth University, was an improvement and gave students definite externally validated credentials for their Dartmouth academic courses. Moreover, the move to giving both Short Career and Medium Career Officers the full two-term Naval Studies package meant that there was a uniform output on to all lists – except Supplementary List Aircrew – for Naval College Entry Young Officers. The introduction of a naval orientated degree course, taking in maritime strategy, strategic studies, international politics, defence economics, information technology and management for seamen and supply officers based at the Royal Naval Engineering College, but taught by a mixture of staff from RNEC, RNC Greenwich and BRNC, was a very promising development. The two-term academic package was a necessary qualification for this course, not actually part of the degree, which was then completed over two, rather longer than usual university academic years. The abolition of the WRNS' own division, Talbot, and the integration of the female officers into the ordinary training patterns was enormous progress. On the other hand the abolition of the separate Special duties Officer Pre-qualifying Course Division, St George, was more a function of declining numbers of SD candidates and a wish to achieve standardisation than genuine educational improvement.

But as the centenary of the decision to build the college at Dartmouth approaches, the future looks very uncertain. The tensions between the educational and the training functions of the College remain unresolved. The decline in the Navy's size and requirement for officers is posing threats to the viability of the three Naval Colleges. The closure of one, RNEC Manadon, has already been confirmed; with it will end in-service education to first-degree standard. The assumption is that there will be enough graduates with the right degrees to supply a much greater proportion of the Navy's future need for officers. This, in turn, suggests that the end of academic training at Dartmouth may be in sight. On the other hand, it could make it necessary to change the direction of officer education. Instead of the main duty of the College's lecturing staff being to provide a basic scientific, technical, strategic and linguistic education for those who do not go to university, it could become that of making good the gaps in officers' education where they have acquired university degrees that do not adequately provide the intellectual skills needed by officers.

It may be that all the Services will, as their sizes decline, come to regret the failure to pick up the Howard-English plan for a tri-Service university. Whether the College will survive into its second century we do not know. Whether the age old argument between those who see officership as a matter of conditioning and character producing leadership, and those who see it as a matter of intellect directing character to achieve leadership will ever be resolved is not knowable. Indeed it is not clear that a resolution is possible – or desirable.

Whatever the answer, for as long as it exists, the Navy will need officers, and somewhere will have to be found to train and to educate them in the ways and requirements of their chosen profession.

Not least of the factors producing that education is the building that is Britannia Royal Naval College, and far from least among the places in the College where the history and traditions of the Royal Navy, with its astonishing record of success at things naval and maritime stretching back to the days of the Anglo-Saxon Kings, is the Gunroom. Here, in a splendid barrel-vaulted room, at least 30,000 people between the ages of thirteen and 35, all of them aspiring to be officers in the Royal Navy, have dined in the last 88 years. The Gunroom suggests to me the inside of the upturned hull of a boat. Its ceiling has since 1979 been magnificently painted with the Royal Coat of Arms of King Edward VII and other heraldic emblems.[18]

Around the walls eleven centuries of naval history look down. Inscribed in gold letters at the top of the panelling are the names of famous naval battles, their dates and the name of an officer associated with the event, usually the commander-in-chief. They begin, just above the door, just behind the president's head at a formal dinner with a victory over the Danes ascribed to Alfred the Great, one of three monarchs mentioned[19] and run on via the Armada, the battles of the Dutch Wars to La Hogue in 1692, and then the great roll of victories in the eighteenth century: Finisterre, Lagos, Quiberon, Les Saintes, the Glorious 1st June, Camperdown, St. Vincent, the Nile, Copenhagen and Trafalgar. The name of Nelson appears three times, although he was not the senior officer

present at Copenhagen. Cochrane is remembered for Aix Roads in 1809, not Lord Gambier; Exmouth for Algiers; and last in the list is Acre in 1840, as the circle of the room clockwise is completed. There, in 1905, the cadet sat down to dine, amidst a statement about the Royal Navy for 1,000 years. The list of battles has not been modernised since 1905, but the list is now accompanied by another circle, of portraits of the Navy's great (or, in one case, not so great) officers. They too form a circle. They begin with Charles Howard, Lord Howard of Effingham, Earl of Nottingham, Lord Admiral of England and commander-in-chief against the Spanish Armada in 1588, and round the room are some of the heroes of the age of sail: Edward Russell, Earl of Oxford, victor of La Hogue in 1692, dressed in armour – which has always struck me as a doubtful asset in a naval battle. Anson is there, in a fascinating portrait painted in 1746, just before the introduction of the naval uniform, dressed in a brown civilian coat. Adam Duncan is there. The victor of Camperdown in 1797 is shown as a young and elegant captain wearing the original naval officer's uniform of the 1748 pattern. Nelson is there and so is Hardy. Also there are some of the dominating figures of the twentieth century: Fisher is there, creator, reformer, and, from his picture, mischief maker; Jellicoe, the only man who could have lost the First World War in an afternoon; Chatfield is there, Beatty's flag captain on that fateful day at Jutland, and greatest of the inter-war First Sea Lords; Andrew Brown Cunningham stands in front of Grand Harbour at Malta. ABC looks quizzical and puzzled rather than the embodiment of his other nickname, 'Tiger'. Michael Le Fanu stands with his hand resting on a model of HMS *Aurora*, in which his genius as a gunnery officer first found expression, and whose tragic early death from leukaemia deprived the nation of a great Chief of the Defence Staff. Mountbatten is there, and last is Lord Lewin. Only three naval officers have been awarded knighthoods of the Garter for purely naval services: Howard is one, Lewis the third. The second, Earl Howe, 'Black Dick' Howe, is, sadly, missing. And the not so great one? The first Lord Dartmouth, who, as commander of the English Fleet in 1688, was the last admiral to fail to prevent a seaborne invasion of England.

This room has been the scene of many formal dinners, splendid occasions when Queens and Princes have been entertained, or annual tributes to the greatest of them all, Nelson, some of whose silver dinner service is permanently displayed there, on Trafalgar night. It has been the scene of more work-a-day formal mess dinners when divisions in the College introduce the young officers to the pleasure and ceremony of the Navy's society. It is a routine place to eat, but there, as on the front of the College, is the Navy's pride, tradition, achievements. There also to be seen is the Navy's future.

NOTES

1. George Goschen, First Lord of the Admiralty, in a speech at Lewes, 26 February 1896. Goschen was picking up on the phrase 'splendidly isolated' used by Sir George Foster in a speech in the Canadian House of Commons in January 1896. A. D. Elliott, *The Life of George Joachim Goschen, First Viscount Goschen 1831–1907*, vol II, pages 206–8.

2. Printed from the Pepysian MSS in H. W. Hodges and E. A. Hughes (eds), *Select Naval Documents*, Cambridge University Press, 1922, 1936 edition, pages 72–3. Another version of this proclamation is printed in J. B. Hattendorf, R. J. B. Knight, A. W. H. Pearsall, N. A. M. Rodger and G. Till (eds), *British Naval Documents, 1204–1960*, pages 296–9, Navy Records Society, vol 131, 1993, where it is dated 22 December 1677.

3. F. B. Sullivan, 'The Royal Academy at Portsmouth' in *Mariner's Mirror*, vol 63, 1977, page 311.

4. HMS *Illustrious*, 74, 1,746 tons builder's measure, the second RN ship of that name, launched at Rotherhithe on 3 September 1803, broken up 1868.

5. HMS *Britannia*, usually referred to as the fourth *Britannia*, although Colledge's list makes her number 5. 1st Rate 120-gun ship, 2,616 tons builder's measure, launched at Plymouth Dockyard 20 October 1820. Fleet flagship in the Baltic, 1854. Training ship 1 January 1859. Broken up 1869.

6. E. P. Statham, The Story of the *'Britannia'*. Cassell & Co., 1904. Commander Statham was a cadet in HMS *Britannia* at the time of her stay in Portland. He entered on 10 December 1861 and passed in March 1863.

7. HMS *Hindostan*, 80, 2nd rate, 2,029 tons builder's measure, 3,242 tons displacement, launched Devonport Dockyard, 2 August 1841; training ship 1864 (Colledge's list errs in giving 1868) transferred to the Tamar as HMS *Fisgard III* in October 1905. Renamed *Hindustan* (sic) in 1920, scrapped 1921.

8. Classrooms.

9. HMS *Prince of Wales*, number 4 in Colledge's list, Screw 1st rate, 121 guns, 3,994 tons builder's measure, 6,201 tons displacement, launched Portsmouth dockyard after twelve years on the stocks, 25 January 1860. She ran her trials, without her rigging, but never saw sea service. Renamed *Britannia* 1869, reduced to accommodation ship 1905. Sold 13 November 1914. Arrived at Blyth for breaking up, July 1916.

10. Sir Aston Webb, 1848–1930. Architect of the principal block of the Victoria and Albert Museum, Royal College of Science, Admiralty Arch, the eastern facade of Buckingham Place, and the surround of the Victoria Monument in front of Buckingham Place. 'As a designer, Aston Webb was distinguished by clear-sightedness and common sense.' (H. S. Goodhart-Rendel)

11. Admiral Count Togo Heihachiro, 1847–1934.

12. Memorandum dealing with the Entry, Training and Employment of Officers and Men of the Royal Navy and of the Royal Marines, Command Paper 1385 of 1902. Signed by Lord Selbourne, First Lord of the Admiralty, on 16 December 1902.

13. The last of the old-scheme cadets who had joined in May 1905 would pass into the fleet after their four-term course in July 1906. The first of the new-scheme cadets would complete the six-term Dartmouth part of the Selborne Scheme course in July 1907. This gap of two entries would have been bridged. Hence the need to keep the old scheme running for nearly three years after the new scheme had begun.

14. N. Pevsner, *The Buildings of England: South Devon*, Penguin Books, 1952, pages 115-65.

15. J. Lodwick, *The Cradle of Neptune*, London, 1951, page 6. The order of the sentences has been rearranged.

16. This memorandum has been printed in J. B. Hattendorf, R. J. B. Knight, A. W. H. Pearsall, N. A. M. Rodger and G. Till (eds), *British Naval Documents, 1204–1960*, pages 972-4; Navy Records Society, vol 131, 1993, where it is dated 25 February 1902.

17. F. B. Sullivan's remark (*op. cit.* page 311) that the argument about the relative merits of the shore-based and sea-based education and training for officers would last 'at least a century and a quarter' is well wide of the mark. Fisher was arguing the case, and the case is being argued today.

18. The ceiling has, ever since 1905, had mouldings of these coats of arms and so on in place, but it was only in 1979, through a legacy to the College from Miss Alice Fawcett-Walker, that the ceiling could be properly painted.

19. The others are Edward III and James II as Duke of York.

INDEX